Mastering Derivatives Markets:

Second Edition

'An invaluable and straightforward guide, full of practical applications.'
– *International Petroleum Exchange*

'Another valuable step on the road to improving competence and confidence in the world of financial derivatives.'
– *Paul Dex, Education Manager, LIFFE*

'A vital book for every new entrant into market.'
– *Christopher Bellew, Director, Prudential-Bache International Ltd*

'Contains just about everything you might ever want to know concerning the derivatives markets. "Mastering Derivatives Markets" is a well written book about a difficult subject.'
– Technical Analysis of Stocks and Commodities, *The Trader's Magazine*

'The best primer yet on the mysteries of derivatives ... A comprehensive step-by-step guide which will be widely welcomed.'
– *Wilf Altman,* Chartered Secretary

Mastering Derivatives Markets:

Second Edition

A step-by-step guide to the
products, applications and risks

FRANCESCA TAYLOR

Prentice Hall
FINANCIAL TIMES

An imprint of **Pearson Education**

London · New York · San Francisco · Toronto · Sydney
Tokyo · Singapore · Hong Kong · Cape Town · Madrid
Paris · Milan · Munich · Amsterdam

Pearson Education Limited

Edinburgh Gate
Harlow CM20 2JE
Tel: +44 (0) 1279 623623
Fax: +44 (0) 1279 431059
Website: www.pearsoned.co.uk

First published in Great Britain 1996

© Francesca Taylor 2000

British Library Cataloguing in Publication Data
A CIP catalogue record for this book can be obtained from the British Library.

ISBN 0 273 65243 5

10 9

Typeset by Pantek Arts Ltd, Maidstone, Kent
Printed and bound in Great Britain by Bell & Bain Ltd, Glasgow

The Publishers' policy is to use paper manufactured from sustainable forests.

The Author

Francesca Taylor is the Principal of Taylor Associates, a financial training company, established in 1993, specializing in derivatives, capital markets and treasury training. She has personally trained in major UK plcs, American and UK banks and 'derivatives houses', both in the UK and world-wide.

Francesca's career in finance/treasury commenced with BICC plc, one of the UK's largest companies, where she learned her basic treasury, FX and money market skills – from the client's perspective. In a typical day she would liaise with banks, transact money market and foreign exchange deals and advise on risk management.

The City beckoned and Francesca joined Midland Bank, becoming Team Leader in the Financial Engineering Group, concentrating on marketing, selling and trouble shooting the whole range of derivatives products to a client list including central banks, major and minor commercial banks, corporates and supranationals. She also spent 12 months with Midland Futures, broking financial futures to a range of major financial institutions. In addition, it was Francesca's responsibility to educate and train Midland's client base in the uses and applications of a growing number of derivative products.

Francesca then became a treasury consultant advising her clients on all aspects of currency and interest rate risk management. Notable clients included major utilities and engineering companies. Following this, she spent some time as an inter-bank swap broker with Sterling Brokers.

Over the course of her career Francesca has followed each of the four major groupings within banking and finance. She has been a corporate, a banker, a broker and a consultant. This leads her to be ideally placed to offer independent training and product education to clients.

Her company, Taylor Associates, has been highly successful since its inception and now offers a wide range of treasury, risk, general finance and complementary soft-skills courses to banks and non-banks alike.

Francesca is a designated speaker for the ACI/FOREX Association, specializing in options, and has spoken at major conferences in the UK, Hong Kong, Singapore, Malaysia and Australia.

She is an Associate Member of the Association of Corporate Treasurers (ACT), holds a Master Degree in Management Science from Imperial College, London and also has a BSc in Geology.

'A derivative is like a razor. You can use it to shave yourself and make yourself attractive for your girlfriend. You can slit her throat with it. Or you can use it to commit suicide.'

Financial Times

CONTENTS

'This book is written for both the new entrant into the City or other associated financial areas, and also for the seasoned professional in financial institutions or companies who requires a refresher on the basics of derivatives.'

FOREWORD

In the first edition of *Mastering Derivatives Markets* I wrote that the US hedge funds were in the media spotlight, as market practitioners saw a possible default chain reaction linking these speculative organizations to major international lending banks. *Was I right or was I right??*

The most high-profile incident of recent years involved one of the larger US hedge funds – Long-Term Capital Management (LTCM), actively trading (among other things) credit spreads on bonds – by buying emerging market bonds and hedging them with short positions in US T. bonds. When Russia defaulted on some of its outstanding borrowings, credit spreads across many diverse bonds rapidly widened as investors sought 'quality'. Prices of US T. bonds shot up and emerging market bond prices fell – end result, huge losses resulting in a US$3.6 billion bailout provided by 14 banks and organized by The Fed.

Even Eddie George, Governor of The Bank of England, spoke of 'the dreaded derivatives', a remark made somewhat ironically in the aftermath of the Barings Bank collapse. Barings was brought down brutally, and with some speed, by the actions of one of its traders, and also by the *in*action of some members of its management team. The full extent of the losses are estimated at around £1 billion, but will probably never be fully admitted – a legend in banking history.

We should not forget the losses of Orange County in California, US$3–5 billion – many times the size of the Barings losses. And, in our own backyard, the Hammersmith and Fulham Local Authority which, in the late 1980s, sold derivatives to City institutions, but could not then fulfil its obligations due under the contracts – resulting in a loss to the Authority of somewhere in the region of £80 million.

Even individuals have suffered. Late in 1998 an independent futures trader (a local) trading on the computerized exchange EUREX heavily overtraded his own position. The exchange claimed not only his collateral, but that belonging to other locals who had also placed their funds with the same bank – on the grounds that the funds were not 'segregated'!

History is littered with examples of financial institutions and companies that have endured deep crises, or indeed collapsed, due to misjudgements. These could be misjudgements due to the price of oil, due to the price of property, due to the gold price and are often misjudgements on the direction of an exchange rate or an interest rate. The fact

> 'The term derivative seems enough to strike fear into the boardrooms of some of our major companies.'

> 'As the role of derivatives in risk management grows, it is essential that the finance and treasury functions within business become increasingly adept at making proper and effective use of these instruments.'

> 'Used correctly, derivatives perform hedging and risk management functions; used incorrectly and speculatively, derivatives can lose you (or make you) large sums of money.'

that these positions were taken with derivative instruments is ultimately irrelevant. The real problem was the original 'wrong view' on the market. To blame the derivative transaction is like saying that it was the bullet that killed the person, when in fact the killer is not the bullet, but the man who fired the gun.

Negative publicity surrounding derivatives means that the uninformed or misinformed company may interpret the use of any derivatives as highly speculative – even when they are used for risk management. The term derivative seems enough to strike fear into the boardrooms of some of our major companies.

In the words of a prominent industrialist, 'As the role of derivatives in risk management grows, it is essential that the finance and treasury functions within business become increasingly adept at making proper and effective use of these instruments'.

To put this whole situation into perspective we need to consider the size of the derivatives market. This is not an easy thing to do. Every journal you pick up quotes a larger total figure. At the time of writing, the total is likely to be in the region of US\$150 trillion (US\$150,000,000,000,000), notional amount outstanding and still growing. *This figure is five times larger than that used in the previous edition of this book.* It includes all derivative instruments in all markets in all countries and currencies, converted into US dollars. Compare this with US\$20 trillion, which is the estimated size of the global equity market and you can begin to see the scale of the issue. Even so, many market practitioners believe the overall position is understated and always will be, as many capital market bond and equity transactions include complex embedded derivatives – *not* included in these figures.

Used correctly, derivatives perform hedging and risk management functions; used incorrectly and speculatively, derivatives can lose you (or make you) large sums of money.

But should every product carry a 'health warning', and, if so, to what extent? Surely the real issue is whether the derivative product is right for the customer. The selling bank must ensure that all its clients fully understand the risks of using derivatives. But what about when the customer wants to sell the derivative to the bank: can you then assume he must know the inherent risks in the product otherwise he would not be considering the sale of it? Can you futher presuppose that because the client has a professional treasury department he is a 'professional'?

There are many arguments for and against further regulation, but they all condense into one question: should clients be protected from derivatives, should certain products be forbidden or restricted in order to protect the 'innocents' from themselves, or, if that is considered too extreme, to what extent should regulation go? Rudolf G. Mueller, Chairman of UBS, London, said: 'We must never lose sight of the guiding principle that willing buyers and sellers should carry responsibility for their own decisions'.

How will e-commerce affect the derivatives markets? Already the lines are becoming blurred between OTC and exchange-traded transactions as on-line dealing is opened up to a wider range of users.

The rivalry between established futures exchanges such as CBOT, LIFFE and the CME was knocked for six when EUREX, the totally electronic exchange, beat them all in terms of turnover.

By special request, this current edition includes three extra chapters: first, on credit derivatives (Chapter 8) – no longer the exotic playthings of investment bankers and hedge funds alike, but now the everyday work horse of the risk manager. This I hope will give an insight into the fairly esoteric world of credit spreads.

Second, risk and risk management (Chapter 9), written by Bernard Cowley – a very important area for anyone interested in more than just how to make money; what risks do these products open up?

Third, first principles of accounting for derivatives (Chapter 10), written by Deborah Morton-Dare, for all of you who need to know things such as how to account for the option premium.

Finally, a completely updated Chapter 11 from Tony Blunden, one of the market's leading international specialists, on the compliance function in a UK derivatives practitioner.

This book is written both for the new entrant into the City or other associated financial areas and for the seasoned professional who requires a refresher on the basics of derivatives. It is written without pages of equations and concentrates on the fundamentals, thereby making it easier to understand. This book will allow you to make considered decisions regarding the use (or otherwise) of these products. The aim is to demystify the subject. Not all derivatives will suit all end-users and not all banks will seek to make a market in all instruments. The key to using derivatives *successfully* is to use them *selectively*. But to be selective you need to be able to distinguish between them and see their individual key features, and to identify which one is most appropriate at that time. The ultimate choice of instrument will also be determined by the risk management culture within the company.

There is now even more jargon used when discussing derivatives. In order to assist the reader further, an updated glossary of terms can be found at the end of the book.

Acknowledgements

I think I can honestly say that preparing this second edition of *Mastering Derivatives Markets* has proved to be even harder than writing the original. Many things have changed in the intervening few years: people move on and become involved in other things, exchanges rise and fall, currencies disappear and the Euro takes their place.

A big thank you to Natasha Keats, Justin, Eva and Nicky at Bridge Information Systems and on the Bridge help-desk (also to Rich Martin who has now moved on). Without them, the many figures in this book would not have been possible. Antoine Kohler at Garban-Intercapital plc and Dave Orchard at Tullets have also kindly given me permission to use their real-time data for this book. The exchanges also allowed their source material to be used, so thanks also to LIFFE, IPE, NYMEX and CME.

Very special thanks also go to those who have helped in updating and advising on the text, notably Lee Oliver, Bridge News, Adrian Maconick, Jenny McLaughlin, International Petroleum Exchange and Warren Edwardes of Delphi Risk Management Ltd. My co-contributors are friends and colleagues and to them enduring thanks for making extra time in their busy schedules. They are Deborah Morton-Dare, Tony Blunden and Bernard Cowley.

Grateful thanks to Richard, Jonathan and Amanda at my publishers, Financial Times/Prentice Hall, who produced the finished article. Finally, thanks to Derek, Alex and Barbara who gave me the time to write this book and ensured things ran smoothly both at home and in Taylor Associates.

'Derivatives have been likened to aspirin: taken as prescribed for a headache, they will make the pain go away. If you take the whole bottle at once you may kill yourself.'

Background and Development of the Derivatives Market

INTRODUCTION

Those of you who are new, or comparatively new to international finance will be forgiven for thinking that derivative products have been around for ages. The word 'derivative' has only been in common usage for about the last nine years or so. Seasoned practitioners in this market will remember the terms, 'off-balance sheet instruments', 'financial products', 'risk management instruments' and 'financial engineering' – all meaning much the same thing, and all now covered by the expression 'derivative'. The term 'derivatives' is simply a new name for a tried and trusted set of risk management instruments. Unfortunately, some market participants, not only the banks who provide a service in these instruments, but also some end-users, have used these derivative products to speculate wildly.

Derivatives have been likened to aspirin: taken as prescribed for a headache, they will make the pain go away. If you take the whole bottle at once, you may kill yourself.

The expression 'derivative' covers any transaction where there is no movement of principal, and where the price performance of the derivative is driven by the price movement of an underlying commodity.

Definition	A **derivative instrument** is one whose performance is based (or derived) on the behaviour of the price of an underlying asset (often simply known as the 'underlying'). The underlying itself does not need to be bought or sold. A premium may be due.

Definition discussed

A true derivative instrument requires no movement of principal funds. It is this characteristic that makes them such useful tools to both hedge and to take risk, and why some years ago, these same instruments were known as off-balance sheet instruments. 'Off-balance sheet' signified that, as there was no movement of principal (e.g. no commitment to lend or take deposits), they did not have to appear on the company balance sheet. There are many types of derivative product and listed in Table 1.1 are some examples, together with their respective 'underlying asset'.

USES OF DERIVATIVES

Derivatives have many uses. A treasurer in a risk-averse organization may simply buy a currency option to hedge his currency risk, while another

Derivative products and their underlying commodities

Table 1.1

Derivative	Underlying
Currency options	Foreign exchange
Interest rate swaps	Government bonds, (e.g. UK gilts)
Interest rate futures	Implied forward interest rates
FT-SE 100 Futures	FT-SE 100 Index
Total return swaps	Credit risk

treasurer in a profit-centred organization may well sell options to speculate and earn premium income. The stories are legion of various companies and individuals losing their shirts in the currency market due to 'unforeseen' circumstances. If they are honest, they simply sold options hoping to keep the premium and 'beat' the market – but they lost!

RANGE OF DERIVATIVES

Exchange-traded versus OTC instruments

A derivative product can be either 'exchange traded', where a contract is bought or sold on a recognized exchange, or it can be over the counter (OTC). An OTC instrument is written or created by a bank (or sometimes corporate and other financial institutions), and tailored to suit the exact requirements of the client.

1. An exchange-traded instrument

This is an instrument that is bought or sold directly on an exchange such as LIFFE (the London International Financial Futures Exchange) or the CBOT (the Chicago Board of Trade). There are still over 30 recognized, regulated exchanges world-wide.

Each exchange-traded product has a 'contract specification', which details precisely the characteristics of the 'underlying', and who is under obligation to do what at maturity. Typical exchange-traded instruments include financial futures and listed options. These have historically been sold by a method of trading known as 'open outcry', which originated on the Chicago exchanges and entails face-to-face contact, hand signals and loud verbal agreements. This style of trading conveys 'price transparency' and allows every market participant to have equal access to the trade at the same price.

From mid-1998 there has been a shift away from open outcry trading towards electronic screen-based trading of exchange-traded derivatives. Many of the exchanges have grouped together into formal and informal alliances, for example:

- **EUREX**   SOFFEX and DTB (Swiss and German exchanges) Chicago Board of Trade and Eurex will launch a joint trading platform in mid-2000.

- **GLOBEX$_2$**   MATIF, SIMEX, CME, BM&F, Montreal Exchange (French, Singaporean, Chicago Mercantile, Brazilian and Montreal exchanges).

In the UK, LIFFE has developed an electronic trading platform called LIFFE CONNECT™ to encompass all the strategies, trades and nuances underpinning the traditional open outcry markets. Whereas the old PC-based trading – APT (automated pit trading) – used to cover about 5 per cent of the daily turnover, screen-based systems world-wide now tend to dominate the market.

On 19 November, 1999 LIFFE closed the pits where the short-term interest rate (STIR) futures were traded by open outcry. Hence forward all STIR trading will be done via computer. This was part of an ongoing plan to take trading on-screen.

2. An over the counter (OTC) instrument

This is a financial instrument that is sold by a bank (usually) to a client and tailored to fit a specific set of requirements. Occasionally, banks will purchase these products from companies or other non-banks, but each buyer and seller must take the credit risk of their counterparty.

An OTC product allows much greater flexibility in terms of expiry date, reference price, amount, underlying commodity, and vast amounts of transactions are executed every day. An OTC instrument can be very simple, in which case it is known as a 'vanilla' product, or it can be exceedingly complex. The price of the trade will be agreed upon between the parties, is confidential and will involve many factors.

Single versus multiple settlement

Derivatives also divide neatly into products where there is a single settlement at or during maturity, and those where there are multiple settlements throughout the transaction (see Table 1.2).

1. Single settlement

A single settlement product can only cover a specific 'tranche' of the underlying. For example, one of the interest rate derivatives is called a

Single and multiple settlement derivatives

Table 1.2

Single settlement	Multiple settlement
Financial futures / FRAs	Interest rate swaps
Interest rate options	Interest rate caps, collars, floors
Currency options	Currency swaps
Energy CFDs	Energy swaps

forward rate agreement (FRA). This is an interest rate derivative used by clients to protect themselves from adverse interest rate movements. Consider a company that needs to cover a US$5 million borrowing for three months which commences in six months' time. It would need to protect an interest rate which will not be set until six months into the future. There will be only one settlement at month 6 when the reference borrowing rate (3-month LIBOR) is settled against the derivative FRA rate.

2. Multiple settlement
Some customers and clients may have borrowings that run for longer periods, where the interest rate is reset to LIBOR every three or six months in line with the current interest rates. In such cases, the derivative chosen must allow for multiple fixings and multiple settlements on specific pre-determined dates.

Premium or non-premium based

Some derivatives require the payment of a premium, others do not. Any product where the buyer (client or bank) has paid a premium allows the buyer himself to decide what course of action to take at or during the maturity. The owner of the product; an option is a case in point, can 'abandon' the instrument if it offers an unfavourable rate: he is not compelled to transact at an adverse rate. Or, should the rate on the derivative be better, he can use the derivative instrument. He will always choose the alternative that offers him the best outcome.

'Derivatives is simply a new name for a tried and trusted set of risk management instruments.'

A premium-based instrument will guarantee for the client a worst or best case outcome, whereas a non-premium-based instrument offers an absolute rate which cannot be improved upon.

In general, anything you pay a premium for you can walk away from.

LIQUIDITY AND CREDIT RISK

Liquidity is an important concept in any tradable instrument, especially derivatives. It is an indicator of how likely one is to be able to sell or to buy the instrument at a particular point in time. Liquidity is undoubtedly far greater with exchange-traded products, and hundreds of thousands of contracts are bought and sold each day on the major exchanges. The chance therefore of finding willing buyers and sellers at a particular time and price is very good. Liquidity in the 'vanilla' OTC instruments is also good, but will be spread among many types of similar but non-identical transactions. As a result of this, as deals become more complex, liquidity will start to dry up, resulting in some deals being so complex and so 'structured' that there is really nil liquidity.

A frequently used expression in the market is that there is a price for buying, a price for selling, and a price for selling quickly.

Credit risk is another important factor. It is the risk that the counterparty to the deal may go into liquidation or default in some way before the contract matures, thus making it impossible for them to fulfil their obligations. Credit risk is lower with exchange-traded products as the clearing house (which is separate from the regulated exchange) becomes counterparty to every trade, reducing exposure to individual clients.

MARKET VOLUMES

Each contract whether exchange traded or OTC will have a 'notional value'; often known as the nominal principal amount (NPA). This is the amount of the underlying commodity whether financial, commodity or equity based, covered by the derivative. For example an interest rate option with an NPA of £5 million will cover a hedging or trading transaction of £5 million, but will not be the vehicle to lend the money or take the deposit. This is assumed to be transacted separately.

The notional value of OTC interest rate and currency swaps increased ten-fold from 1986–1992. This growth is much faster than in other segments of the market. In 1986 the notional value of interest rate and currency swap contracts was equal to about 25 per cent of the assets of international banks reporting to the Bank for International Settlements (BIS) in Basle. By the end of 1991 it was more than 100 per cent. Figures suggest that at least 50 per cent of bank exposure to derivatives is against other banks, as more and more institutions use the derivative markets for

> 'Liquidity is an important concept. A frequently used expression in the market is that there is a price for buying, a price for selling, and a price for selling quickly.'

their own risk management purposes. The BIS has identified a slowdown in the turnover growth of traditional banking markets, such as spot FX, while the market in futures options and swaps continues to grow rapidly.

The most recent survey by the BIS on the global OTC derivatives market shows that:

as at June 1999:	the total estimated notional amount of outstanding OTC contracts stood at US$81.5 trillion
as at December 1998:	the total estimated notional amount of outstanding OTC contracts stood at US$80 trillion (US$80,000,000,000,000)
as at June 1998:	the total estimated notional amount of outstanding OTC contracts stood at US$72 trillion.

From June to December 1998, the increase represents a rise of 11 per cent in only six months. But by June 1999 the position had stabilized – due fundamentally to the reduction in currency contracts which can be linked to the introduction of the Euro in January 1999. Also, interest rate swaps grew at a slower rate but this was more than made up for by an increase in the use of FRAs and interest rate options.

Another spectacular area of growth is in the commodity derivatives market. These products assist companies to reduce their exposure to price changes in energy (oil, gas, kerosene, bunkerfuel etc), or bullion (gold, silver and platinum), and even electricity. The embryo energy derivatives market was estimated at US$3 billion in 1986, and had reached approximately US$10 billion before the Iraqi invasion of Kuwait in 1990. It is now believed to total in excess of US$200 billion.

'Derivatives can be used for risk management or speculation, for risk mitigation, or risk taking.'

Introduction to Derivatives

Different types of derivatives

'Underlying' markets

Main implications of dealing with derivatives

Users of derivatives

Uses of derivatives

DIFFERENT TYPES OF DERIVATIVES

A derivative product can be used for risk management or speculation, for risk mitigation, or risk taking. The instrument itself can be bought or sold on an exchange or over the counter (OTC). There may be a premium payable for the product or it may be zero cost, and it may have one settlement or many. There are many variations to the basic 'vanilla' derivative, but essentially they break down into three key financial techniques, shown in Table 2.1.

Table 2.1

Derivatives: key financial techniques

	OTC	Exchange traded	Premium due
Futures	FRA	✔	No
Options	✔	✔	Yes
Swaps	✔	✕	No

You will notice that an instrument known as an FRA is included in the table. This is, in effect, an 'OTC financial future', where the financial future which comprises the 'raw material' is packaged to make it more user-friendly. Premiums are required only for option-based derivatives, and these are priced through a sophisticated computer model with multiple inputs. If a client chooses to transact an option for risk management purposes, then by paying a premium for his option, he is giving himself the chance to profit, as well as purchasing insurance for the transaction. Where there is no requirement to pay a premium such as on a swap or future, then a risk manager will be unable to profit, but will still have affected his insurance nonetheless. The old business adage 'You get what you pay for' is very relevant. An option gives a specific level of insurance as well as giving the customer the chance of some profit. He or she is assured of a guaranteed worst case, if the insurance is invoked, but his best case will be dependent on how far the market has moved in his favour. If the market improves, the client will 'abandon' the option and transact directly in the underlying cash market at a better rate.

Non-premium-based instruments 'lock' the client into a specific insurance rate, which is fixed for the duration of the transaction, and where the client is obligated to transact. He is unable to walk away from his commitments, whatever his personal circumstances.

'UNDERLYING' MARKETS

Each of these financial instruments can work in an 'underlying market'. The five primary derivatives markets, together with their relevant market share as at June 1999, are:

- interest rates (67%)
- foreign exchange (18%)
- equity (2%)
- commodity (0.6%)
- credit (not known).

Source: BIS, Basle

Recently, derivatives have developed into other areas, notably insurance, property, pollution credits, weather and earthquakes. However, many of these are applied techniques and are still proprietary, so fall outside the scope of this book.

MAIN IMPLICATIONS OF DEALING WITH DERIVATIVES

1a. Bank and customer credit risk – OTC transactions

OTC deals can result in a possible two-way cash flow on the settlement date, from either the bank to the client or vice versa, dependent on who has sold (or written) the instrument and in which direction the market has moved. The seller of the instrument must fulfil his obligations under the contract, this can result in cash payments to the purchaser. For example, with options, the purchaser's only obligation is to pay for the product, and this is all he can lose, whereas the seller must risk manage the resulting position.

> 'Derivatives can enhance the service offered by a bank to a client.'

Where clients take out or buy options as 'insurance' or risk management, there is no risk to them, other than that they may be unwilling or unable to pay the required premium, and if the client does not pay his premium he has no insurance. But where a client sells the derivative to a bank or other counterparty, he will receive the premium, and then he is opening himself up to commercial risk, and he will then have the responsibility for risk managing his derivative position. This is where many companies and banks have made losses. They sell an instrument for premium income which they regard as a profit. This is not the case; the premium should go towards the costs of risk managing the hedge position on the derivative. It is also easy to forget that by selling a derivative, the client or bank is giving himself an obligation to transact in the future at a specific price. A professional trader can tell if he has made a profit on the derivative that he sold to a client only at maturity – if there is any money left from the original premium payment. Unless an identical product was first bought from the market and then on-sold.

It is not just financially naive, but absurd to run derivatives positions without some hedging. But many speculators do just that.

Consider a company who have taken a view that interest rates will not go up. This is not a risk management position but a speculative trade, and an option derivative is 'sold' accordingly. This means that if interest rates stay the same or go down, the company will make money. But if they go up, the company will lose money. As the company did not perceive that rates could go up, this was not seen as a possible outcome, so no hedging was undertaken. Eventually if rates go up, they will suffer a loss which could be substantial.

A professional trader in the market may have the same view on interest rates, but is unlikely to run the position 'naked' or unhedged. If rates do turn against him and go up, he will either have an offsetting position to cover himself or another trade. He may not have been able to keep all of the premium but may have used some of it to buy himself insurance on his derivative position. His potential loss or downside is therefore limited.

1b. Choosing your counterparty

When a client is looking for a suitable bank with which to transact OTC business in derivatives, one question he must ask himself is: 'Am I comfortable with the credit risk of the counterparty bank? In simple terms, if I transact a five-year derivative product, am I confident that if the bank is due to pay me some money on a future date, that they will pay it, and pay it on time?' The client will essentially be taking a five-year view on the creditworthiness of the bank. Likewise, if a client wants to sell a ten-year derivative to a bank, the bank must be comfortable that if they purchase the product from the client, then the bank will receive any payment(s) due to them under the derivative in the future. They will be taking a ten-year view on the client. It is exceptionally difficult to forecast for one year, let alone ten years forward, so a whole department has grown up in the banks devoted to this subject – the credit department. For further details on credit risks on derivatives, see Chapter 8.

It is this concept of credit risk that is beginning to drive the market. Most of the big players in this market have got 'Double or Triple A'* ratings in their own right, and it is just as common for the clients to rate the banks, as it is for the banks to rate the customer. Consequently, if a client is asking for competitive prices, if the prices are all much the same, he will try and deal with the counterparty bank who has the best credit rating.

* A Standard & Poors rating conveying the best type of credit risk.

2. Bank and customer credit risk – exchange-traded transactions

The concept of credit risk does not vanish when you look at exchange-traded transactions. The risk is still there, but all the counterparties are the same. They all turn out to be the clearing house. In London, the London Clearing House (LCH) is owned by its members and regarded as being a very good risk. Whether you are buying or selling an exchange-traded instrument, it does not matter who is the client/bank on the other side of the transaction, your risk is always the clearing house.

3. Client relationships

Derivatives can enhance the service offered by a bank to a client. They can offer not only an extra dimension of risk management, but also permit a bank to continue dealing with a client where existing credit lines are 'full'. These are the lines that the bank credit department will allow for a particular client and will reflect the bank's appetite for his business. If the line is full, it means that the bank can transact no more business with that client. For example, if a customer wishes to transact some forward foreign exchange, but there is no more room available on the credit line, then it may be possible to sell him a currency option, without breaking the 'line' (assuming the client is willing to pay the premium). He will have the same level of hedging or risk management, but now he has some profit potential (although he must now pay a premium). The bank has no extra risk, once they have received the required premium. Offering a service in derivatives can also entice clients away from other banks, and other mainstream banking business may follow.

4. Gearing

Derivatives are often said to offer 'highly geared' positions. Just what does this mean? If a trader has a view that a particular currency is going to strengthen, then if he wishes to profit from his view, he could physically buy the particular currency, wait for it to increase in value, and then sell it at a profit. Derivatives offer an alternative. The trader could buy an option to purchase the currency at, say, a premium of 2 per cent of face value. If the currency increased in value, he could sell the option back to the writing bank (or exercise the option), and make the same profit as the original cash position (less the 2 per cent premium). But he has only laid out 2 per cent of principal for the same view on the market. So if his view turned out to be wrong, the most that he could lose is the original premium payment of 2 per cent.

> 'Anyone can sell a derivative (subject to their credit) and anyone can buy a derivative (subject to their paying for it).'

A cash trade would not only need 100 per cent of the amount committed at the beginning, but there is the possibility of substantial losses should the view be wrong. So by using the derivative he could take a position up to 50 times the size (50 × 2% = 100%) for the same original cash outlay, and if he was wrong he could lose the lot. But if he was right he would make 50 times the profits. In market jargon we say this position is *geared* by 50 times. It could offer the market movement multiplied by a factor of 50 times. A serious profit, if you are right. If you are wrong, all that is at risk is the premium (but that in turn may be substantial).

NB: It is rumoured that LTCM, the US hedge fund, had positions that were 100 times geared.

5. Compliance and regulation

Compliance is a term that came into being at the time the Financial Services Act was enacted in 1986. Banks needed senior staff whose role was to ensure that their banking business did not contravene any government or other regulations.

In the UK several financial regulators oversee different sectors of the financial markets. The government is introducing new laws to merge the existing self-regulatory organizations (SROs) into one organization known as the Financial Services Authority (FSA).

The first of these laws came into effect on 1 June, 1998 when the FSA took on responsibility from The Bank of England for the supervision of banks and wholesale money markets.

The three key SROs which will ultimately be merged into the FSA are:

- SFA: The Securities and Futures Authority regulates about 1,300 firms involved in all the City markets, i.e. stock market, Eurobonds, futures (financial and commodity), and also corporate finance specialists. About half of the firms are overseas owned.

- IMRO: The Investment Managers' Regulatory Organisation regulates about 1,100 fund managers, unit and investment trust managers and trustees, pension fund managers and managers of unregulated collective investment schemes.

- PIA: The Personal Investment Authority regulates about 4,000 firms including independent financial advisors, all of whom are involved in advising on and arranging deals for private investors.

For further details on compliance, see Chapter 11.

USERS OF DERIVATIVES

There are many different types of 'users' in this market.

1. Hedgers

These may be anyone from a small to medium-sized corporation with a currency exposure that they wish to protect, to a large multinational with a $500m borrowing that needs interest rate protection, to a French fund manager who is worried about the domestic stock market falling. Hedgers generally will 'buy' the insurance. This is a global market and derivatives easily cross borders.

2. Traders

The banking fraternity predominates here, although not all banks will make a market in all derivative products. Their role is to create the derivative, at a price, sell it to the client, run their positions at a profit, and hedge themselves. Traders will also speculate in the inter-bank market.

3. Private clients

Individuals who have funds 'under management' with one of the large financial institutions may use derivatives to enhance their yield, or maybe to take out speculative positions. Decisions may be taken by the banker or the individual in concert or in isolation.

4. Arbitrageurs

Individuals or banks who try and identify price discrepancies and profit from them. This is not confined solely to the derivatives market.

Anyone can sell a derivative (subject to their credit), and anyone can buy a derivative (subject to their 'paying' for it).

- Companies can sell derivatives to banks for income, and take on risk, or they can purchase derivatives and pay someone else to take their risk.
- Banks can write derivatives and sell them to clients for profit, or they can purchase them from clients for their own strategic or speculative purposes, or they can trade them inter-bank.

Typical derivatives users include:

- supranationals (World Bank, European Development Bank, African Development Bank, etc.)
- governments
- government agencies
- banks (for their own or client positions)
- financial institutions
- companies
- high net worth individuals
- private clients
- hedge funds.

USES OF DERIVATIVES

A selection of applications for derivatives includes:

- taking on credit risk without the loan
- protecting against a possible dollar devaluation (or any other currency)
- profiting from a potential increase in the value of the Euro (or any other currency)
- protecting a stock market portfolio from a downturn in the stock market
- taking a view on the upswing of the Nikkei (or any other) stock index
- protecting an interest rate exposure for five years at a fixed insurance rate
- choosing a FX rate to use when submitting a foreign currency tender
- enhancing the yield on a non-performing investment
- offering a fixed rate mortgage product
- insuring against an upward movement in interest rates
- fixing an investment rate now, when the investment does not start until a future date
- speculating as a private client on the foreign exchanges with minimal risk.

'There are a whole range of interest rate derivatives which can be used to cover anything from an overnight exposure to one lasting 75 years.'

Interest Rate Derivatives

INTRODUCTION

There are a whole range of interest rate derivatives, which can be used to cover anything from an overnight exposure to one lasting 75 years (honestly!). Some of these products have only one reference fixing within their timescale, whilst others are capable of multiple fixings. Generally, the longer the maturity of the underlying transaction, the more likely it is that the product needs to have multiple fixings. The range of instruments is shown in Table 3.1.

Table 3.1

Range of interest rate derivatives

	Settlement	
Interest rate derivative	Single	Multiple
Financial futures	✓	
Forward rate agreements (FRAs)	✓	
Interest rate options	✓	
Interest rate caps, collars floors		✓
Interest rate swaps		✓
Interest rate swap options (swaptions)	✓	

Interest rate derivatives can be used to hedge (risk manage), or to take risk (speculate).

What is interest rate risk?

The risk is either of increased funding costs for borrowers, or of reduced yields for investors. Short-term volatility, and the unpredictability of interest rates led the banks and the financial exchanges to create 'an explosion' of financial instruments. Each of these instruments has a different set of characteristics for hedging interest rate risk on both loans and deposits, in different global currencies in both the short and the long term.

The main choices facing a borrower or depositor are the following:

- Do nothing – and wait.

- Fix the rate of interest by means of an option-type product, where a premium is due.

- Fix the rate of interest by means of a zero-premium product, such as an FRA or a future.

Before a definitive choice can be made, it is necessary to look at the maturity of the underlying transaction and the range of instruments available to cover the risk. In an interest rate market, the maturity profile in any currency is generally subdivided as shown in Figure 3.1 and Table 3.2.

The maturity profile

Fig 3.1

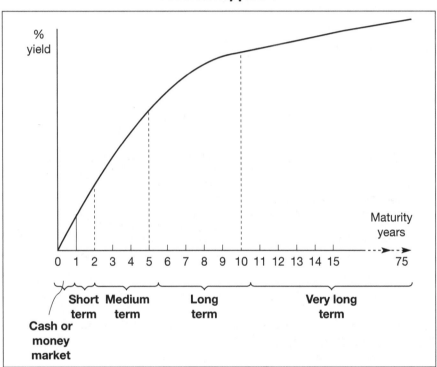

How the maturity profile is subdivided

Table 3.2

0–1 years	Cash or money market
1–2 years	Short term
2–5 years	Medium term
5–10 years	Long term
10–75 years	Very long term

Fig 3.2

Scope of operation of interest rate derivatives

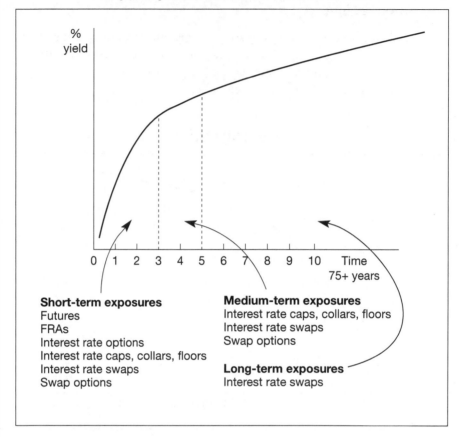

Risk management techniques also follow a similar pattern, as shown in Figure 3.2 and Table 3.3.

Table 3.3

Pattern of risk management techniques

0–2 to 3 years	Financial futures, FRAs, interest rate options caps, collars, floors, swaps, swap options
3–5 years	Caps, collars, floors, swaps, swap options
5–10 years	Swaps and to a lesser extent caps
10–75 years	Swaps

Once the maturity of the underlying exposure extends beyond 24 months, realistically the derivative needs to cater for multiple fixings, leading to swaps, interest caps, and the other products just mentioned.

YIELD CURVES

A yield curve is a graphical expression of interest yields against time. In the USA this is known as the 'term structure of interest rates'. It is usually drawn using the gross redemption yield on risk-free instruments such as government bonds, e.g., UK gilts and UK treasury bills, or US treasury bills and US treasury bonds. The shape of the yield curve (see Figure 3.3) is an important consideration when choosing whether or not to use derivatives. An upward sloping yield curve (positive) is one where, as the maturity lengthens, interest rates increase as investors seek higher yields for locking up their money for longer periods at fixed rates. A downward sloping yield curve (negative) is one where as the maturity lengthens, the less reward the investor gets and the cheaper borrowing becomes. This type of curve is usually an indicator of reducing inflationary tendencies. A flat yield curve indicates a stable inflationary environment – not necessarily a zero inflation rate.

Different types of yield curve

Fig 3.3

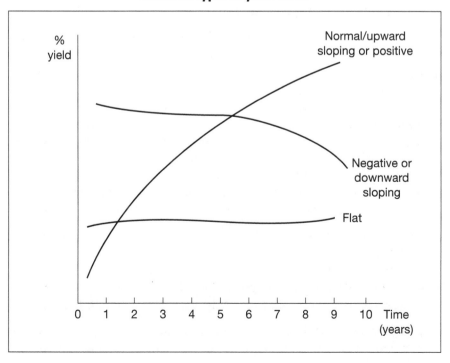

SINGLE SETTLEMENT INTEREST RATE DERIVATIVES

This section will concentrate upon single settlement interest rate derivatives. These are instruments which have only one settlement/fixing during the life of the transaction and are typically used to hedge or trade shorter maturities. The instruments consist of:

- financial futures
- forward rate agreements (FRAs)
- interest rate options (IROs).

FINANCIAL FUTURES CONTRACTS

Introduction

Futures have been around in various guises for over 100 years. Originally based on agricultural commodities, there are now many different varieties. In the early 1970s futures became respectable, with the opening of 'regulated exchanges' around the world. The two oldest exchanges are both American and both based in Chicago:

- Chicago Mercantile Exchange (CME)
- Chicago Board of Trade (CBOT).

In the 1980s other countries followed suit and opened their own national exchanges, each trading their own specific brand of domestic and international contracts.

Not all futures contracts trade on all exchanges and many have contracts specifically designed for their own domestic market. Some futures contracts are international and offered globally around the world. Some even have their administration systems linked, and are known as 'fungible'. This means that you can open a position in one financial centre and close it in another; for example it is possible to sell a Eurodollar future on the CME and close out the position by buying it back on SIMEX in Singapore.

During 1998 the big futures exchanges in terms of traded volumes were:

1 Chicago Board of Trade (CBOT) – keynote contract, US treasury bond (T. Bond)
2 London International Financial Futures and Options Exchange (LIFFE) – keynote contract, German government bond (Bund)
3 Chicago Mercantile Exchange (CME) – keynote contract, Eurodollar.

LIFFE opened in 1982 and 15 years later, in June 1997, ranked the second largest in the world, turning over in excess of a million contracts per day.

Who would have believed that these vast institutions of marble and steel, home to thousands of employees every day would, in effect, have to almost close their doors a matter of just a few years later?

Floor-based trading is people intensive and people cost money. For some years there have been rumblings about the need for technological changes and the demise of open outcry. But it took EUREX, the entirely digital exchange created in 1997 from the Deutsche Terminbörse (DTB), in Germany, and SOFFEX, the Swiss exchange, to crystallize people's hopes and fears.

In January 1999 the trading volumes at EUREX overtook those of the Chicago Board of Trade, long regarded as the 'Rolls-Royce' of exchanges. LIFFE as well as the CBOT, CME and many other smaller exchanges will have to adapt or die.

The adaptation continues in 2000 and it is not yet clear whether EUREX itself will survive, or whether it simply acted as a catalyst for change.

(Any reader seeking a more in-depth look at these changes is recommended to read *Capital Market Revolution* by Patrick Young and Thomas Theys, (1999), published by Financial Times/Prentice Hall.)

The financial future is the building block for interest rate exposure management techniques (derivatives). Futures are primarily used by banks, other financial institutions and large multinational companies to hedge and trade interest rate positions. Some smaller companies will use futures from time to time, but there are some economies of scale that may make futures expensive for an occasional small user. Many types of futures exist globally, and this book will focus on those of a financial nature.

The five largest financial exchanges in terms of current traded volume in 1999 were:

1 EUREX
2 Chicago Board of Trade (CBOT)
3 Chicago Mercantile Exchange (CME)
4 Matif/Paris Bourse
5 London International Financial Futures Exchange (LIFFE).

Confusion abounds regarding the format used by the exchanges when they release their data to the market. So much for 'transparency'.

On 2 August, 1999, EUREX announced that it had traded 35.6 million contracts in July, and in the six months from January to July 1999, trading amounted to 213 million contracts.

The following day, 3 August, 1999, EUREX announced (for the seventh consecutive month) higher volumes in Bund futures –14.2 million – compared to the CBOT, which traded 6.4 million US treasury bond futures.

The day after that, on 4 August, 1999, LIFFE announced the nominal value of contracts traded was £194 billion per day during July 1999.

To put this in context, a press article from Lee Oliver at Bridge News (by kind permission of BridgeNews, a unit of Bridge Information Systems) follows.

BRIDGE FOCUS: CONFUSION CLOUDS DERIVATIVES EXCHANGES' MARCH DATA

DATE: April 13,1999
By Lee Oliver, Bridge News

London–Apr 13–Recently published figures for March from Europe's 3 leading derivatives exchanges make interesting, if slightly confusing reading. With competition between the 3 exchanges extremely fierce, each is determined to highlight its successes and outdo its rivals.

However, differences in reporting monthly figures make comparisons extremely difficult.

EUREX, the German/Swiss exchange, was, as usual, the first to issue figures for March when it reported that it had become the first exchange ever to trade more than 30 million contracts in a month. The exchange saw its volume soar to a record 33.8 million contracts traded, beating its previous figure of 28.25 million contracts set in September, 1998.

Turnover, in terms of contracts traded, rose by an annualized 74.0%.

The Exchange said impressive growth was posted across its range of products, but much of the success stemmed from the popularity of the Bund future, a contract based on German 10-year government bonds.

The London International Financial Futures and Options Exchange, (LIFFE), which has taken to headlining its activity in terms of the nominal value of its contracts traded, was the next to report. However, in terms of the number of contracts traded, LIFFE reported an annualized decline of 44.0% with just 11.9 million lots changing hands.

The Paris-based MATIF was the next to step up to the plate. It reported an impressive monthly surge in contracts traded of 20.0%, as volume rose to 16 million lots turned over. In March 1998, MATIF managed a turnover of just 6 million contracts.

Many industry watchers were surprised by the strong pick-up in activity from what most consider is becoming more and more of a peripheral player.

But, under closer scrutiny, all of the 3 exchanges' figures need to be taken with a liberal pinch of salt.

By reporting in terms of contracts traded, EUREX was clearly Europe's, and probably the world's, leading derivatives exchange.

However, EUREX's reported turnover made no mention of the smaller contract size of its blue riband Bund future as a result of Economic and Monetary Union (EMU).

The euro-denominated Bund is only 4/5 the size of the Deutsche mark-denominated contract, which ceased to exist at the start of March.

But EUREX would still have had a record month even if it had accounted for this factor.

However, the figures from MATIF have caused considerable controversy and debate within the market.

In terms of the number of contracts traded, MATIF appeared to have raced past LIFFE and assumed the position of the number 2 European derivatives exchange.

MATIF's surge in volumes was based on the success of its equity products. Reported volume of the exchange's CAC-40 long-term option was a staggering 6.1 million lots.

But after much probing, MATIF admitted that the tick size of this product was a modest 1 euro. In comparison, LIFFE's FTSE options have a tick size of 10 sterling, or 14.92 euro. MATIF denied it was indulging in creative accounting by reducing the size of its contracts.

However, there seems little point in comparing different exchanges if their products have such different nominal values. Therefore, **LIFFE's** decision to headline its figures in terms of nominal value traded appears fully justified.

The annual decline in the number of contracts traded at **LIFFE** stemmed from 2 major factors:

The first was the total migration of Bund futures dealing to EUREX. LIFFE can do little about this, which is a harsh reality of competing in a global marketplace.

However, the second factor which has also had a significant impact on the number of contracts traded at LIFFE, stemmed from EMUs introduction.

Before the launch of the single currency, euromark futures, based on the 3-month Deutsche mark money market deposit rate, had a contract size of 1 million Deutsche marks. Its replacement, EURIBOR, had a contract size of 1 million euro, virtually double the size of the old euromark short-term interest rate product (STIR).

The nominal value of **LIFFE's** key STIRs has doubled, and this has resulted in a decline in the number of contracts traded.

This detail is not immediately apparent if figures are reported in terms of the number of contracts traded. Therefore, not surprisingly, **LIFFE** is now keen to report its figures in terms of nominal value.

A **LIFFE** official said: 'Reporting in nominal value terms is probably closer to the relevant facts'.

LIFFE's turnover in nominal value terms was 5.16 trillion stlg (7.7 trillion euro) in March.

Both **EUREX** and **MATIF** were happy to report their figures in a similar manner. **EUREX** said it traded a nominal 4 trillion euro, while **MATIF** slipped back to third spot with a nominal 622 billion euro dealt.

Few would seriously believe that **LIFFE** is currently more successful that **EUREX**. Reporting figures in this manner clearly also fails to tell the whole story. The relative sizes of the different exchange's contracts also distorts the figures when they are reported in nominal value terms.

For instance, **LIFFE's** most actively-traded product, **EURIBOT**, has a nominal value 10 times the size of **EUREX's** Bund. But the commission charged for trading EURIBOR is not 10 times that for trading Bunds.

And calculating the nominal value of equity products traded is largely dependent on the level of the cash index on which the contract is based. The nominal value is derived from multiplying the contract's tick size, volume trade and level of the cash index.

Therefore, the higher the cash index on which the equity products are based, the greater the reported nominal value traded. If a particular stock index moves significantly, it will have a major impact on the reported nominal value traded at any one exchange.

So what is the fairest way to report the figures so comparisons can be made about various different exchanges?

A spokesman for **EUREX** said: 'It is common to compare the number of contracts traded. However, that neglects the fact that contract values can differ from exchange to exchange.'

He added: 'If you want to make comparisons, perhaps the best way would be to compare growth rates.

'However, this is only valid if like-with-like comparisons can be made. If an exchange alters its contract sizes, this type of comparison is invalid.'

What seems clear is the exchanges – particularly the less successful ones – are getting more and more adept at putting a spin on their numbers.

Reporting in terms of contracts or nominal value traded clearly does little to reveal the true health of a derivatives exchange.

At a time when the market is generally pressing for greater transparency, perhaps the best way to report would be to do so in terms of revenue generated.

Whether all exchanges would agree, remains to be seen.

Bridge News, a unit of Bridge Information Systems
Tel: +44-20-7842-4218

However, whatever the pros and contras of electronic tradings when a client decides to look at using futures to hedge or take interest rate risk, he/she must choose whether they wish to protect a long-term interest rate such as that applying to a UK gilt or a US treasury bond with a 10- to 15-year maturity, or a short-term interest rate such as 3-month LIBOR.

In London the available futures on LIFFE cover:

- Short-term rates   Euribor, Eurolibor, Sterling, Euroswiss, Euroyen (TIBOR and LIBOR)
- Long-term rates   UK government bond (5 year and long gilt)
  (fixed income)   Italian government bond
        Japanese government bond
        German government bond
- Synthetic swaps   EuriborFinancedBond (5 and 10 year)
- Equity products   –   FT-SE 100 and FT-SE 250
        European indices:
           FT-SE Eurotop 100 and 300, FT-SE
           Eurobloc 100,
           FT-SE EstarsIndex
           MSCI
- Commodities   Cocoa, coffee, sugar, wheat, barley, potato
        BIFFEX (freight index).

Definition   *A **financial futures contract** is a legally binding agreement to make or take delivery of a standard quantity of a specific financial instrument, at a future date, and at a price agreed between the parties through open outcry on the floor of an organized exchange.*

Definition discussed

To understand futures fully we need to open up this definition. With a financial future, each contract has its own specification – a type of contract description. This is so that both buyers and sellers of the future know what is expected of them and what obligations they must perform. Each future will also have a fixed 'contract amount' to make it easy to determine how many futures are required for the hedge/trade. It is not possible to trade in parts of contracts: you have to sell/buy whole numbers of futures contracts. The contract specification determines the specific financial instrument in question, and the trade will come about as willing buyers and willing sellers come together to transact business. Futures trade on every business day except public holidays, and prices will fluctuate with supply and demand. The price agreed between two traders today will be for 'delivery' on a particular date in the future. The term 'delivery' is still used although most of these contracts are no longer physically delivered (perhaps 1 to 2 per cent will go to delivery). There is usually a cash settlement of the differences between the buying and the selling price. Delivery now denotes contract expiry.

Method of trading – 'open outcry'

For some time, the method of trading adopted by most of the exchanges around the world was based on the Chicago method of 'open outcry': Colourful to watch, very professional, conveying 'price transparency' by allowing every trader equal access to the same trade at the same price. Technically the meaning of open outcry is that your bid or your offer is good 'while the breath is warm'. What this actually means is that each trader on the exchange will shout out what trade he is trying to execute. He is not able to just shout it once and assume everyone has heard him, he must keep shouting. If he stops shouting, it is assumed that he no longer wishes to execute his trade at that price level. Everyone around him is also shouting, resulting in a lot of noise without too much clarity. The consequence of this is that not only do traders have to shout continuously what trades they are trying to fill, they must also 'hand signal' their trades, in case a trader a long way away cannot hear clearly. The hands and the mouth must say the same thing. Traders cannot just trade with hand signals and they must take examinations to comply with the requirements of the respective exchanges (see Figure 3.4).

'The financial future is the building block for interest rate exposure management techniques (derivatives).'

To simplify matters, the exchange requires that if you wish to trade in a certain futures contract you must physically stand in a 'pit' designated solely for that contract. This is a smallish area which is often hexagonally shaped with two or three small steps leading down into the centre. On a busy day the pit may hold 100 traders; on a quiet day the same pit may hold only ten traders.

Method of trading – electronic trading

As already noted, in the last few years there has been a shift away from 'open outcry' trading towards the order-driven screen based trading familiar to users of the stock exchange. New technology now makes it possible to reach more people with more products than ever before.

Fig 3.4

Four basic hand signals

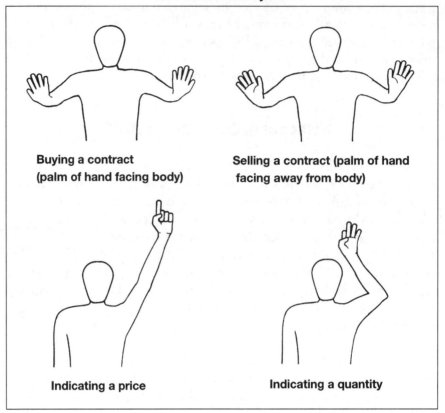

Buying a contract
(palm of hand facing body)

Selling a contract (palm of hand
facing away from body)

Indicating a price

Indicating a quantity

Source: Chicago Mercantile Exchange

In the late 1990s the first shots in the electronic vs open outcry conflict were fired by the DTB (Deutsche Terminbörse) in its battle, with London-based LIFFE, for market share in the lucrative German government bond futures. DTB offered to its clients screen-based trading from the clients' own offices. Initially, the critical factor in choosing between the traditional open outcry markets and screen-based trading was down to speed and cost, with those in favour of screen trading claiming that open outcry markets were outdated, cumbersome, slow and expensive, citing research which showed very significant cost savings. They claimed that trading through the DTB was many times cheaper than trading the same contract on LIFFE.

Now the cynics argue that the real reason the major banks want to trade on-screen is so that they can offer more enhanced services to their top customers through electronic trading than they ever could before, thus earning for themselves more fee income with lower risk.

In any event, traders (from mostly non-UK banks) voted with their feet and soon the DTB had the higher turnover in the fiercely competitive government bond futures markets.

In self-defence, LIFFE developed its own electronic trading platform called LIFFE CONNECT™, and on 22 November, 1999, such is the pace of change, all STIR contracts were moved to on-screen trading.

The development of the electronic marketplace has been aided by the rush for the major derivatives exchanges to consolidate. On 24 June, 1999, the Chicago Board of Trade finally agreed to proceed with an alliance CBOT-EUREX which should be fully operational by mid-2000.

One of the key aspects of the new electronic market is anonymity. Traders will not know whose orders they are trading against, which is, of course, completely different from the open outcry market.

The system will match orders in the central order book and the matching criterion used will be one of the following:

1 Price and time priority:
   • highest bid/lowest offer has priority over other orders in the same contract
   • first order at a price has priority over others
2 Price and pro-rata:
   • highest bid/lowest offer has priority over other orders in the same contract
   • all orders at a price have the same priority, orders are filled in proportion to their volume.

Short-term futures contracts

Key features

Market
Futures are traded on a regulated exchange with standard contract sizes and specific delivery dates. Trades are executed by a member firm or broker physically on the floor of the relevant exchange or via a computer terminal.

Contracts
Different contracts are available in major currencies on each exchange. They cover both the long and short ends of the yield curve and some exchanges offer contracts on equities, equity indices, and even electricity.

Pricing
It is a competitive auction-based market and prices are quoted on an index basis as a bid offer spread. For example, if the three-month implied interest rate from December to March is 8 per cent, then the futures price is quoted as:

$$100.00 - 8.00 = 92.00$$

Market operations

Both buyers and sellers must put up minimum levels of collateral for each open contract that they hold. This is known as 'initial margin'. The actual level is calculated by the relevant exchange in conjunction with the clearing house. The method used to calculate the level is the standard portfolio analysis of risk (SPAN) system. This was originally developed by the CME to monitor how risky particular positions had become. The level of initial margin is quoted as so much per open contract, say £750 per contract, and can change if market volatility changes. Initial margin will be returned with interest when the position is closed out.

Positions are 'marked-to-market' on a daily basis by comparing the level on the client's trade and the settlement price on the day. Profits or losses are crystallized daily. If a position loses money during the day, the client must pay his losses that day. If the position is in profit on that day, the client will receive his profit payment that day. These daily payments are known as 'variation margin'.

Credit risk

Once a trade is executed on the floor of the regulated exchange (virtual or physical), it is entered into a matching system. In London this is known as the Trade Registration System (TRS), and it is used by both the International Petroleum Exchange (IPE) and LIFFE. Once a trade has been successfully matched, the London Clearing House (LCH), which is a separate entity to the exchange itself, provides the clearing mechanism for the futures trades. It is the Clearing House who will call for margin from market participants and their brokers, and ultimately each trade will eventually end up as a trade between the buyer/seller and the Clearing House. This is illustrated in Figure 3.5.

Availability

There are a number of different financial futures contracts, and it is advisable to check with the exchange in question exactly which contracts they offer.

Using short-term interest rate futures

To illustrate more clearly how this works, the contract specification of the three-month sterling contract is shown in Table 3.4. This is known colloquially as the 'short' sterling contact.

The clearing process

Fig 3.5

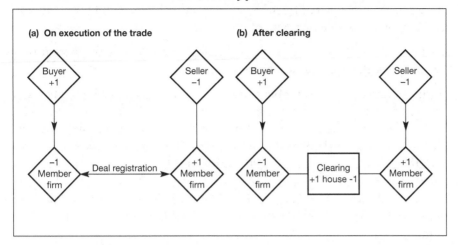

(a) On execution of the trade   (b) After clearing

Three-month sterling (short sterling) interest rate future – abbreviated contract specification

Table 3.4

Unit of trading	£500,000
Delivery months	March, June, September, December
Delivery day	First business day after the last trading day
Last trading day	11.00 hrs, third Wednesday of the delivery month
Quotation	100 minus rate of interest
Minimum price movement	0.01% known as a 'tick'
Tick value	£12.50
Trading hours	08.05 – 18.00
Trading platform	LIFFE CONNECT

Source: LIFFE

What exactly are we trading?
The short sterling interest rate future is based on a notional 8-month deposit transaction. Notional because the future will not actually lend the client the money.

The price agreed in the pit between the traders sets the interest rate for the deal. Each single contract has a notional value of £500,000, and you can buy or sell whole numbers of contracts.

Note: All futures contracts settle to LIBOR not LIBID even though they are notional deposit transactions.

Futures contracts are available to mature in March, June, September and December, for the next five years. These are called the 'delivery' months.

The delivery date is the actual date in the month when the contracts expire (like the settlement day on a FRA). The third Wednesday in the month is usually around the 19th, 20th or 21st of the month, and it is on this date that the financial futures price is finally settled at the exchange delivery settlement price (EDSP). It is only on this date that the actual 3-month LIBOR fixing (at 11.00 hours) will match the futures price.

In the market, futures traders are acting on behalf of speculators, hedgers and arbitrageurs. Some may believe that rates will increase, others that rates will decrease. The bid–offer spread quoted will reflect the market view of what 3-month LIBOR will be on the delivery date. Not what it is today, but what it will be in the future. This is known as the implied forward rate or the implied interest rate. Obviously some traders may think that interest rates in the future will be higher, some may think they will be lower. The actual interest rate will not be known until the delivery date when the 3-month LIBOR fixing will match the underlying futures price.

All short-term futures contracts are quoted on an 'index basis'. If the market believes that the 3-month LIBOR on 20 June 2001 will be 6.27 per cent, then the future will be trading at that point in time at 100.00 – 6.27 = 93.73. This may seem confusing, but futures contracts are designed so that you can 'buy low, sell high' and make a profit. This method of price quotation reverses the behaviour of futures prices. If a trader anticipates that interest rates are going to fall, he would expect the futures price to rise. Therefore he would want to buy the future now and sell it when it was higher, making a profit on the difference between the rates. How much profit he will make depends on how many 'ticks' he has made, each tick representing a market movement of 0.01 per cent.

A futures trading transaction

At the beginning of October a trader feels that sterling interest rates will fall as year end approaches. The current 3-month LIBOR rate today is, say, 6.25 per cent, the implied forward interest rate is 6.15 per cent, so the futures markets are already discounting (or assuming) a fall in rates. She wishes to make a profit from predicting a short-term downward movement in rates; her trading amount is £5 million.

Action

Buy 10 December 3-month sterling interest rate futures at the current trading level of $100 - 6.15 = 93.85$.

Outcome

On the third Wednesday in December, the price for the DEC futures contract is 95.35 in line with the current 3-month LIBOR rate of 4.65 per cent. The trader decides to close out her position, so she will need to sell ten futures contracts, at the closing level of 95.35.

Profit or loss?

The view on the market was correct and interest rates did fall. Our trader has made a profit.

Opening futures level	93.85 (bought)
Closing futures level	95.35 (sold)
Profit	**1.50, or 150 ticks**

What is this profit worth in real money?

The trader has made a profit of

10 contracts × 150 ticks × £12.50 each tick

a total of £18,750.

If our trader had put on the same trade, but the view on the market was wrong, and interest rates had increased rather than decreased, she would have lost a number of ticks on the position, as she would have originally bought the futures at the same level of 93.85, but she would have then sold them lower down, resulting in a loss.

Tick values

Each tick on each futures contract has a monetary value: in the case of short sterling futures, it is £12.50. Where does the £12.50 come from? It is the notional contract size multiplied by the length of time of the three-month notional time deposit underlying the contract in years (i.e., 3/12) multiplied by the minimum tick size movement of 0.01 per cent.

$$£500,000 \times 0.01\% \times 3/12 = £12.50$$

The trading units (contract sizes) and tick values for short-term contracts currently traded are shown in Table 3.5.

Table 3.5 **Trading units and tick values for short-term futures contracts**

Contract	Trading unit	Tick value	Tick size
Three-month EuroLibor	€1,000,000	€12.50	0.005
Three-month Euribor	€1,000,000	€12.50	0.005
Three-month EuroYen	YEN 100,000,000	YEN 1,250	0.005
Three-month EuroSwiss franc	Sfr 1,000,000	Sfr 25	0.01
Three-month sterling	£500,000	£12.50	0.01

Source: LIFFE

Market structure

Each futures exchange is set up in a similar way. Members of the exchanges are those firms who have joined the 'club' and in effect paid a membership fee. The specific nature of their membership will allow them to trade futures or options or both, and will be a determining factor on how many people can be employed trading for that member company. Membership is not restricted to domestic companies and most exchanges around the world have a complex mix of nationalities and cultures, banks, institutions and others.

In an open outcry market, trading members of staff of the member firms are entitled to wear distinctive coloured jackets, the idea being that if a trader is dealing across a pit with another member firm, he may not know the individual in question, but he will recognize the jacket. Non-trading members of the firm who may be in a support role will wear a different coloured jacket. In London this is an orange-yellow colour, and these staff are known as 'yellow jackets'. Traders who are self-employed wear a plain red jacket and are known as 'locals'. These are the individuals who are buying and selling futures (or options) for their own account, adding liquidity to the market. The exchange also employ their own people who are known as 'pit observers'; their role is to ensure, first, an orderly market, and, second, that trading is conducted 'professionally'. These personnel are dressed in blue and are equally distinctive. The open outcry method of trading can get very enthusiastic when busy, and everyone needs to have equal access to the price. The pit observers can 'police' trading to ensure that this happens.

There is a very real possibility that open outcry trading may cease altogether in some centres.

Market operations – open outcry

Fig 3.6

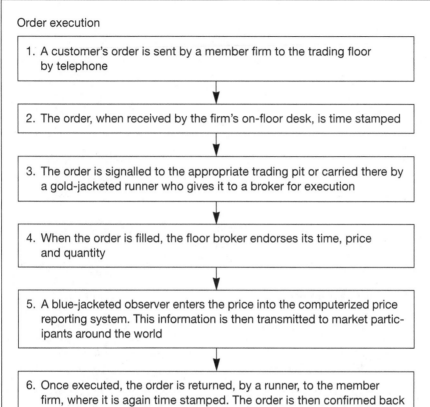

Source: Chicago Mercantile Exchange

Market operations – electronic trading

Using LIFFE CONNECT™ as an example – the new market will be anonymous and order driven with orders being automatically matched.

All orders will be received by the 'trading host', which provides the matching, trade reporting and price dissemination. To access the host, participants will need the appropriate trading application. Many independent software vendors (ISVs) such as Reuters and EasyScreen have developed their own applications.

Some examples of electronic trading follow.

Figure 3.7 shows when an order is submitted, the system's actions are dependent on the type of order entered and whether or not there is an order already in the central order book that the new order can match with.

In this example assume a central order book that already has a limit order to pay 94.25 for 500 MAR00 BTP futures.

Fig 3.7

A simple price/time priority matching trade

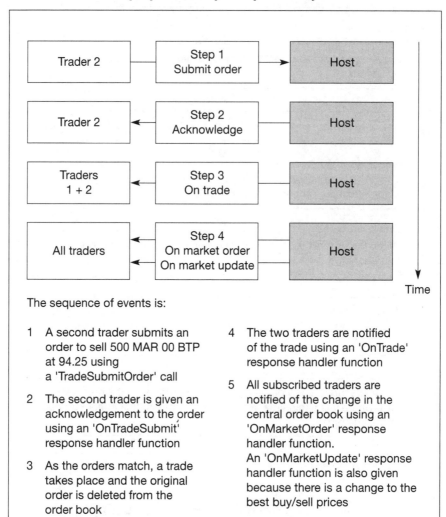

The sequence of events is:

1   A second trader submits an order to sell 500 MAR 00 BTP at 94.25 using a 'TradeSubmitOrder' call

2   The second trader is given an acknowledgement to the order using an 'OnTradeSubmit' response handler function

3   As the orders match, a trade takes place and the original order is deleted from the order book

4   The two traders are notified of the trade using an 'OnTrade' response handler function

5   All subscribed traders are notified of the change in the central order book using an 'OnMarketOrder' response handler function. An 'OnMarketUpdate' response handler function is also given because there is a change to the best buy/sell prices

Source: LIFFE

Given the same market situation as in Figure 3.7, the sequence is more complicated if the second trader wants to sell only 300 lots and at 94.30

A partially filled order

Fig 3.8

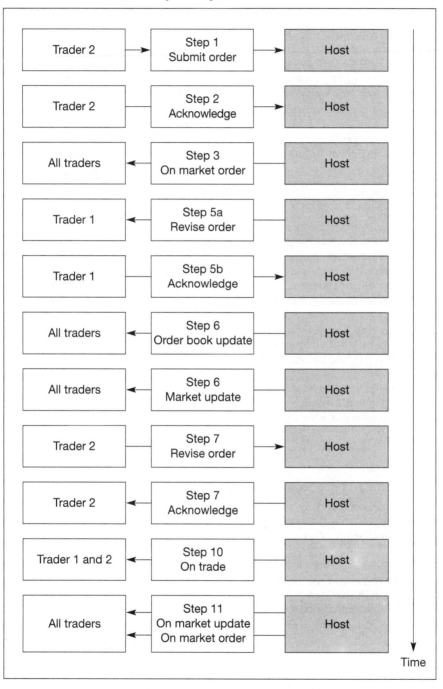

Fig 3.8

Continued

The explanation of this sequence of events is:

1 A second trader submits an order to sell 300 MAR 98 BTP at 94.30. The system puts the order into the central order book

2 The system sends an acknowledgement of the order to the second trader using a 'OnTradeSubmit' response handler function

3 All subscribed traders are notified of the order book update using an 'OnMarketOrder' response handler function, and a 'MarketUpdate' because a best buy/sell price has changed

4 The orders do not match, and both orders are kept in the central order book pending further trader action

5 The first trader revises the order, to pay 94.27, using a 'TradeReviseOrder' call and gets an acknowledgement using an 'OnTradeRevise' response handler function

6 All subscribed traders are sent an 'OrderBookUpdate' and a 'Market Update' because a best buy/sell price has changed

7 The second trader revises the order, to sell at 94.27, using a 'TradeReviseOrder' call and gets an acknowledgement using an 'OnTradeRevise' RHF call

8 As the orders now match in price, a trade takes place for 300 lots at 94.27

9 The order to sell 300 lots is deleted and the central order book shows the residual order to pay 94.27 for 200 lots

10 Both traders receive an 'OnTrade' response handler function

11 All traders receive both an 'OnMarketUpdate' and an "OnMarketOrder' response handler function

Continued

Fig 3.8

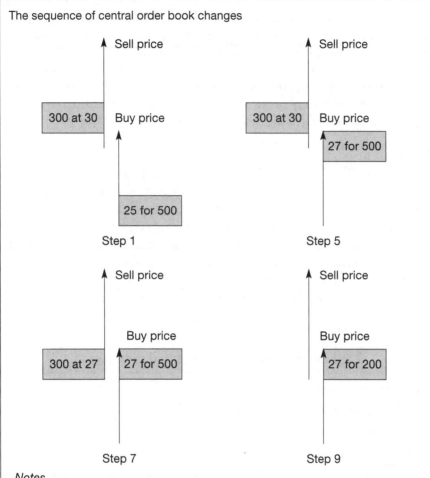

The sequence of central order book changes

Step 1 — Sell price / Buy price: 300 at 30, 25 for 500

Step 5 — Sell price / Buy price: 300 at 30, 27 for 500

Step 7 — Sell price / Buy price: 300 at 27, 27 for 500

Step 9 — Sell price / Buy price: 27 for 200

Notes

1. It is possile for a trader to have more than one order at the same time, in the same market. These are distinguished using a host-supplied 'order-id' which the system then returns with any relevant response handler function.

2. In general, trading is done simultaneously in several different markets. The automated market references are used to distinguish them.

3. Where more than one trader is competing for an order at a specific price, preference is given to the order with the earliest time stamp for price/time priority contracts. Pro-rata contract orders all have the same priority, orders receive trade allocations based upon the proportion of the market volume each order represents.

Source: LIFFE

Matching

With electronic trading, the two sites of the deal are automatically matched. With open outcry trading there must be a buyer and a seller for the trade to take place. Once these two parties have dealt across the pit, the trade details are passed to a yellow jacket for input into the trade registration system (TRS). This is an integral part of the clearing mechanism. TRS ensures that each trade has the 'other half'. Occasionally there may be an unmatched trade and it is the responsibility of each member firm to resolve these discrepancies.

Clearing

Once all the details are noted and matched, the clearing house interposes itself between buyer and seller. All LIFFE's contracts are cleared by the London Clearing House (LCH), which is independent of the exchange (see Figure 3.9). In effect it becomes seller to every buyer and buyer to every seller. Although it is not a principal itself and never initiates a trade, after every trade it takes on the other side's counterparty risk. It is this characteristic that makes futures so popular with market participants. The LCH's own credit exposure is, in turn, covered by margin. Any bank

Fig 3.9

The London Clearing House as central counterparty

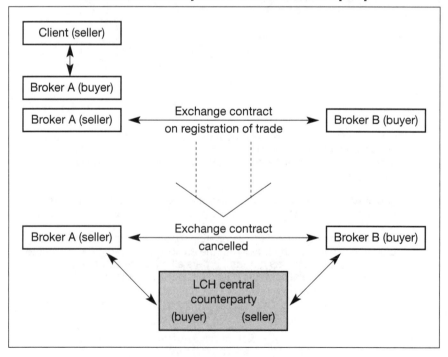

Source: LIFFE

can deal with any other bank or individual, whatever their credit standing in the market. They know that once the trade is electronically matched or confirmed through TRS, then 'cleared', their only counterparty risk is to the clearing house. Removing this counterparty risk ensures swift trading without the need to check on each party's credit risk. All that remains is to agree the size of the trade and the price. This feature also enhances liquidity.

Initial margins

The only way that the clearing house is able to take on the credit risk of both counterparties is that each of them is required to put up margin or collateral at the time of trading. This is known as initial margin.

Assume the initial margin is £750 per contract on the short sterling future. If a client had opened a position of 30 contracts, he would need to deposit with the exchange 30 × £750 or £22,500. Both buyer and seller of the contracts would put up the same amount of security. This effectively insulates the clearing house; whatever direction the market moves in, the clearing house has funds in advance to pay off daily losses, should they be incurred. The extent of the daily losses should not exceed the initial margin. For example, £750 per contract represents a possible loss on a day of 60 ticks or a 0.6 per cent movement in the implied interest rate. If the clearing house felt that there was potential for a greater loss due to excessive volatility in the market, it would call for increased initial margin payments from everyone with outstanding open positions. The SPAN computer program used to calculate margin amounts uses the term 'scanning risk' for initial margin.

Variation margins

At close of business every day, each open position on the exchange is marked-to-market and compared with the day's official settlement price. If the position is in profit, the margin account will be credited with the profit. If the position has made a loss, the margin account will be debited by that amount. These payments are known as variation margin as distinct from the initial margin that was deposited when the original position was opened. Since these payments are paid/received in cash, variation margin calls are normally made in cash.

If a client has a position which is making losses on a daily basis, there will be variation margin calls against him every day. This should prevent very large losses being run up as they are paid off daily and cannot accumulate. But Barings Bank collapsed, notwithstanding this type of safeguard is in place on all exchanges. When a trading position continually loses money, the losses are paid daily, so that funding of the position is required. When a trader calls for more and more funding due to variation margin movements, it should raise questions. If the funding of the variation margin is not forthcoming, the clearing house will start to close out the position. Barings continued to fund substantial loss-making positions on a daily basis in a falling market.

Consider a client who has taken a view that interest rates will fall. In fact he is wrong and they rise. On each day of his open position he will make a loss that he must fund on a daily basis. If the original trade was for ten contracts and initial margin was £750 a contract, on Day 1 he would put up £7,500. At close of business that day, let's say his position has moved against him by 20 ticks per contract:

$$(20 \times 10 \times £12.50 = £2,500)$$

The LCH will debit his margin account by that amount, leaving a balance of only £5,000. At an initial margin of £750 per contract, this balance of £5,000 will support only six futures contracts. If he does not respond to the variation margin call by adding a further £2,500 to replenish his margin account, he will not have enough initial margin to maintain his position, and the exchange will close out any unmargined outstanding contracts.

Some traders regard the initial margin as a 'stop loss'. If a trader never tops up the initial margin account, then that is all the money he can lose on the position. However, with the Barings position, the variation margin from the losses was continually funded, resulting in greater and greater losses as the market continued to fall.

Example

Hedging with short-term sterling interest rate futures

14 February
The treasurer of a large UK company is committed to borrow £15 million on 22 June. He has no requirement for the cash today, but he has invested in a strategic venture that requires £15 million for a period of three months from 22 June. He believes that sterling interest rates will rise and is worried about the eventual borrowing rate he will incur. The 3-month LIBOR in the market today is 5.5 per cent and he feels rates will rise higher than this. The current June future is trading at 94.20 implying a future 3-month LIBOR of 5.8 per cent for the June date, so the market is already anticipating an interest rate rise. The treasurer decides to hedge using futures.

14 February – Action
Treasurer sells 30 June short sterling futures at the current level of 94.20, and puts up the appropriate level of initial margin.

Over the next few months until 22 June, the treasurer receives/pays daily variation margin as the market moves.

22 June – Action

The treasurer borrows his money from the inter-bank market at a 3-month LIBOR rate of 6.7 per cent. The same morning he lifts his hedge, and closes out his futures position. To do this, he will buy back the futures contracts at the prevailing market rate of 93.30, and receive back his initial margin plus interest.

Profit or loss?

Total profit on the futures trade is 90 ticks (94.20 – 93.30) on each of 30 contracts:

$$(30 \text{ contracts} \times 90 \text{ ticks} \times £12.50 \text{ tick value} = £33,750)$$

This is not a profit overall, simply a profit on the futures 'leg' of the transaction. In the cash markets the treasurer has borrowed his £15 million at 6.7 per cent, a higher rate of interest. We need to establish whether the profit on the futures trade is enough to offset the extra interest paid on the loan.

Cash market loan

Equation 1. The amount of interest the treasurer would have paid at the original LIBOR rate of 5.5 per cent:

$$\frac{£15,000,000}{36,500} \times 91 \times 5.5 = £205,684.93$$

Equation 2. The amount of interest the treasurer would have paid at the rate of 5.8 per cent, the implied interest rate already in the market – implied by the futures price:

$$\frac{£15,000,000}{36,500} \times 91 \times 5.8 = £216,904.11$$

Equation 3. The amount of interest the treasurer actually paid at the final LIBOR of 6.7 per cent:

$$\frac{£15,000,000}{36,500} \times 91 \times 6.7 = £250,561.64$$

The extra amount of interest the treasurer had to pay was £33,657.53 [Equation 3 – Equation 2]. We use Equation 2 as it reflects market sentiment for future interest rates. If we had used Equation 1, we would have been simplistically assuming that the treasurer could borrow the money in the future, but still at today's rates. This is not a realistic assumption.

To offset against this extra outgoing, the futures trade made a profit of £33,750, neatly locking the treasurer into an insurance rate of 6.7 per cent. This hedge was nearly 100 per cent effective.

As all short-term interest rate futures trade in much the same way, the same hedging techniques can be used in other currencies.

Example

Hedging with short-term EuroLibor interest rate futures

2 May

The treasurer of a European multinational needs to protect the value of a forthcoming €50,000,000 deposit. The funds are the proceeds of a divestment and are expected in mid-September when the paper work is finalized. On receipt, the treasurer will invest them in a three-month time deposit. The company is worried that Euro interest rates will fall between May and September, and that they will be disadvantaged. The funds will be placed 'offshore', and a Euro-interest rate will need to be protected.

The current 3-month LIBOR rate for Euro is 3.3 per cent, and the treasurer believes that rates will fall below this. The current September future is trading at 96.88, an implied forward rate of 3.12 per cent. The market is already anticipating an interest rate reduction, so the treasurer decides to hedge using futures (see Table 3.6).

Table 3.6

3-month EuroLibor interest rate future – abbreviated contract specification

Unit of trading	€1,000,000
Delivery months	March, June, September, December
Delivery date	First business day after the last trading day
Last trading day	11.00 hrs, two business days prior to the third Wednesday of the delivery month
Quotation	100 minus rate of interest
Minimum price movement	0.005% – a 'half-tick'
Tick value	€12.50
Trading hours	07.30 – 18.00
Trading platform	LIFFE CONNECT 16.15 - 18.00

Source: LIFFE

2 May – Action

The treasurer buys 50 September EuroLibor futures at the current level of 96.88, and puts up the appropriate level of initial margin.

Throughout the next few months until mid-September the interest rates fluctuate and the treasurer receives/pays daily variation margin as the market moves.

20 September – Action

The treasurer receives €50 million and places it on deposit immediately for a period of three calendar months at a 3-month EuroLibor rate of 3.0 per cent. The same day he closes out his futures position. To do this he will sell back the futures contracts at the EDSP (exchange delivery settlement price) of 97.00, which exactly matches the LIBOR fixing rate. He will also receive back his initial margin plus interest.

Profit or loss?

The total profit on the futures trade is 12 ticks or 24 half-ticks (97.00 – 96.88) on each of 50 contracts:

$$(50 \text{ contracts} \times 24 \text{ ticks} \times €12.50 \text{ tick value} = €15,000.00)$$

This is not a profit overall, simply a profit on the futures 'leg' of the transaction. In the cash markets the treasurer has invested his €50 million at 3.00 per cent – a worse rate of interest. We need to establish whether the profit on the futures trade is enough to offset the loss of interest income on the investment.

Cash market investment

Equation 1. The amount of interest the treasurer would have received at the rate of 3.12 per cent, the implied interest rate already in the market:

$$\frac{€\,50,000,000}{36,000} \times 90 \times 3.12 = €\,390,000$$

Equation 2. The amount of interest the treasurer actually received at the final LIBOR of 3.00 per cent:

$$\frac{€\,50,000,000}{36,000} \times 90 \times 3.00 = €\,375,000$$

The shortfall of interest was € 15,000 [Equation 1 – Equation 2] (it is important to note that the market was already discounting lower interest rates in the futures prices).

To offset against this lack of interest receivable, the futures trade made a profit of € 15,000, neatly locking the treasurer into an investment rate of 3.12 per cent. This hedge was 100 per cent effective.

Practical considerations

If a client wants to trade or hedge with futures, how does he go about it? First, he will need to set up documentation, and that associated with futures is particularly arduous. A prospective user of futures will need to put in place one set each of the documents with the exchange and the clearing house, and one set with the futures broker, all of which must be checked by the company lawyers.

If a client is not a member of the relevant exchange, a broker will be required to transact the trades in the futures pit on behalf of the client. He will be acting entirely on instructions received, and will charge a fee for his services. Once the documentation is agreed with the broker, the level of brokerage must be agreed. This will depend upon many things, but especially the volume of business that is anticipated, and the level of service required of the broker. Some clients want a service which is 'execution only', others prefer a full service offering advice, execution, clearing, and perhaps a listening service on to the exchange so they can hear what is going on. Once this has been agreed, the client is now ready to deal. There is a specific order for the information flow on an exchange (see Figure 3.10).

Wherever the client is around the world, he can phone his futures broker and place his bid or offer. The broker will telephone the order on to the floor of the exchange, where one of his firm's yellow jackets will take the details, fill out a ticket which will be time stamped to reduce the possibility of disagreements later, and pass the order to the appropriate trader in the futures pit. The order may be filled immediately or it may take some time. Once the order is executed, the details are passed back by the trader to the yellow jackets who again time stamp the ticket and input it into the trade registration system. At this point the 'fill' details are communicated back to the client. Once the deal is successfully matched, it will then be cleared through the clearing system. Initial margins must be posted at close of business on that day, and maintained until the position is closed out. Variation margin must also be paid/received, until the position is closed out.

To trade and hedge with futures sucessfully, it is important to have an information link. The types of companies who offer these services are Bridge, Reuters, and many others. The costs of the various services will again be dependent on the client's individual requirements, but one should not underestimate how important fast and accurate data are. Currently, infrared modems allow mobile telephones to access the Internet and real-time data. Unheard of five years ago!

One should never forget futures are the fastest way to make or lose lots of money!

How a trade is made

Fig 3.10

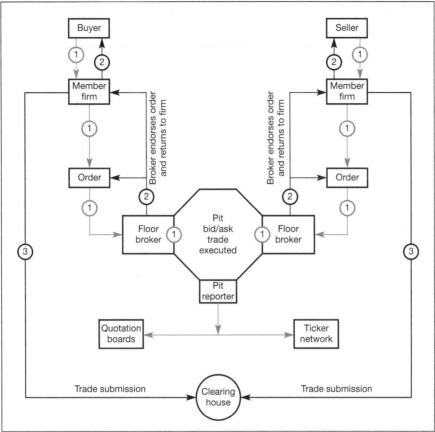

Source: Chicago Mercantile Exchange

Conclusion

Futures offer banks and other financial institutions excellent hedging and trading opportunities. Unfortunately, most companies do not have the time or the resources necessary to manage a portfolio of futures contracts efficiently. In addition to the documentation mentioned (most of which runs to a minimum of ten pages long), the user must also install systems to monitor his margins and accounting. He will also need to manage basis risk, and must agree to accept the settlement dates and the specific sizes of contracts that are fixed by the exchange. These will rarely match his own company exposure.

Financial futures are recognized as being 'unfriendly' to the occasional user. Consequently, it was only a matter of time before the banks 'packaged' financial futures into a more friendly product, known as FRAs or forward rate agreements.

FORWARD RATE AGREEMENTS

Introduction

Earlier we introduced the concept of the 'implied forward rate'. For example, imagine a businessman who is about to go away on an extended business trip, miles away from telephones and information systems. He has a medium-term loan which will be re-fixed to the 6-month LIBOR rate in one month's time. He will be unable to call the bank on the loan re-fixing day to confirm the rate as he may well be in a meeting. What he needs to know today is the rate that will be applicable for his transaction. In effect, he wants to know the rate in advance. The 6-month LIBOR rate today may be an indicator of what rate he will achieve, but it is by no means a certainty. Interest rates in one month's time could be higher or lower than today, and this element of uncertainty is what the businessman would like to avoid. The bank can determine the customer's loan rate without resorting to derivatives, although they do make life a lot easier.

In Figure 3.11 X per cent is the rate we are trying to calculate. The bank can do this by borrowing the money for the full seven months and

Fig 3.11

Implied forward rates

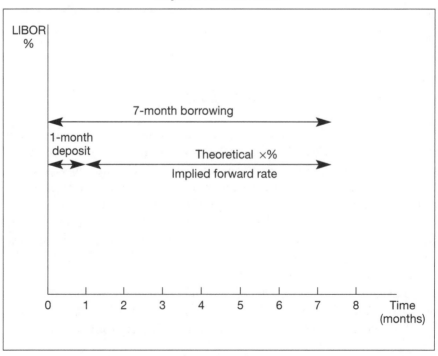

investing it back for one month as the client does not need it straight away. By borrowing long and lending short, the bank has created a *synthetic forward borrowing* enabling it to quote a forward/forward rate of interest. However, it has transacted both the loan and the deposit physically in the cash markets. This ties up the bank's credit lines and also requires the bank to hold extra capital for the capital adequacy requirements as specified by the Central Bank for cash transactions. This money is in effect on permanent deposit.

In simple terms, because both transactions are in cash there is little or no profit margin for the bank, as the added cost of the capital adequacy requirement, as laid down by the Bank of England makes this use of bank assets uncompetitive.

The concept of fixing interest rates into the future was well received, and other financial techniques were thus developed to allow the forward/forward interest rate to be calculated, but without the commitment from the bank to lend or take the money. With no movement of the cash principal the instrument is taken 'off-balance sheet', no longer attracting the onerous capital adequacy requirements that made it so uncompetitive in the first place. The Central Bank still requires an element of 'cover' on this new transaction, but it is a much smaller amount than that previously needed; something in the region of 1/100 of the amount. This new product is called the FRA or forward rate agreement, and it offers more profit opportunities for bankers than the original forward/forward loans. It is also known by some market practitioners as an OTC future. The FRA (pronunciation to rhyme with 'bra') is quite simply a forward/forward loan or deposit given without the commitment to lend or take the money. To many users these are 'packaged' financial futures.

A **forward rate agreement** *is a legally binding agreement between two parties to determine the rate of interest that will be applied to a notional loan or deposit, of an agreed amount to be drawn or placed, on an agreed future date (the settlement date) for a specified term.*

Definition

Definition discussed

One of the parties is a 'buyer' of the FRA, the other a 'seller'. The buyer agrees notionally to borrow the money at the FRA rate, and the seller agrees notionally to lend the money at the FRA rate. On the settlement date the difference between the FRA rate and the prevailing LIBOR rate will be settled by one party to the other in cash. The terms 'seller' and 'buyer' are used only to determine who is the borrower and who is the lender of the money, not necessarily who is providing the service. Banks can be sellers and buyers and so can customers.

We need to clarify the components. The FRA contract is legally binding and neither party can walk away. The two parties are the 'buyer' and the 'seller' of the FRA, both of whom are able to hedge against future interest rate movements. Usually one of the parties is a bank, and the other can be a corporate, financial institution or another bank. The FRA rate of interest will be that calculated on the forward/forward basis plus a profit margin, for the particular maturity required and can be derived from the financial futures markets. This FRA rate is applied to a notional loan or deposit amount. This is an important concept, because it shows that the FRA can hedge or trade an amount equivalent to, say, £5 million, but will not actually lend or take deposit of the £5 million.

Currency, amount and length of transaction must be specified. The underlying loan or deposit transaction being hedged must commence in the future at a forward date which needs to be specified. It cannot commence today. There is no uncertainty today about, say, the 3-month LIBOR; we know the rate, it was fixed in the market at 11 a.m. this morning. Products like FRAs and futures are used to hedge or trade an implied interest rate during this 'uncertainty period', before the rate is fixed in the market at 11 a.m. on the specific date. If there is no uncertainty period, no hedge is required.

As this product is based on a notional amount, the assumption is that if there is a loan or investment underlying the deal, then that it is with another part of the bank or another bank entirely. The FRA will not lend the money or take the deposit. This is an important point: anyone can buy or sell an FRA subject to their credit lines – the bank providing the service in FRAs has not got the time or the inclination to check whether this is a hedge or a trade, they are not policemen. The bank 'selling' the FRA will not differentiate on price between a FRA used to hedge or a FRA used to trade. On the settlement date, a cash sum equivalent to the difference in the FRA rate and the actual LIBOR fixing rate will be exchanged. It is impossible to tell at the outset of the FRA who will pay whom the cash settlement – that will only be clear at maturity. It could be the bank paying the client or vice versa.

FRAs

Insurance

The bank will guarantee (or insure) a rate of interest for a transaction which starts on a future date. The client is legally obligated to transact at that rate, so is 'locked' into the FRA interest rate; if rates move adversely, he will be protected and receive a cash settlement equivalent to the difference between the FRA rate and the LIBOR fixing, but if rates move in his favour he will be unable to profit, as he is committed to pay back a cash settlement to the other party.

Cash settlement

Principal amounts are not exchanged. The differences between the FRA rate and the ruling market rate (LIBOR) will be settled by the parties.

Profit potential

For a hedger – nil. If interest rates move in the client's favour, any difference must be repaid to the other party. For a trader, any cash received under the FRA is a profit.

Flexibility

If the FRA is no longer required, a reversing transaction may be transacted to close out the position.

Zero cost

To a hedger, but zero profit potential. The FRA will guarantee an *absolute rate of interest*, not better or worse.

Market structure and operations

FRAs are over the counter (OTC) instruments, and are quoted by many banks around the world. There is no requirement for them to be traded on an exchange as with futures. Each market participant will take the counterparty credit risk of the other. This is a significant point, as at the outset of the FRA trade, it is not clear who will cash settle with whom. The bank could pay the client or the client could pay the bank. So at Day 1 there is a potential two-way cash flow.

For a bank to quote a FRA rate, basic information relating to the trade is required. Consider our businessman who was going on a business trip. His underlying loan was to be re-fixed in one month's time for a period of six months (see Figure 3.12). In market jargon, this would be described as a 1s–7s exposure, possibly requiring a 1s–7s FRA to cover it. The exposure exists now, but the underlying transaction starts in one month and finishes in seven months therefore the duration must be six months. To price this we also need to know the amount and currency of the underlying loan, say £5 million. In this case, our man will ask for a 1s–7s borrower's FRA, or he could say he wishes to 'buy' the FRA.

Important dates on an FRA transaction

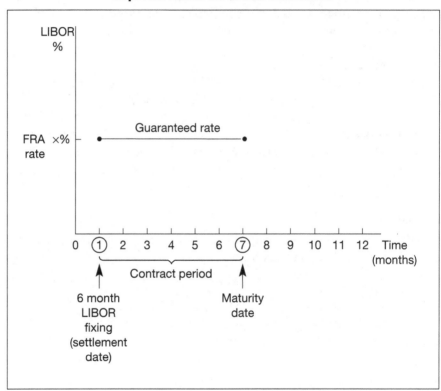

FRA

FRA	A forward rate agreement sometimes called interest rate insurance.
Buyer/ borrower	The party wishing to protect itself from a rise in interest rates, or profit from a rise in rates.
Seller/ lender	The party wishing to protect itself from a fall in rates, or profit from a fall in rates.

Future rate, agreed rate, guaranteed rate	The FRA rate agreed between the parties at the outset of the of the transaction.
Settlement date	The start date of the underlying loan or deposit, when cash settlement is made.
Maturity date	The date on which the FRA contract period ends.
LIBOR	London inter-bank offered rate. The rate at which banks lend funds to each other.
LIBOR fixing	The mean interest rate quoted by specified reference banks.
LIBOR fixing date	The date when the LIBOR is checked at 11 a.m. This is the same day as the settlement date for sterling, and two business days before for currency deals.
Contract period	The period running from the start to maturity of the underlying loan or deposit.

Hedging with sterling FRAs

Example

Our businessman who is about to go on his business trip wishes to hedge a £5 million sterling borrowing which will take place in one month's time. The maturity of the underlying borrowing is six months. This, then, is a 1s–7s transaction. In order to comfort himself that the price quoted by his bank is competitive he will put up one of the screens provided by brokers who offer a service in FRAs, before he calls the bank. An example of a Telerate page is shown in Figure 3.13.

Strategy

Our businessman asks his bank for an FRA price to protect a six-month borrowing out of the specific rollover date, i.e., a 1s–7s. The market price for that period is 6.55 per cent. The client agrees to the rate, no money changes hands, and he is now fully protected against an adverse interest rate movement. Confirmations will be sent by both the client and the bank. These should be checked for errors as soon as they are received, preferably by a 'third' party.

Fig 3.13

GBP Short Swaps

01/07 09:30 NYC	[GARBAN INTERCAPITAL LONDON]		4914

GBP SHORT SWAPS 07/01 14:30 GMT

3M FRAS		GM FRAS		12M FRAS		SHORT SWAPS	
1 × 4	6.30-6.26	1 × 7	6.55-6.52	1 × 13	6.99-6.96	6MA3	6.41-6.38
2 × 5	6.43-6.40	2 × 8	6.68-6.65	2 × 14	7.08-7.05	9MA3	6.62-6.59
3 × 6	6.55-6.52	3 × 9	6.79-6.76	3 × 15	7.16-7.13	1YA3	6.84-6.81
4 × 7	6.67-6.64	4 × 10	6.89-6.86	4 × 16	7.24-7.21	15MA3	6.95-6.92
5 × 8	6.79-6.76	5 × 11	6.99-6.96	5 × 17	7.31-7.28	18MA3	6.95-6.92
6 × 9	6.88-6.85	6 × 12	7.08-7.05	6 × 18	7.37-7.34	1YS/S	6.75-6.72
9 × 12	7.15-7.12	9 × 15	7.30-7.27	9 × 21	7.49-7.46		
12 × 15	7.26-7.23	12 × 18	7.40-7.37	12 × 24	7.56-7.53		

GBP 3M IMM		GBP GM IMM		GBP 12M IMM		GBP IMM	
2 × 5	6.46-6.44	2 × 8	6.72-6.69	3 × 15	7.10-7.07	MAR/MAR	7.10-7.07
5 × 8	6.83-6.81	5 × 11	7.04-7.01	6 × 18	7.34-7.31	JUN/JUN	7.33-7.30
8 × 11	7.08-7.06	8 × 14	7.28-7.25	9 × 21	7.48-7.45	SEP/SEP	7.47-7.44
11 × 14	7.30-7.28	11 × 17	7.40-7.37	12 × 2	7.56-7.53	DEC/DEC	7.56-7.53

[FOR FURTHER INFORMATION CALL 020 703 8050 OR CALL BRIDGE DIRECT DEALER ICAP]

Source: Garban-Intercapital plc (*courtesy*: Bridge Information Systems)

NB: *The client will need to look for the 1 × 7 data. Both sides of the price are shown on this screen. Our client is a borrower in the underlying market, so he will be on the high side of the FRA quote, i.e., 6.55 per cent. An investor would be on the lower side of the price.*

Outcome

Assume the 11 a.m. LIBOR fixing in one month's time is 8 per cent: this is the reference rate against which the FRA will be cash settled. This is the day when the customer will confirm the borrowing rate on his loan. It is known as the settlement date as this is the day when settlement is received. The hedge the businessman has with the bank will now come into operation. As the LIBOR rate of 8 per cent (Ⓐ in Figure 3.14) is above the FRA rate of 6.55 per cent, the bank will refund the difference to the company, discounted back for early settlement.

NB: *The amount of the settlement is paid at the beginning of the loan, not at the end when the client will pay his interest. The client is getting his refund earlier than he needs it, so the amount is discounted at the LIBOR fixing rate on the FRA. The reasoning here is that the customer should be indifferent as to whether he gets the full amount at maturity, or a smaller amount at the beginning which he can place on deposit. The interest and principal together will add up to the original amount as if it had been paid at maturity. A fairly complicated settlement formula is used to calculate the amounts.*

If the LIBOR market rate had been say 6.37 per cent (Ⓑ in Figure 3.14), then the company would have refunded the difference to the bank, also on a discounted basis. So for nil cost, the company has obtained full interest rate protection, at a rate of 6.55 per cent, although agreeing to give up any profit.

FRA settlement formula:

$$\frac{(\text{LIBOR} - \text{FRA rate}) \times \text{amount} \times \text{period (in days)}}{\text{Year} \times 100} \times \frac{1}{1 + \left[\dfrac{(\text{LIBOR} \times \text{period})}{(\text{Year} \times 100)}\right]}$$

LIBOR	11 a.m. fixing rate
FRA rate	Rate agreed between the parties and confirmed on the confirmation
Amount	Full amount of the transaction
Period	Number of days of the underlying transaction
Year	365 days for sterling, 360 for most other currencies

The first part of the formula works out the cash settlement, the second part of the formula discounts it, as the funds will be received early.

Using the formula, we can calculate the amount of the settlement and who will receive it.

1. If rates had been 8 per cent on settlement:

$$\frac{(8.00 - 6.55) \times £5,000,000 \times 181 \text{ days}}{36,500} \times \frac{1}{1 + \dfrac{(8.00 \times 181)}{36,500}}$$

£35,952.05 × 0.96184 = £34,580.12

The borrowing rate of 8 per cent was above the FRA rate when the deal was finalized so the bank will compensate the client with the amount of £34,580.12. This will go towards the higher interest costs he must pay.

2. If rates had been 6.37 per cent on settlement:

$$\frac{(6.37 - 6.55) \times £5,000,000 \times 181 \text{ days}}{36,500} \times \frac{1}{1 + \dfrac{(6.37 \times 181)}{36,500}}$$

£4,463.04 × 0.969379 = £4,326.38

Fig 3.14

Example of sterling FRA settlement amounts

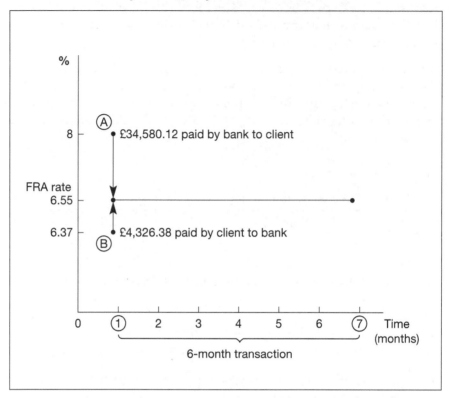

The borrowing rate was below the FRA rate when the deal was finalized, so the client will compensate the bank with the amount of £4,326.38 (see Figure 3.14). A negative number signifies that the payment goes in the opposite direction.

Example

Hedging with Eurodollar FRAs

A European treasurer wishes to hedge the income on an investment. He will be receiving US$10 million in two months' time, and he is concerned that interest rates may fall before he receives his funds, and before he has a chance to place them on deposit. He anticipates placing them on deposit for three months. He decides to hedge using FRAs, as they are zero cost and will guarantee for him a fixed rate for the period.

This, then, is a 2s–5s transaction. The treasurer puts up the Telerate screen shown in Figure 3.15. The underlying transaction is an investment so the company will need to deal on the lower side of the price at 6.18. The company would need to 'sell' the FRA.

Indication of US dollar FRA levels

Fig 3.15

Tullett and Tokyo Global

Forward Rate Agreements

1 × 4	6.11	14:16
2 × 5	6.18	14:28
3 × 6	6.26	14:39
4 × 7	6.37	14:32
5 × 8	6.49	14:37
6 × 9	6.57	14:41
7 × 10	6.65	14:36
8 × 11	6.72	14:36
9 × 12	6.87	14:36

Int Rate Caps Vols

1 YR	11.50	12:20
2 YR	15.37	12:21
3 YR	17.25	12:21
4 YR	17.87	12:21
5 YR	18.12	12:21
7 YR	18.00	12:21
10 YR	17.25	12:22

07-Jan-00 14:42 LDN

USD Derivatives

Forward Rate Agreements

1 × 7	6.32	6.36	14:32
2 × 8	6.39	6.43	14:41
3 × 9	6.47	6.51	14:37
4 × 10	6.57	6.61	14:37
5 × 11	6.66	6.70	14:36
6 × 12	6.78	6.82	14:36
12 × 18	7.03	7.07	14:37
18 × 24	7.17	7.21	14:37
12 × 24	7.23	7.27	14:37

Index on page 6600
Symbols on page 6601

Fwd/Fwd Caps Volatilities

1Y × 2Y	16.50	17.50	12:20
2Y × 3Y	18.80	19.80	12:21
2Y × 4Y	18.80	19.80	12:21
3Y × 5Y	18.90	19.90	12:21
4Y × 7Y	17.62	18.62	12:21
5Y × 10Y	16.50	17.50	12:21

IRS - Annual

1 YR	6.59	6.63	14:38
2 YR	6.89	6.93	14:38
3 YR	7.01	7.05	14:40
4 YR	7.06	7.11	14:42
5 YR	7.15	7.19	14:39
6 YR	7.20	7.24	14:39
7 YR	7.24	7.28	14:42
8 YR	7.28	7.32	14:39
9 YR	7.32	7.36	14:40
10 YR	7.35	7.40	14:43

(c) BRIDGE

Source: Tullet & Tokyo Liberty plc
(*Courtesy*: Bridge Information Systems)

Strategy

The treasurer will ask one of his bankers for an FRA price to protect a three-month investment starting in two months' time, i.e., a 2s–5s. The market price for that period is 6.18 per cent. The client agrees to the rate, no money changes hands, and the company is now fully protected against an adverse interest rate movement. Confirmations will be sent by both the client and the bank.

Outcome

Assume the 11 a.m. LIBOR fixing in two months' time is 5.90 per cent: this is the reference rate against which the FRA will be cash settled. This is the day when the customer will confirm the investment rate on his deposit. As this is a Euro-currency FRA (non-sterling), settlement will be made two business days later. The hedge the company has with the bank will now come into operation.

(a) As the LIBOR rate of 5.90 per cent (Ⓐ in Figure 3.14) is below the FRA rate of 6.18 per cent, the bank will refund the difference to the company, discounted back for early settlement.

(b) If the LIBOR market rate had been say 6.45 per cent (Ⓑ in Figure 3.14), then the company would have refunded the difference to the bank, also on a discounted basis.

So for nil cost, the company has obtained full interest rate protection, at a rate of 6.18 per cent, although agreeing to give up any profit.

1. If rates had been 5.90 per cent on settlement:

$$\frac{(5.90 - 6.18) \times \$10,000,000 \times 90 \text{ days}}{36,000} \times \cfrac{1}{1 + \cfrac{(5.9 \times 90)}{36,000}}$$

$$-US\$7,000 \times 0.98546 = US\$6,898.22$$

The actual LIBOR rate was below the FRA rate when the deal was finalized, so the bank will compensate the client with the amount of US$6,898.22. This will go towards the shortfall of interest.

2. If rates had been 6.45 per cent on settlement:

$$\frac{(6.45 - 6.18) \times \$10,000,000 \times 90 \text{ days}}{36,000} \times \cfrac{1}{1 + \cfrac{(6.45 \times 90)}{36,000}}$$

$$US\$6,750.00 \times 0.984131 = US\$6,642.88$$

Example of a Eurodollar FRA hedge

Fig 3.16

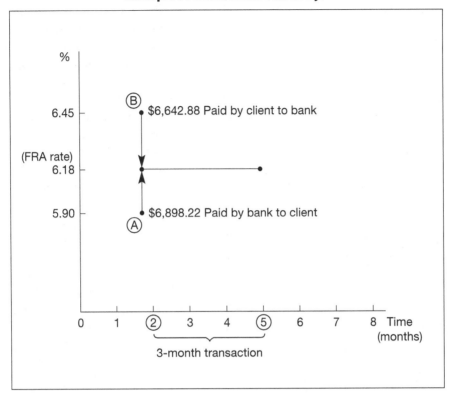

The actual LIBOR rate was above the FRA rate when the deal was finalized, so the client will compensate the bank with the amount of US$6,642.88 (see Figure 3.16). This will go against the increased interest income on the deposit.

Practical considerations

A forward rate agreement does not require the payment of a premium, and as such will guarantee for the buyer an 'absolute' rate of cover. However, should a client wish to transact one of these for the first time, it will be necessary to contact the bank to arrange for an appropriate credit line. This will be required because the FRA allows for a 50/50 chance of a cash flow in either direction on settlement, either from the bank to the client or vice versa. It is obviously the potential risk that the client will not repay the bank when he is supposed to. The credit department of the bank will normally require the last three years' annual reports to aid them in deciding whether to grant the facility. It is usual to set the credit line up in advance of dealing.

It is advisable to consider different banks from those who may offer mainstream banking facilities, if only to spread the risk. Some clearing banks offer an excellent service in derivatives, as do some UK, Japanese, European and US houses.

It is always worth having credit lines with more than one FRA provider, as banks will quote different rates on different days. If the bank has an off day, have at least one other bank you can call for a price.

The FRA market is heavily brokered, and a broker can offer a very useful service, in both an information and a dealing capacity. However, a broker will not be a counterparty to the deal, but will put together willing buyers and sellers of the FRA for a small commission. Remember, if a broker finds you a good price, you cannot deal on it unless you have a credit line already in place with the counterparty bank.

It may be worth seeking competitive quotes for individual transactions in excess of £5 million or US$5 million. Smaller deals are available, but may be at a slightly worse rate.

Clients can transact for any period over one month including broken dates (non-calendar), as long as the start date of the FRA is ideally at least two weeks forward, and the end date is not more than 60 months. FRAs are most readily available for multiples of three-monthly periods, e.g., 3s–6s or 6s–12s, but it is worth checking with your bankers for other periods. Unusual periods such as 1s–2s and 0s–1s are possible, but at a price.

Availability

FRAs are normally available in marketable amounts, from £5 million or US$5 million, in most major and some minor currencies. Some banks will make prices in smaller transactions for their own clients, sometimes as low as £500,000. It should be recognized that rates for smaller value transactions are likely to be worse than the rates for a 'marketable amount'.

Documentation

The FRA market started in 1983, and by 1984 it was clear that many banks were trading in this new instrument. In 1985, to ensure there was a measure of uniformity in the market, the British Bankers' Association (BBA) endorsed the documentation that has now become the market standard. These are known as FRABBA (FRA British Bankers' Association) terms and conditions, and are written for the inter-bank market. Copies of the documentation can be obtained from the BBA direct. It is becoming increasingly popular for market participants to include FRA transactions on their ISDA documentation.

Table 3.7 compares financial futures and FRAs.

Comparison between financial futures and FRAs

Table 3.7

	Financial futures	FRAs
Documentation	Detailed, relates to exchange, broker and clearing house	Standard agreement 'FRABBA'
Margins	Initial and variation	None
Amounts	Fixed contract sizes	Any amount from £1 million
Maturity	Fixed contract dates	Any date up to five years
Liquidity	Can be problems in the back months	Good
Flexibility	Can be closed out at any time	Reversing FRA to settlement date
Restrictions	On dates, amounts, and 3-month runs	None
Bid/offer spreads	0.01–0.02 ticks	0.03-0.10 per cent
Basis risk	Between futures price and LIBOR	None
Credit risk	Margin monies placed with broker, who then places them with the exchange	With the counterparty, for cash settlement of differential
Credit lines	Not required	Required for interest rate differential

BASIC OPTION CONCEPTS

Introduction

An option contract is the only derivative instrument that allows the buyer (holder) to 'walk away' from his obligations. This is in contrast to both the financial future and the FRA (in the interest rate market) and forward foreign exchange transactions (in the currency markets). The FRA, futures and forward FX all provide the client with an obligation of a guaranteed rate. In effect these products provide certainty, whatever the resulting market conditions. In contrast, option contracts allow the holder the best of both worlds; insurance when things go wrong, and when things go right, the ability to walk away from the instrument (or guarantee), and the ability to deal at a better rate in the market.

Options are available in many markets including interest rates/fixed income, currency, equity and commodity. Unfortunately, options do not come free of charge: a premium is due, usually paid upfront. The option allows a degree of flexibility, it does not completely remove all the risk, (all losses *and* all profit). Instead it allows a degree of risk management which is not total; controlling the risk rather than removing it completely.

Options also illustrate the concept of 'asymmetry of risk'. The most that an option buyer (holder) can lose is the original premium that he paid, whereas the most he can profit is unlimited. The extent of the profit will be governed by how far the market has moved in his favour. A seller (writer) of options, in contrast, can only hope to keep the premium, but the extent of his losses are potentially unlimited.

The buyer or holder of the option is the one who has paid the premium, and he/she is the party with the right to either buy or sell the underlying asset. Once the premium is paid, he has no further obligations under the contract. He can use the option, or not, depending on the rate of the option compared to the underlying rate in the market. The buyer will always choose the alternative which gives him the best outcome.

The seller or writer of the option has much heavier obligations. Once he has received the premium he must start to risk manage the position. In fact, hedging the option position will start immediately the deal is concluded, whereas the premium will not be received for two business days. The seller's obligations are to have 'the underlying' ready. If the option is a call, the seller must be ready to deliver the underlying. If the option is a put, the seller must take delivery of the underlying. The buyer can ask to make or take 'delivery' of the underlying, either at maturity or on any business day during the life of the transaction. This will depend upon how the option contract was originally designed.

Options can be bought or sold on an exchange in which case they are known as exchange traded or 'listed'. Alternatively, they can be tailored to fit the exact circumstances of the client, when they are known as over the counter or OTC. Options can be transacted in any one of the undelying primary markets, interest rates, currency, equity and commodity. Whatever the underlying commodity, all options are distinguished by the key phrase, 'the right, but not the obligation'. This separates an option from every other instrument.

> *An* **option** *gives the buyer the right, but not the obligation, to buy or sell a standard quantity of a specific financial instrument at a specific rate on or before a specific future date. A premium is due.*

Definition

There are a great variety of options, not only those based on a financial commodity. There are options on such diverse things as orange juice, pork bellies, grain, live hogs, etc. The first commonly used option-pricing model was written in the early 1970s by Fisher Black and Myron Scholes, and published in *The Journal of Political Economy*. Their treatise contained many new descriptive words that are now in everyday usage – at least among options users and providers. Before we go any further, let's look at some of this terminology.

Basic option

Terminology

Call option The right (not the obligation) to buy the underlying.

Put option The right (not the obligation) to sell the underlying.

Exercise Conversion of the option into the underlying transaction or commodity.

Strike price Guaranteed price chosen by the client, which can be described as:
– at the money (ATM)
– in the money (ITM)
– out of the money (OTM).

Expiry date Last day on which the option may be exercised, up to 10 a.m. New York time (the cut-off time is currency specific). Two business days before the value date if denominated in currency.

Terminology Value date	The date when the underlying is settled or delivered.
American option	An option which can be exercised on any business day up to and including the expiry date.
European option	An option which can be exercised on the expiry date only.
Premium	The price of the option.
Intrinsic value	Difference between the strike price and the current market rate (depending upon whether the option is American or European style).
Time value	Difference between the option premium and the intrinsic value, including time until expiry, volatility and cost of carry.
Fair value	Combination of intrinsic value and time value, as calculated by the option pricing model.
Volatility	Normalized annualized standard deviation of the underlying reference rate.

Terminology discussed

Calls and puts

It is possible for the bank or the customer to have bought or sold the option contract itself. It is also possible to have options to buy the underlying and to sell the underlying. This results in a possible four-way price. It is because of this that we use the terms call and put.

Jargon: The client has bought a call option on the US dollar against sterling.
Reality: The client has bought the right to buy US dollars with sterling.

Jargon: The bank has sold a put option on the FT-SE 100 Index.
Reality: The bank has given someone else the right to sell the FT-SE 100 Index to them.

Jargon: The client has bought a put option on the sterling three-month future.
Reality: The client has bought the right to sell the sterling three-month future.

Jargon: The bank has sold a Euro call option against US dollar.
Reality: The bank has sold someone else the right to buy Euro from them with US dollars.

Exercise

This is how to convert the option which at inception is simply a piece of paper into the 'underlying commodity'. The term also denotes the physical movement of the underlying, unless the option is to be cash settled, bought back by the writing bank or sold for intrinsic value.

Strike price (or exercise price)

This is the rate chosen by the client. Options are not like FRAs, forwards or futures where the current rate in the market is pre-determined. Instead the client can choose a rate that may be better or worse than the current market rate. This is called the strike of the option. The strike rate must be compared to the current market rate to establish whether the client's rate is better, or worse, or the same. Each option product has its own 'benchmark' rate against which the strike is measured. Some of the benchmark rates are:

- currency options – outright forward FX rate
- interest rate options – FRA rate (implied forward rate)
- interest rate caps, floors (a series of options) – swap rate
- traded energy options on futures – energy futures price.

For example, if a customer wishes to fix the borrowing rate on a future loan commitment with an interest rate option that has the characteristics of a 3s–6s, then the 3s–6s FRA rate is the benchmark.

Consider FRAs for a moment: assume the FRA rate is 6.75 per cent. If the client chose a rate on the interest rate option that was identical we would say the option was **at the money (ATM)**: it is at the same rate as the FRA. If he had chosen a rate that was better for him immediately, say 6.5 per cent, we would say the option was **in the money (ITM)**: it is better than the FRA rate. If he had chosen a rate that was worse for him, say 7 per cent, the option would be described as **out of the money (OTM)**: worse than the FRA rate.

Any strike on any option can be described using this method. Naturally, an ITM option which gives an advantage to the client will be more expensive than an option that is OTM or ATM. Likewise an OTM option which gives the client a lesser degree of protection will cost less than an option which is either ITM or ATM.

At the money (ATM)	Same rate as the benchmark.	**Terminology**
In the money (ITM)	Better rate than the benchmark.	
Out of the money (OTM)	Worse rate than the benchmark.	

Expiry date

This is the last day when the buyer of the option can exercise the option into the 'underlying asset'. After this date the option will lapse. The expiry date will be agreed at the outset. It is not uncommon for options to have guide cut-off times. These are currency specific, and will often relate to a particular centre, for example, 10 a.m. New York or 10 a.m. Tokyo time. This is necessary, because most banks providing a service in options run their positions as portfolios, and manage their option risks across many option books and many currencies. So if a client exercises his option with the bank, the bank will settle with him, and may then have to exercise an option they purchased from someone else, and so on.

There is no linear relationship between time to expiry and premium due (see Figure 3.17). A four-month option will not necessarily cost twice the premium of a two-month option although it will certainly cost more.

Value date

This is the date when the underlying commodity is cash settled or delivered. For example, a sterling interest rate option written by a UK bank will have the expiry date and the value date the same. This is the same for dollar-based options written by an American bank, etc. With currency options, the settlement or delivery of the currency will result in a two-business-day value period (except US$/Canadian dollars with one business day).

Fig 3.17

Non-linear relationship of option premium vs maturity

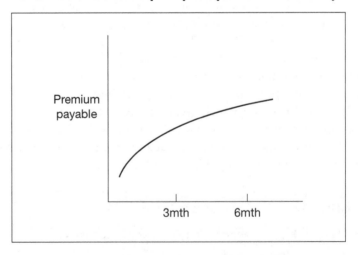

American options

These can be exercised into the underlying commodity (or cash settled if previously arranged) on any business day within the transaction period up to the expiry date. It must be a business day in both currencies.

European options

These can be exercised only on the expiry date, but they can be sold back to the writing bank for fair value at any time. The names originally came from the side of the Atlantic these options were traded on.

Both American and European options can be sold back to the writing bank for *'fair'* value at any time.

Premium

This is the price of the option as determined by the option pricing model. It comprises two components, intrinsic value and time value.

Intrinsic value

When the client chooses the strike on the option, the pricing model will compare that rate with the option benchmark rate. If the option strike is advantageous we say it is in the money (ITM). Intrinsic value is a measure of how much it is ITM.

Consider a client who wishes to buy some shares in BRIX plc. Assume the market price today is £5.00 a share. If she buys a call option on BRIX with a strike of £4.80 the option will be 20 pence in the money. This option has 20 pence intrinsic value. If she buys the call option with a strike of £5.00 it will be ATM and there would be zero intrinsic value. Equally, she may decide to purchase the call option with a strike at £5.10, this is 10 pence OTM. But it is impossible to have negative intrinsic value, so here the intrinsic value would again be zero.

This comparison between the strike and the benchmark rate works similarly whether the option is American or European style. The only difference is that the benchmark is slightly different. With an American option the benchmark is the current spot rate, as the client can exercise on any business day. But with a European option the benchmark is the current forward rate (to the expiry date), as the client can only exercise on the expiry date.

For the technically minded, an option's intrinsic value is measured by the present value of the amount by which it is in the money. That is the present value (PV) of the difference between the strike of the option and the forward price of the asset. The present value is used, because we have an expiry date in the future.

Time value

The seller of the option will demand a premium in excess of the intrinsic value, as he must manage the risks he has taken on, some of which are very complex. The risks include, volatility, time to expiry, cost of carry, etc.

Consider a trader wishing to purchase an option on Grape plc. Grape is trading in the market at £7.30 per share. If the option required is a call option at a strike of £7.20 with an expiry date in three months' time, there would be 10 pence intrinsic value in the option. However, the total premium for the option is 45 pence per share; then 10 pence is accounted for by the intrinsic value. The remaining 35 pence is the time value, or some traders regard this as risk premium. The reason a trader is prepared to pay an extra 35 pence for the option is because he believes that the share price will move by more than 35 pence within the next three months. Time value will decay through time, as the chance that the option will be exercised lessens.

Fair value

Fair value is the result of the premium calculation performed by the option-pricing model. The figure is a breakeven figure for the writer of the option. The premium that the client pays for the option may be adjusted upwards to allow for a profit margin.

Volatility

This is a measure of the degree of 'scatter' of the range of possible future outcomes for the underlying commodity. A volatility input is only required for options. If you wish to speculate on the level of volatility you will need to trade options. The reason that we need an input for volatility is because of one of the key underlying assumptions in the pricing models. The model assumes that underlying financial data such as exchange rates and interest rates behave within a log-normal distribution. Normal distributions are typically found in nature, for example the height of trees, the weight of children, the length of snakes, etc., are all distributed normally. The volatility input into the model helps generate a prediction of how the particular rate will move in the future. Not necessarily what the rate will be as a number on a specific date in the future, but how the exchange rate or interest rate will get there; will there be a large degree of scatter around a theoretical average or will there be very little movement? The best way to explain this is by using an example from nature.

Imagine data are being collected on the height of king penguins in Antarctica. One hundred penguins will be measured and then the data will be analyzed. Once we have the data, we can calculate the average height of the penguins: this is called the mean.

Many years ago a German scientist by the name of Gauss did some mathematical research. It showed that if you had data taken from a population with a normal distribution, once you had calculated the mean you could calculate certain 'confidence limits'. He worked out that if you took the mean +/– something called a standard deviation, you could ensure that 66 per cent of all the data readings would fall between these limits. He then further predicted that if you took the mean +/– two standard deviations, you could guarantee that 95 per cent of all the data would fall within these wider limits.

Let's assume the penguins have been measured, the mean has been calculated at 1m, and the standard deviation computed at a figure of 10 per cent. This would give us a normal distribution as shown in Figure 3.18.

Possible analysis of the height of king penguins

Fig 3.18

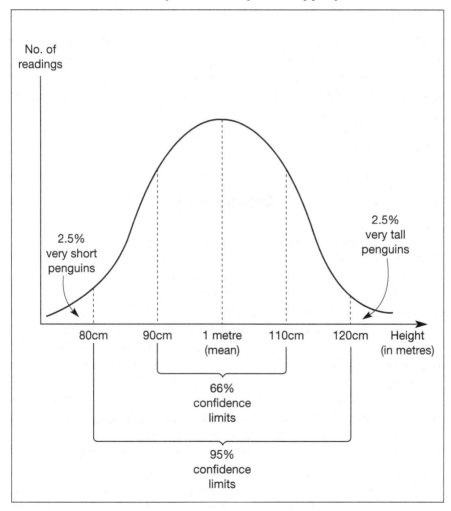

Once you have the data, it is not too difficult to do the calculations: anyone who has studied statistics will recognize the shape of the distribution.

How does all this fit in with options and option pricing? Standard deviation and volatility are the same thing.

The statistical definition of volatility is, 'the normalized, annualized standard deviation of the returns of the underlying commodity'. The biggest problem in using volatility is trying to predict what the volatility level will be in the future, before there are any data to back it up.

For example, a trader trying to price a currency option in three-month US dollar/Yen, has to guess the shape of the normal curve. Will it be steep with low volatility, and most readings about the mean, or will it be very flat, with high volatility and many readings widely scattered? In fact, he is trying to guess how volatile the exchange rate will be in advance. Not an easy thing to do (see Figure 3.19).

Historical data will give an idea of the level of volatility, but will not necessarily be much help in predicting a future value of volatility. The market operates using the concept of 'implied volatility'. This is where it is possible to take data from a premium already quoted, and get the model to work backwards to deduce the volatility. The relationship between volatility and premium is linear; as volatility increases so does the premium (see Figure 3.20).

Option pricing

Most option pricing has evolved from the original model written by Black and Scholes in the early 1970s. There has been a fair amount of tinkering with the basic formula to make it work with interest rates and currency, but its essential element confirms that financial data move in the same way as nature, and that the normal distribution is a fair way of looking at it. Options are actually based on a log-normal distribution which is very different to a straight normal distribution to a statistician, but for our purposes, it is close enough to be viewed similarly.

The option pricing model itself is based on a 'black box' concept (see Figure 3.21), whereby a number of inputs are requested, and then the model calculates the premium. Whichever input you do not give the model, it will take the data from the other inputs and work backwards. This is how we mostly determine the 'implied volatility'. It means the volatility implied in the price. This price can come from a premium that another bank has quoted, or it can come from a price which refers to an exchange-traded option contract. Here, price transparency ensures that everyone can see the premium being quoted and traded, because the Bridge and other information networks are transmitting the data around the world.

The effect of different volatility levels on the shape of the normal curve

Fig 3.19

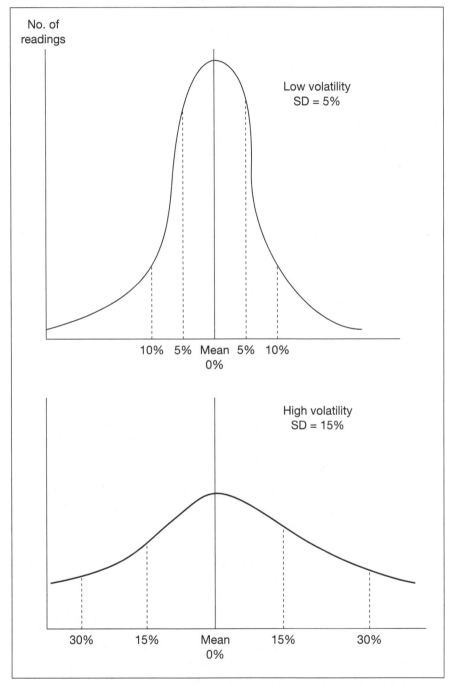

Fig 3.20

Linear relationship of option premium vs volatility

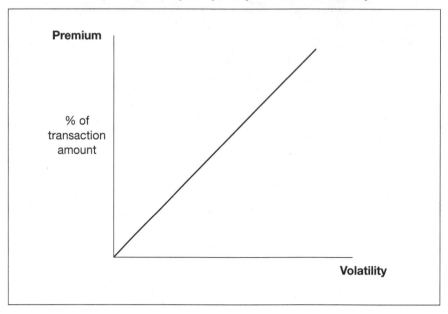

Option mechanics

The most straightforward way to go about understanding the way options work is to draw the profit and loss profile (P/L) of the transaction at expiry. Consider the price of gold; if a trader bought physical gold bullion today in the expectation of the gold price rising, the P/L profile would look like the one shown in Figure 3.22.

The trader has bought the gold at US$250 per ounce. If gold appreciates in value, the position will start moving into profit. But if the gold price weakens, the same position would move into loss. This is an unhedged position, with an equal probability of profit or loss.

Alternatively, instead of running this risk, an option could be purchased that at the same level of US$250 per ounce would allow the same 1:1 profit opportunity, but where the only potential downside would be the loss of the premium paid. This would be a call option on gold: the trader has bought the option, so he is 'long' the call (see Figure 3.23).

The attraction of the options lies in the limited downside risk represented by the premium, compared to the unlimited downside on the physical bullion position. Both have upside potential, although the premium cost of the option must not be forgotten.

The profile of the option resembles that of the unhedged position, except that it starts from a negative position reflecting the premium paid. It is important to take into account the premium on the option and any

Variable inputs for option premium calculation

Fig 3.21

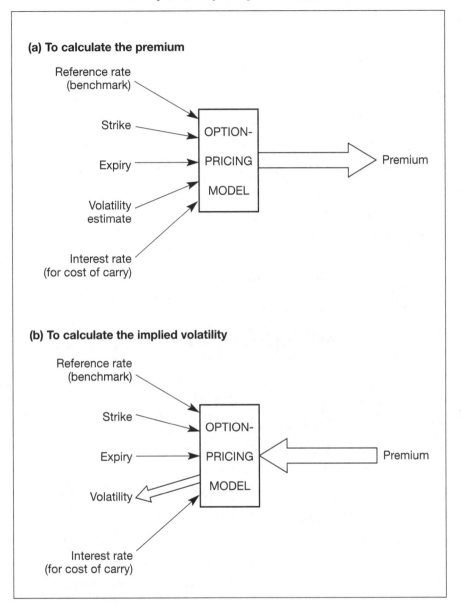

(a) To calculate the premium

Reference rate
(benchmark)

Strike

Expiry

Volatility
estimate

Interest rate
(for cost of carry)

OPTION-
PRICING
MODEL

Premium

(b) To calculate the implied volatility

Reference rate
(benchmark)

Strike

Expiry

Volatility

Interest rate
(for cost of carry)

OPTION-
PRICING
MODEL

Premium

associated holding or funding costs. An option purchaser may need to fund (borrow) the option premium, and an option writer must deposit the premium, so the deposit interest rate that the trader obtains must be factored into the final option premium.

The bank writing the gold call option would have a mirror-image position, where it had received the premium (see Figure 3.24).

Fig 3.22

Profit/loss profile of physical gold position

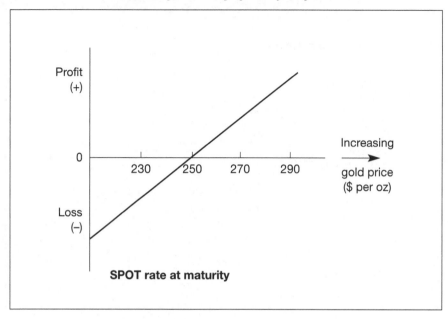

Fig 3.23

Profit/loss profile of long call strategy

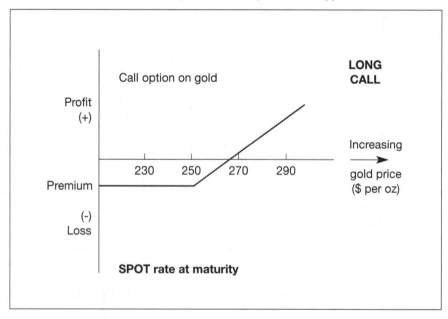

With this position, the bank that has written the option is 'short' the call option; all it has taken in is the premium, yet its potential for loss is high.

Profit/loss profile of short call strategy

Fig 3.24

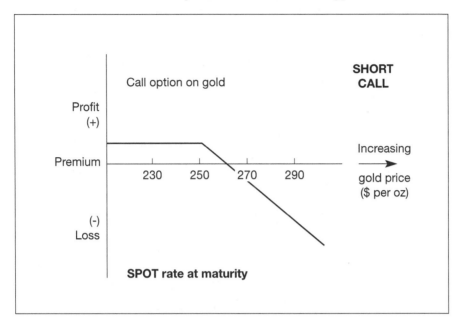

The trader has just changed his mind about the direction of the gold price. He now feels that it is going to weaken, so with his new trade he needs to buy a put option on gold (see Figure 3.25).

Profit/loss profile of long put strategy

Fig 3.25

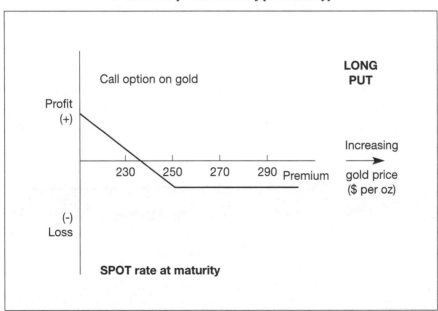

Fig 3.26

Profit/loss profile of short put strategy

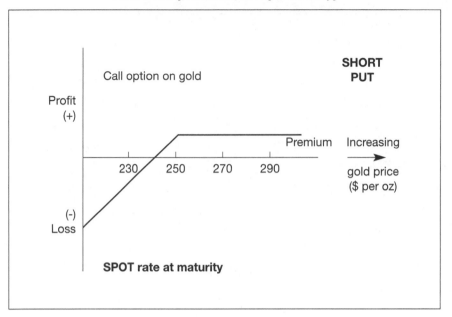

This P/L profile shows again that the holder of this option can lose only his premium, but can profit as long as the market moves in his favour. In comparison the writer of the option whose P/L profile is shown in Figure 3.26 is 'short' the gold put option, and, could lose a considerable amount.

In all, there are four basic building blocks in options: calls and puts; bought and sold.

The four strategies, long call, short call, long put, short put, are shown in Figures 3.23, 3.24, 3.25, 3.26.

These four strategies will allow the user to build some very complex strategies by using the options either singly or in combination. Even the most elaborate strategies can be broken down into their component parts which by definition must include these components of calls and puts, bought and sold.

INTEREST RATE OPTIONS (IROs)

Introduction

An interest rate option (IRO) is a derivative which is used to hedge either single periods of interest rate exposure, eg. a three-month period from 1 February, or a series of sequential periods, such as three months from 1 February, and from 1 May, and from 1 August. In the latter case, a series of IROs will be needed, known as a 'strip'. It is also possible to hedge this type of longer exposure with a 'strip' of FRAs or a 'strip' of financial futures. Some market practitioners know these derivatives collectively as interest rate guarantees

There are two different types of interest rate options: those traded on a regulated exchange and OTC options that are custom tailored for the client. This section will focus on OTC interest rate options.

> An **interest rate option** *gives the buyer the right, but not the obligation, to fix the rate of interest on a notional loan or deposit for an agreed amount for an agreed period on a specific future date. A premium is due.*

Definition

Definition discussed

This option gives the prospective borrower or lender the chance to fix the rate of interest that will apply to their forthcoming transaction. The option instrument will let the client choose the guaranteed rate, the writing bank will then guarantee that rate if/when required by the customer. Because this insurance is optional, and the client is not obligated to take the cover, a premium is required. The premium must be paid upfront the same day, if it is a sterling or domestic currency interest rate option, and within two days, if it is a foreign currency interest rate option transaction. Take a US dollar interest rate option written by a UK bank in London. The buyer of the option has no obligation to lend to or borrow from the writing bank. On expiry, the bank will make a cash payment to the customer to compensate for the extent (if any) to which the option strike rate is more advantageous than LIBOR.

In these circumstances the customer is the buyer of the option and must pay the premium, the bank is the seller or writer of the option, and must have the 'underlying' ready in case the client needs it. The underlying in this case is the loan or investment at a particular interest rate. However, this instrument is cash settled, and at expiry, a cash lump sum will be paid equivalent to the difference between the two interest rates.

Interest rate options are similar to FRAs and financial futures, and can be used to fix the rate of interest on a forthcoming transaction.

Interest rate options

Insurance protection

The client pays a premium to insure against adverse interest rate movements. The bank in return agrees to guarantee a fixed rate of interest if/when required by the client.

Profit potential

The risk of adverse interest rate movements is eliminated, while at the same time, the buyer retains the potential to benefit from favourable interest rate movements. The option can be allowed to lapse if interest rates move in the customer's favour.

Sell back

Interest rate options can be sold back to the writing bank, for residual or fair value if they are no longer required. They are not transferable, there is no secondary market.

Cash settlement

The underlying principal funds are not involved. The client is not obliged to deposit with or borrow from the same bank. On exercise, the bank will pay the difference between the option strike rate and the current LIBOR, discounted back for as the early settlement.

Cash market linked

No basis risk. This means hedging 'apples with apples', not 'apples with pears'. A 6-month LIBOR transaction can be hedged with a 6-month LIBOR derivative. With futures there is a limitation, in that each future is linked to a 3-month LIBOR. If you are hedging a 6-month LIBOR, then the futures hedge would not be very efficient. It would be necessary to buy twice the amount of futures contracts for a 6-month exposure, and two 3-month LIBORs do not make a 6-month LIBOR.

Premium determinants

Once a client is comfortable with the concept of options he will need to seek an indication price from an option trader or through the bank's corporate sales desk. The amount of premium that a client must pay to buy an interest rate option is determined by five factors:

- underlying price
- strike price
- maturity
- call or put
- expected market volatility.

(a) Underlying price vs strike price

With interest rate options the underlying benchmark rate against which the strike price is measured is the appropriate FRA rate. Strikes are therefore referred to as follows:

		Terminology
At the money (ATM)	where the strike is equal to the current FRA rate.	
In the money (ITM)	where the strike is more favourable than the FRA rate, and the option premium is higher than that for an ATM option.	
Out of the money (OTM)	where the strike is worse than the FRA rate and the option premium is lower than that for an ATM option.	

(b) Maturity

The longer the time to expiry, the higher the probability of large interest rate movements, and the higher the chance of profitable exercise by the buyer. The buyer should be prepared to pay a higher premium for a longer dated option than a short-dated option. The premium, however, is not proportional to maturity.

(c) Call or put

This is important for determining whether the option is in, at, or out of the money. With interest rate options, the terms 'call' and 'put' have been replaced by 'borrowers' and 'lenders' options respectively.

(d) Expected market volatility

The higher the volatility the greater the possibility of profitable exercise by the customer, so the option is more valuable to the company, therefore the premium is higher. With interest rate options, it is not too difficult to establish a level of implied volatility. The procedure would be to find the nearest exchange-traded interest rate future, then find the option on the future, see where the price is, and use that as an input to make the pricing model work backwards.

Various market factors may lead to an increase in the option premium: these include events such as government intervention, imposition of new taxes, exchange controls, politics, or illiquidity in the market. In general terms, anything that may destabilize an interest rate or a currency will lead to an increase in volatility, so the option premium will increase.

Terminology

Interest rate options

Strike price	Specified interest rate where the client can exercise his right to cash settlement.
Borrowers' option	An option used to hedge against a rise in interest rates, or to speculate that interest rates will increase.
Lenders' option	An option to hedge against a fall in interest rates, or to speculate that interest rates will fall.
Exercise	Take-up of the option on expiry.
Expiry date	The date when the option may be exercised, two business days before the value date if in currency, or same day if in sterling.
Value date	The date of (settlement) payment.
Premium	The price of the option, as determined by the option-pricing model.
Intrinsic value	Difference between the strike price and the current market rate.
Time value	Option premium minus intrinsic value, reflecting the time until expiry, changes in volatility, and market expectations.

Example

Hedging with sterling interest rate options

1 May

The treasurer of a medium-sized UK company has a number of loans at variable rates linked to LIBOR. His view is that interest rates will decrease, but the finance director believes the next move will be upwards.

An interest rate option can cater for both eventualities, and not leave them exposed. If rates increase, the IRO will refund the difference; if interest rates fall, the treasurer will abandon the option, and the loan will be transacted at a lower LIBOR rate. One particular £5 million loan has a rollover in six months' time (on 1 November), when the LIBOR will be re-fixed for the next six months.

Current financial data:
6-month LIBOR is currently 5.25 per cent
6s–12s FRA is 5.10 to 5.00 per cent

Action – 1 May

The treasurer asks for an indication price for a borrower's option to protect (or guarantee) the present LIBOR level of 5.25 per cent. This will insure the rate of 5.25 per cent, and should interest rates fall, he will be able to profit by dealing at the lower borrowing rate – by abandoning the option cover. This will be a 6s–12s borrower's interest rate option (IRO).

NB: This is an OTM option: although it is the same level as the current LIBOR, it is out of the money compared to the FRA rate by 0.15 per cent (5.25 per cent–5.10 per cent).

The bank quotes an indication rate of 16 bp pa – 16 basis points per annum. A basis point is 0.01 per cent. To establish the premium due for this option, a small calculation must be done, based on the actual number of days for the option is required for. In this example, the loan rollover is six calendar months away. Assume there are 180 days in the period; after this the loan rate will be confirmed, so there is no more uncertainty. It is necessary to hedge only the uncertainty period.

$$\frac{£5,000,000 \times 180 \text{ days} \times 0.16}{36,500}$$

This comes to £3,945.21 payable upfront, and the treasurer proceeds with the transaction. The treasurer believed that the underlying six-month interest rate could increase or decrease by 1 per cent in the six-month period before the LIBOR was re-fixed. In which case there are a list of possible outcomes (see Figure 3.27), the extremes of which are:

1 November

(1) If the 6-month LIBOR is 6.25 per cent, the treasurer will exercise his option, giving him a net borrowing cost of 5.41 per cent.

We get this from the guaranteed interest rate on the option, but we must then take into account the option premium of 16 bp. As both the option premium and the LIBOR are quoted on an annualized basis, we

Fig 3.27

Effective borrowing costs for a sterling interest rate option

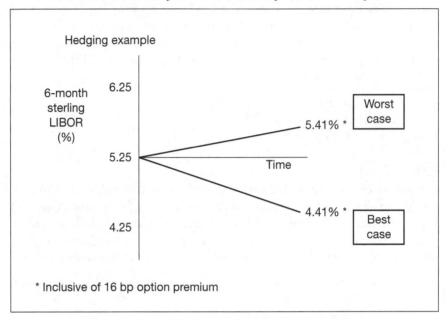

Hedging example

6-month
sterling
LIBOR
(%)

6.25

5.25

4.25

Time

5.41% * Worst case

4.41% * Best case

* Inclusive of 16 bp option premium

can add up the two figures to arrive at a breakeven rate of 5.41 per cent. (2) If the 6-month LIBOR had fallen to 4.25 per cent, the option will be allowed to lapse, and the borrowing will be funded at the new lower rate of 4.41 per cent (inclusive of premium).

The treasurer has insured against an adverse interest rate movement for a limited and known cost, and preserved his right to benefit if the cash interest rates move in his favour. This option has guaranteed for the client a worse rate. If rates go higher than the option strike of 5.25 per cent, the client will always exercise the option. So in practice the worse rate is 5.25 per cent. But if the treasurer is lucky, and interest rates fall, then he will abandon the option and borrow at the cheaper rate. There is no limit to the amount of profit he can make on the deal, the extent of the profit is limited only by how far the market moves in his favour (see Figure 3.28).

Using Eurodollar interest rate options to hedge an investment

10 April

The treasurer of a small European bank based in Paris is concerned that dollar interest rates will soon fall. He will place a six-month fixed-term deposit of US$25 million on the money market in three months' time, but is worried that by the time the funds arrive, and he can place the

Sterling interest rate option example

Fig 3.28

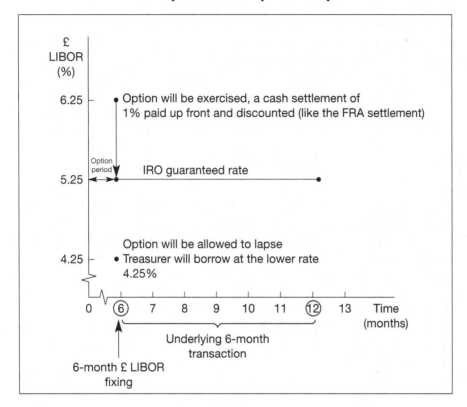

deposit, interest rates will have already fallen. The bank's economist disagrees with that view, and believes that rates will either stay the same, or go up.

Current financial data:
6-month LIBOR is currently 6.25 per cent
3s–9s FRA is 6.12 – 6.07 per cent

Action – 10 April
The treasurer asks for an indication price for a lender's option to protect (or guarantee) the present LIBOR level of 6.25 per cent. This will insure the rate of 6.25 per cent, and should rates rise, he will be able to profit by dealing at the higher investment rate. This will be a 3s–9s lender's IRO.

NB: *This option is slightly ITM: although it is at the same level as the current LIBOR, it is in the money compared to the FRA rate by 0.18 per cent (6.25 per cent – 6.07 per cent).*

The bank quotes an indication rate of 55 bp p.a. – 55 basis points per annum. A basis point is 0.01 per cent. Remember this includes 0.18 per cent of intrinsic value. To establish the premium due for this option, a small calculation must be done, based on the actual number of days that the option is required for. In this example, the investment will be placed in exactly three calendar months' time. All Eurodollar calculations are based on a 30-day month and a 360-day year. In three months' time, the investment rate will be agreed in the market, so there is no more uncertainty. It is only necessary to hedge the uncertainty period from now until month three.

$$\frac{US\$25,000,000 \times 90 \text{ days} \times 0.55}{36,000}$$

This comes to US$34,375.00 payable in two business days' time. The bank treasurer assumes that the underlying six-month interest rate could increase or decrease by 1 per cent in the three-month period before the funds are available to invest. There is a list of possible outcomes (see Figure 3.29), the extremes of which are:

Action – 10 August
(1) If the 6-month LIBOR is 5.25 per cent, the treasurer will exercise his option, at 6.25 per cent giving him a net investment rate of 5.7 per cent.

Fig 3.29

Effective investment rates for a Eurodollar interest rate option

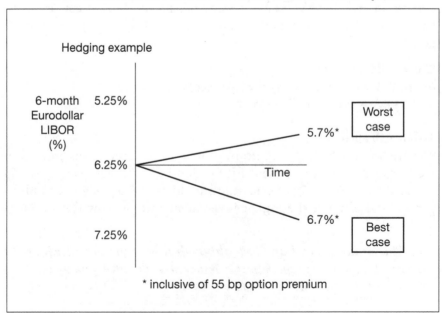

Hedging example

6-month Eurodollar LIBOR (%)

5.25%

6.25%

7.25%

Time

5.7%* — Worst case

6.7%* — Best case

* inclusive of 55 bp option premium

We get this from the guaranteed interest rate on the option, but we must then take into account the option premium of 55 bp. As both the option premium and the LIBOR are both quoted on an annualized basis, we can subtract 55 bp from 6.25 per cent to arrive at a breakeven rate of 5.7 per cent.

(2) If the 6-month LIBOR has risen to 7.25 per cent, the option will be allowed to lapse, and the investment will be placed at the higher rate of 6.7 per cent (inclusive of premium).

The treasurer has insured against an adverse interest rate movement for a limited and known cost, and preserved his right to benefit, if the cash interest rates move in his favour. This option has guaranteed a worse case rate for the client who happens to be a bank. If rates go lower than the option strike of 6.25 per cent, the client will always exercise the option. So, in practice, the worst rate is 6.25 per cent. But, if the client is lucky, and interest rates rise, then he will abandon the option and invest at a better rate (see Figure 3.30). There is no limit to the amount of profit he can make on the deal, the extent of the profit is limited only by how far the market moves in his favour.

Hedging a Eurodollar investment with interest rate options

Fig 3.30

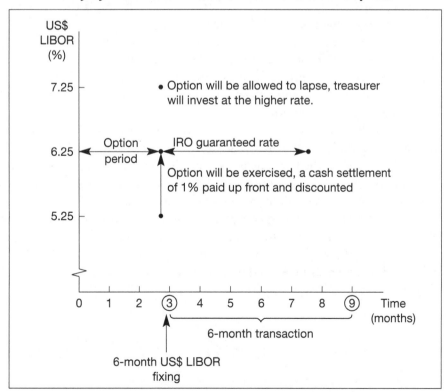

Availability

IROs are normally available in amounts from £2 million. However, some banks will make prices in smaller transactions for their own clients, sometimes as low as £500,000. Clients can transact for any period over one month, including broken dates (non-calendar dates, not whole month periods), as long as the start date of the IRO is at least about two weeks forward, and the end-date is not more than three years. IROs are usually for multiples of three-monthly periods, e.g., 3s–6s or 6s–12s, and are available in all major currencies. If the option is no longer required it may be sold back to the writing bank for residual or fair value.

Practical considerations

The real value of options is that the client can actively manage his interest rate risk. Not only by choosing an instrument that can be abandoned if the market improves, but also by choosing an instrument where one can select the rate of interest; this can be ITM or OTM or ATM. The premium will be calculated according to many different parameters, but the client will always pay up if he chooses an ITM option, as the intrinsic value is a major component of the price.

There is no such things as a free lunch. If a client needs an ITM option, he will pay for it with a more expensive premium.

Most interest rate options are European style, whereby they can be exercised only on the expiry date. This is the date when the underlying borrowing or investment transaction commences.

Occasionally, it is possible to defer the payment of the premium, and pay at maturity of the option. This would need to be arranged specifically with the credit officers at the bank, as in practice the client is asking the bank to loan him the money for the premium. The bank may wish to do this, but the interest rate for the loan of the premium is likely to be fairly high.

It is always worth seeking competitive quotes for these products. But please bear in mind that not as many banks make prices in IROs as they do in, say, 'vanilla' OTC currency options.

Table 3.8 compares FRAs and interest rate options.

Comparison between FRAs and interest rate options

Table 3.8

	Interest rate options	FRAs
Margins	None	None
Premium	Yes	No
Amounts	Custom tailored from £500,000	Custom tailored from £1 million
Maturity	Any date up to five years	Any date up to five years
Liquidity	Fairly good	Good
Flexibility	Exercise at expiry or sell back to writing bank	Reversing FRA to settlement date
Restrictions	None, completely custom tailored	None
Bid/offer spreads	0.10–0.15 per cent	0.03–0.10 per cent
Basis risk	None	None
Credit risk	With the bank for cash settlement of the differential	With the counterparty for cash settlement of the differential
Credit lines	Not required unless option is sold	Required for interest rate differential

'The market for longer dated derivatives has increased enormously: 'long' can now mean periods up to 40 and, in some cases, up to 75 years. The only limiting factor is credit lines.'

Multiple Settlement Interest Rate Derivatives

4

INTRODUCTION

The interest rate derivatives that we have considered so far have involved a single period of interest rate exposure: for example, a 3s–6s FRA will cover the three-month period commencing in three months' time. Once the appropriate cash settlement has been paid/received under the FRA, it has no further use. Likewise, an interest rate option, once it has been cash settled or abandoned, has no further use. However, sometimes the underlying transaction period that needs to be covered may be extended, or it may need to have more than one re-fix or rollover during its lifetime. Where these types of exposures need to be covered, there are two alternatives (see Figure 4.1):

Fig 4.1

Different ways of hedging a longer maturity risk

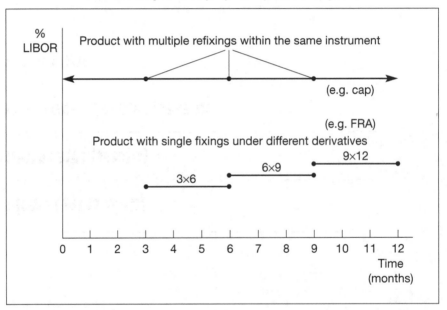

- Construct a 'strip' of products to cover sequential periods, for example 3s–6s, then 6s–9s, then 9s–12s, etc.
- Construct a product that allows multiple fixings, for example a two-year option product with re-fixings or rollovers every three months on pre-determined dates. Swaps could also be used (see later).

The limitation with the first solution is that each individual three-month slot of time will have a different level of interest rate cover. If a borrower wishes to cover his exposure in a rising interest rate market, with a positive yield curve, the cover with a FRA will be achieved at higher and higher rates. In Figure 4.2 we have taken prices from the sterling FRA data in Figure 3.13, which show the variable levels of cover.

NB: *The reason we have not included a 0 ×3 FRA is because the three-month rate today is already known to us. It was fixed at 11 a.m. this morning at the LIBOR fixing.*

FRA rates for a strip 3 × 6, 6 × 9, 9 × 12

Fig 4.2

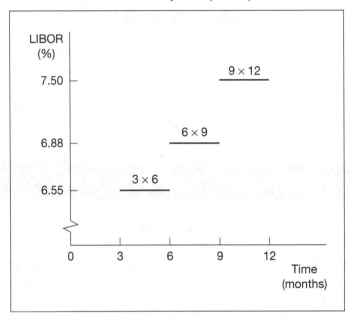

The market for longer dated derivatives has increased enormously: 'long' can now mean periods up to 40 and, in some cases, up to 75 years. The only limiting factor is credit lines. Many users of longer dated interest rate derivatives prefer to have a single 'guaranteed' level of interest, rather than a lot of different rates for different periods. Banks now provide a service in longer dated derivatives that are 'built' from shorter dated products, and linked together to provide a guaranteed level at the same rate, throughout the insured period. In essence there are two types of longer term products that are constructed in this way, interest rate caps and interest rate swaps.

Interest rate caps

An interest rate cap is a series of individual interest rate options with each time period specially tailored. The strike rates or strike prices of each option will be identical. A premium is due, and will cover the entire maturity of the underlying transaction. The client need take up his 'insurance' only if the rate on the interest rate cap is more favourable than that currently available in the market on the rollover date. There is no obligation for him to transact, and he has profit potential in that if on a particular rollover date, the rate in the market is more advantageous, he can abandon the option, and deal at the better rate.

Interest rate swaps

This is similar to a series of sequential FRAs, but all at the same interest rate. It is a zero-cost derivative, meaning that the client is obligated to transact, whatever the market conditions on each of the rollover dates. As such, it fixes the rate of interest for the whole maturity, but for the hedger allows no profit potential. More later.

INTEREST RATE CAPS AND FLOORS

Introduction

An interest rate cap is the term for an option derivative used to cover a longer term borrowing exposure. Interest rate floors are identical, except that the underlying transaction is a deposit or investment rather than a loan. A premium will be required. Typically, maturities are in the two-to five-year range: much longer than this and the premiums can become prohibitive. Each cap or floor will need to have multiple settlements (fixings), with dates that are pre-agreed at the outset.

- A strip of borrower's options = an interest rate cap.
- A strip of lender's options = an interest rate floor.

Definition

> An **interest rate cap** is an agreement that gives the buyer (or holder) the right, but not the obligation to fix the rate of interest on a notional short- or medium-term loan at a specific rate (the strike) for a specified period. The bank will guarantee a maximum funding cost for the client if/when he requires it. The bank will reimburse the holder of the option for any excess funding costs over the agreed strike rate. A premium is due, payable upfront.

> *An* **interest rate floor** *is an agreement that gives the buyer (or holder) the right, but not the obligation, to fix the rate of interest on a notional short- or medium-term investment at a specific rate (the strike) for a specified period. The bank will guarantee a maximum investment rate for the client if/when he requires it. The bank will reimburse the holder of the option for any interest shortfall over the agreed strike rate. A premium is due, payable upfront.*

Definition

Definitions discussed

To clarify the picture we need to open up these definitions. As with all option contracts we have a buyer and a seller of the option itself. Mostly, but not always, the option writers or sellers will be the major banks. Usually, the buyer of the option is a corporate or a financial institution looking to risk manage its position. These derivative products are simply a series of individual options. The terms 'caps' and 'floors' are merely to identify whether the option product is on an underlying loan or investment. This is always done from the perspective of the buyer of the product, and replace the terms 'call' and 'put'. The amount of premium due for these option-based products is calculated by an option-pricing model and the premium quotation itself is most often quoted on a 'flat basis'. This means that if the premium is quoted at 0.9 per cent flat, the premium payment will be 0.9% multiplied by the principal amount. If the client wants to cover a £5 million loan, the cost would be £5 million × 0.9% = £45,000, due same day if in sterling, but two business days later if the cap were in a foreign currency. Care needs to be taken if the client is getting a number of banks to quote for the transaction: some may quote on a 'flat' basis, but, occasionally, others may quote in 'basis points per annum'. In both cases, premiums are paid upfront.

Once the premium has been paid by the buyer to the seller, the buyer (or holder) of the option has no further obligations. On each rollover date, he will simply compare the strike on his cap or floor with the relevant LIBOR fixing for the day and exercise his cover if it is advantageous for him to do so. In contrast, the writing bank will receive the premium, and is then obligated to hedge the banks' position, and must have the 'underlying asset' ready for when the client needs it, if he needs it. With caps and floors there will be a cash settlement on each of the fixing dates (in arrears). If the client has bought the interest rate cap or floor, he will never need to settle with the bank (except for the premium). Instead, where the underlying market has improved he will abandon the option in favour of a better rate in the money markets.

In order to ascertain if a cap or floor is ATM, ITM, or OTM, a benchmark rate is used to compare the strike on the product with current market rates. In this case, the equivalent underlying interest rate swap rate is used.

As caps and floors are multiple settlement products, the FRA reference rate that we used for single interest rate options is no longer relevant.

Key features

Caps and floors

Multiple exercise
A time series of either borrowers or lenders interest rate options with the same strike rates.

Insurance protection
The client pays a premium to insure against interest rate risk.

Profit potential
A cap or floor reduces the cost of adverse interest rate movements while retaining profit potential. The cap or floor can be allowed to lapse (abandoned), if the market has moved in the client's favour.

Cash settlement
Principal funds are not involved. The client is not obliged to deposit with or borrow from the same bank. On exercise, the bank will pay the difference between the strike rate and the relevant LIBOR. Settlement is in arrears, and is paid at the end of that particular three- or six-month period.

Cash-market-linked
There is no basis risk, because both the underlying cash transaction and the hedge are priced from the same market, i.e., LIBOR.

Premium determinants

The amount of premium payable for a cap or a floor is dependent on the same inputs that affect the pricing on interest rate options, notably:

• strike price
• underlying price

- maturity
- expected market volatility.

(a) Strike price vs underlying price

With interest rate caps and floors, the underlying price or benchmark rate is the appropriate interest rate swap rate, taking into account the correct side of the swap, i.e., payer's or receiver's side as appropriate (see section on *interest rate swaps* at the end of this chapter). It is against this reference rate that the client's strike rate is measured. Strike rates are therefore referred to as follows:

At the money (ATM)	Where the strike rate is equal to the current swap rate.	**Terminology**
In the money (ITM)	Where the strike rate is more favourable than the swap rate, and the option premium is higher than that for an ATM option.	
Out of the money (OTM)	Where the strike rate is worse than the swap rate and the option premium is lower than that for an ATM option.	

(b) Maturity

The longer the time to expiry or maturity, the higher the probability of large interest rate movements, and the higher the chance of profitable exercise by the client (buyer). The buyer should be prepared to pay a higher premium for a longer dated option than a short-dated option, although the premium is not proportional to maturity.

(c) Expected market volatility

The higher the volatility, the greater the possibility of profitable exercise by the holder, making the cap or floor more valuable with a higher premium as a result. In general terms, if there is high volatility in the market, then there is a strong likelihood of erratic interest rate movements; therefore there is a good chance that one of these movements may happen close to a LIBOR fixing date, and the client may therefore require compensation (dependent on the direction of the move). Various market factors may lead to an increase in the option premium, and these include events such as, government intervention, imposition of new taxes, rumours and expectations, or illiquidity in the market. In general terms, anything that may destabilize an interest rate or a currency will lead to an increase in volatility, so the option premium will increase.

Interest rate cap and floor

Strike price	Specified interest rate where the client can exercise his right to cash settlement.
Interest rate cap	A series of options to hedge against a rise in interest rates, or to speculate that interest rates will increase.
Interest rate floor	A series of options to hedge against a fall in interest rates, or to speculate that interest rates will fall.
Multiple exercise	Take-up of the option on various fixing dates.
Rollover date	The date when the option may be exercised, two business days before the value date if in currency, or same day if in sterling.
Value date	The date of the cash payment (settlement).
Premium	The price of the option, as determined by the option-pricing model.
Intrinsic value	Strike rate minus the current market rate.
Time value	Option premium minus intrinsic value, reflecting the time until expiry, changes in volatility, and market expectations.

Hedging with a sterling interest rate cap

15 September

A UK company managing director has approved the acquisition of a troublesome competitor. The treasurer needs to borrow £10 million for two years, he believes that rates will fall during the period, but is concerned at the weakness of the exchange rate, which might actually cause interest rates to move against him in the short term. The funding will come from the money markets and is linked to 6-month LIBOR. This, however, could leave the company exposed to rising rates.

Action – 15 September

The treasurer asks his bank for an indication cap price as follows:

Term	Two years
Rollovers	6-monthly LIBOR
Face value	£10 million
Strike	1 per cent away from the current swap rate (1 per cent out of the money)
Premium	1.65 per cent of face value = £165,000 payable upfront

This will give full protection starting at a rate of 5.65 per cent (worse than the two-year semi-annual swap rate by 1 per cent). After checking that this premium is in line with that quoted by other market operators, the treasurer proceeds with the transaction (see Figure 4.3).

Hedging with a sterling interest rate cap

Fig 4.3

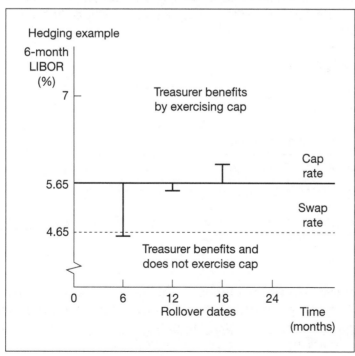

Outcome

On each of the six-monthly rollover dates commencing 15 March, the bank will settle with the company the amount by which the 6-month LIBOR exceeds the cap strike price. If the LIBOR has not risen above the cap strike price, then the treasurer will re-fix his loan at a more advantageous rate, and will keep all the benefit.

An **interest rate floor** *is identical in operation to an interest rate cap, and protects the buyer by fixing the minimum deposit rate on an investment as shown in the following example.*

Example

Hedging with a US dollar interest rate floor

1 November

A French company has just divested one of its US subsidiaries. It received US$25 million, and is about to place this on a 12-month deposit linked to floating rate three-month money (London inter-bank bid rate). The treasurer needs to be sure that the investment rates are competitive, but he cannot wait until rates improve as his company does not allow him to speculate on the deposit rates. The company believes that rates will improve during the period, but is concerned that short-term volatility may affect the interest rate. The actual cash investment will be placed in the Euro-currency money markets and is linked to 3-month LIBID. This could leave the company exposed to falling interest rates. The treasurer is aware that any derivative he uses to hedge his position will be linked to LIBOR not LIBID.

Action – 1 November

Term	12 months
Rollovers	3-month LIBOR
Face value	US$25 million
Strike	At the money
Premium	1.00 per cent of face value = US$250,000 payable within two business days

The treasurer asks his bank for an indication floor price as follows:
This will give full protection starting at a rate of 5 per cent, the same as the equivalent 12-month US dollar quarterly swap. The company decides to hedge its transaction at this rate (see Figure 4.4).

Hedging with a US dollar interest rate floor

Fig 4.4

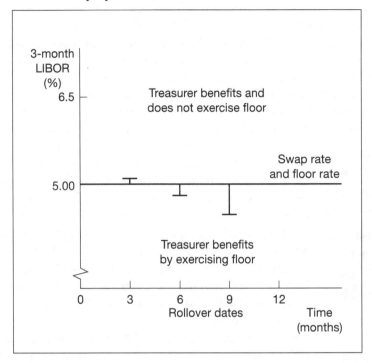

Outcome

On each of the three-monthly rollover dates, the bank will settle with the company the amount by which the floor rate exceeds the 3-month LIBOR. If interest rates do not fall but rise, the treasurer will be able to re-fix his investment at a better rate.

Practical considerations

When a client purchases a cap or floor, his only responsibility is to pay the premium required. Once this has been paid, he has no further obligations. However he could choose to pay the premium by selling another option product to the bank, in effect by trying to create a reduced cost strategy. He would then be opening himself up to possible risk (see the next section on *interest rate collars*). It is because of this risk that the banks take a very different view of client credit risk, depending upon whether the client wishes to buy the derivative, sell it outright or both.

The examples we have examined so far in this chapter involve a client buying the interest rate protection. Technically, the bank who sells the product to the client has no credit risk. Under the terms of the cap and floor agreement, the client can walk away from the product anyway, so if the client has got into difficulties, and needs to walk away, in terms of the credit risk it is the same. The client is not committed to pay anything to the bank anyway, so the bank is still in the same position.

However, if the client is a little more adventurous, he may have sold the product to the bank in return for premium. This will cause the credit department more concern, as by taking the premium the client is undertaking to 'deliver the underlying', should the purchasing bank require it. If for some reason, the client does not hedge his position, and the bank calls up to exercise its cap or floor, the client will not be in a position to deliver, and may have got himself into a serious loss position. As a consequence a bank may be prepared to sell caps and floors to their clients, but generally will not purchase these products from their clients, unless the credit risk is either collateralized or a credit line is in existence.

> 'An interest rate cap is the term for an option derivative used to cover a longer term borrowing exposure. Interest rate floors are identical, except that the underlying transaction is a deposit or investment rather than a loan.'

On a practical note, it is vital to match the cap and floor LIBOR settlement dates to the underlying rollover dates for the loan or investment, otherwise the LIBOR on the derivative may settle a day adrift from that on the underlying deal, and this may well involve losses.

When seeking prices for these products it is always worth 'going competitive', except when the principal amounts are too low (less than £1 million, or US$1 million or equivalent). In addition, different banks may credit assess customers in different ways, and so seek different cover.

Availability

Interest rate caps and floors are generally available in amounts from £5 million, and for periods up to seven years, although the majority of business is written in the two- to five-year range. They are also available in most major currencies, with both the strike rate and the rollover frequency selected by the client. Smaller transactions may be available at some banks.

INTEREST RATE COLLARS

Introduction

In the previous section, we looked at how to cover or 'insure' the interest rate on a medium- or longer term exposure by using option-based products. In that case, the client would need to purchase a cap or a floor, depending upon whether he wished to hedge a loan or an investment. But whatever he decided to do, he would have to pay a premium. Option cover where the client has the right to walk away from the 'insured' level will always carry a charge. In some cases, especially where the underlying transaction may be for a number of years, the premium due for this cover can be considerable.

Reducing the premium

There are a number of ways in which the client can reduce the premium payable on the cap or floor. The first alternative is usually to go 'out of the money'. Instead of having insurance at today's interest rates, where you would get an immediate payout, consider insurance about 0.5 per cent away (worse). The market then has to move further against you before you start to get reimbursement. This is similar to a motor insurance policy with, say, a £100 excess. In that case you are still insured, but for every claim you will cover yourself, or self-insure the first £100, and if the total claim is under £100 you receive nothing from the insurance company.

It is possible to design caps and floors that are out of the money, but it should be borne in mind that you can never go so far out of the money that the option cover costs you nothing! For a borrower or an investor, even if the option is only 0.25 per cent out of the money, the premium will still be lower. But, in some cases, the client may be looking for a greater premium reduction, or is not prepared to go sufficiently out of the money. Then we need to investigate other ways of paying the premium; in other words still pay the premium, but not with money. That begs the question, how else can the client pay the premium? The only available alternative is for the client to agree to give up some of his potential profit, should the interest rates move in his favour. It must be stressed that interest rates may not move in the client's favour, and that it is only a potential profit that the client is giving up. If rates do not move in the

> 'An interest rate collar reduces the risk of adverse interest rate movements while retaining the client's ability to benefit from part of any favourable movement.'

client's favour then he has given up nothing, and he still has his insurance cover, although he will have achieved the cover at a reduced cost.

The mechanics for the client giving up some profit potential involve him buying the option cover he requires and guaranteeing his insured rate (and protecting his downside), and simultaneously selling a similar second option back to the bank. This second option will have a strike rate exactly at the point where the client has agreed to give up any further profit. On the first option the premium is paid, but this will be offset by the second option where premium is received by the client. The resulting net premiums can be positive, negative or zero, depending on exactly how much profit potential the client is willing to give up.

> **Definition**
>
> *An **interest rate collar** is a contract between a bank and a client, whereby if the client's funding cost is greater than an agreed level, he will be reimbursed down to that level. If the client's funding costs fall below a second agreed level, the client agrees to repay any extra benefit to the bank. An upfront premium is payable, but will be lower than that for a cap or floor and can be zero.*

Definition discussed

If we take the case of a borrower who wishes to cover the variable interest rate on his loan for a period of say, three years, at a strike of 7 per cent but at reduced cost, the deal mechanics would be as follows.

The borrower would first confirm what level of insurance he wanted on the transaction. Assume he has already been quoted for a cap that is 0.5 per cent out of the money, but for him the premium quoted by the bank is too expensive given his interest rate outlook. The bank has quoted a premium of 1.3 per cent flat for the whole period, paid upfront. If he does not wish to go further out of the money, but still wants a cheaper alternative, then we have to look at these other ways of how he can pay the premium.

Let us assume that over the life of the borrowing transaction the client believes that interest rates may fall but only by say 1.5 per cent. He can then put that in writing, in effect guaranteeing to the bank that should rates fall below this rate of 5.5 per cent (7 per cent – 1.5 per cent), then he will take no further profit. The way he does this is to sell an interest rate floor to the bank at a strike of 5.5 per cent. Again, let us assume that the bank will pay him a premium of 0.8 per cent flat. This can go to offset the original premium that he paid on his interest rate cap at 7 per cent. The resulting net premium has now fallen, from a level of 1.3 per cent, to 1.3% – 0.8% = 0.5%.

If we go back to the definition, the original agreed strike level is 7 per cent, and if there are any LIBOR fixings throughout the life of the loan that are above that rate then the bank will compensate the client for any difference, on a cash settlement basis (in arrears, not upfront like in the FRA and interest rate options). If there is a LIBOR fix between the level of cap and floor (between 7 per cent and 5.5 per cent) then the client will be able to re-fix his loan at a lower rate than that he had insured through the cap. This is how the client makes a profit, by borrowing at a cheaper rate. But if there is a LIBOR fix of say, 5 per cent, which is below our second agreed level of 5.5 per cent, then the client can only profit down to his agreed level of 5.5 per cent, he will be unable to profit by the extra 0.5 per cent, – this is the 'opportunity cost' of doing this deal.

An interest rate collar can also be used to hedge the yield on investments, in which case the client will buy the floor option and offset the premium by selling a cap.

Interest rate collars

Multiple exercise

A cap and a floor transacted simultaneously, with pre-agreed LIBOR fixings. The cap and floor can be exercised on each LIBOR fix.

Insurance

The client pays a premium to insure against interest rate risk. The premium will be lower as part of the risk is accepted by the client. He also agrees to share part of the profit with the bank. The net premium may be zero.

Profit potential

A collar reduces the risk of adverse interest rate movements while retaining the client's ability to benefit from part of any favourable movement.

Cash settlement

The principal funds are not involved. The client is not obliged to deposit with or borrow from the same bank. On each rollover date, the bank will pay the positive difference between the collar strike rates and the relevant LIBOR fix.

Cash market linked

No basis risk, because both the underlying cash transaction and the hedge are priced from the same LIBOR market.

Hedging with a sterling interest rate collar

A large US corporation has a European subsidiary which will shortly be placing a £10 million deposit. The parent company has insisted on a three-year maturity with three-month fixings. The treasurer of the subsidiary company is concerned that interest rates may become more volatile, and does not wish to be 'locked in' to an insurance rate. Rather, he wants a product like an interest rate floor, where he can walk away from the cover, should the underlying interest rates in the market be more beneficial. However, he does not wish to pay full price for the risk management strategy: instead he is investigating zero- or reduced-cost solutions. To get an idea of current rates, he puts up a Telerate page from one of his brokers (see Figure 4.5).

Our treasurer will need to buy the floor and sell the cap. The current at the money rate is just about 6.75 per cent; the treasurer wants to purchase the floor at 6.5 per cent (slightly OTM), giving a premium payable of 1.18 per cent, against this, he is prepared to give up any further profit above 7.5 per cent; so he will also sell the cap at 7.5 per cent. For that he will receive a premium of 1.09 per cent, making a net cost of 1.18% – 1.09% = 0.09%.

The total cost of this collar transaction is 0.09% × £10 million = £9,000, due the same day.

This is not quite a zero-cost transaction but has reduced the premium significantly. If the client had wanted a zero-cost transaction he would have requested the bank to work out the strike of the second option – it can sometimes be too difficult and time consuming to try and establish the zero-cost line by trial and error. The bank would price the floor, work out the premium required, then make the pricing model work backwards, put in the premium and the expected volatility and the model will calculate the corrrect strike on the cap for that premium.

Strategy

The treasurer could purchase either of the following interest rate collars:
1.

Term	Three years
Rollovers	Three-monthly – linked to LIBOR
Face value	£10 million
Strike rate	Cap 7.5 per cent Floor 6.5 per cent
Premium:	0.09 per cent nett

Indication of sterling cap and floor levels

Fig 4.5

01/07 11:21 NYC [GARBAN-INTERCAPITAL LONDON] 4945 07/01 05:09 GMT

STERLING CAPS AND FLOORS

[CAP PRICES (BASIS POINTS)]

	6.25%	6.50%	6.75%
1YR/3	24-26	16-18	10-12
2YR/3	122 128	100 105	80 86

	6.50%	7.00%	7.50%
3YR/3	208-219	151-163	109-120
4YR/3	319 330	246 258	189 201
5YR/3	417-432	330-345	261-276

	7.00%	7.50%	8.00%
7YR/3	481 505	392 415	320 343
10YR/3	683-718	571-606	479-514

[FLOOR PRICES (BASIS POINTS)]

	6.25%	6.50%	6.75%
1YR/3	15-18	25-28	38-40
2YR/3	39 44	56 62	78 84

	6.50%	7.00%	7.50%
3YR/3	108-118	174-185	255-266
4YR/3	190 201	279 291	385 396
5YR/3	279-294	390-406	520-535

	5.50%	6.00%	6.50%
7YR/3	733-768	343 364	473 495
10YR/3	462-491	619-651	806-841

[IMPLIED VOLS]
[ATM]
[CAPS/FLOORS]

1YR	13.0-15.0
2YR	17.7 19.2
3YR	19.7-20.7
4YR	20.7 21.7
5YR	22.0-23.0
7YR	22.2 23.2
10YR	22.0-23.0

[TELEPHONE 44 171 588 7558 OPTIONS INDEX ON DOW JONES PAGE 4940]

Source: Garban-Intercapital plc (*courtesy*: Bridge Information Systems)

2. Or, alternatively, a similar collar:

Strike rate	Cap 7.5 per cent
	Floor 7.0 per cent
Premium	0.76 per cent nett

Figure 4.6 illustrates how the collar is used.

Outcome

On each of the rollover dates, the LIBOR is fixed at 11 a.m. and compared to each of the collar rates.

(i)   If LIBOR is below the floor, the bank will reimburse the difference.

(ii) If LIBOR is between the cap and Floor rate, the client transacts in the cash market, neither option will be exercised.

(iii) If LIBOR is above the cap rate, the client must give back any extra benefit to the bank.

Fig 4.6

£ hedging example using a collar

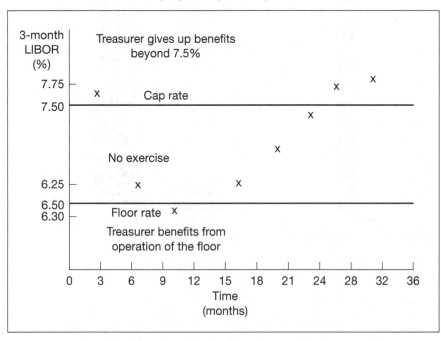

Availability

As these interest rate collars are composite products made up of combinations of caps and floors, their availability will be identical. The only real difference is that one product is bought and one is sold; both transactions need to be carried out simultaneously.

Practical considerations

To implement a collar strategy, it is possible to execute each of the transactions with a different bank. It may happen that on one particular day, a bank may have competitive prices in caps not floors or vice versa. By contacting two different banks and asking for a selection of cap and floor prices, it is possible to 'mix and match' the hedge, so that neither bank knows the strategy is a collar; all that each bank sees is the product that they themselves have been asked to execute. When the premiums of both the cap and the floor net to zero, the product is frequently called a zero-cost collar. But is it really zero cost, or is it simply zero premium where the cost is merely being paid another way?

As one of the components on the collar is an option sold by the client to a bank, a credit line will be required (see Chapter 8 for *credit risk*).

Within the family of option-based interest rate derivatives, there is an element of confusion. When these products were originally designed some years ago, each of the larger banks called their product something different to try and make it stand out from the crowd. Each bank was hoping that its name would become the generic name for the instrument.

1. Single settlement interest rate options
are also known as:

- interest rate insurance
- interest rate guarantees (IRGs)
- options on FRAs.

2. Multiple settlement interest rate products, caps and floors
are also known as:

- interest rate insurance
- interest rate guarantees (IRGs).

3. Reduced premium strategies using caps and floors
are also known as:

- zero-cost (or reduced) cost collars
- zero-cost (or reduced) cost cylinders.

INTEREST RATE SWAPS

Introduction

As mentioned in the section on caps and floors, there are two different ways in which a client can protect himself against a longer term interest rate exposure. First, there are the interest rate caps, floors and collars, and second, the interest rate swaps. The first group of products are option based and require a premium to be paid, although not necessarily with cash. The payment of this premium gives the purchaser 'the right but not the obligation' to borrow or lend at a particular rate. But there is no compulsion. If there is a better rate elsewhere, the option product can be abandoned.

In contrast, the swap group of products are zero cost, and will tie the client into a legal obligation where he must transact at the guaranteed interest rate on the swap on his particular dates, whatever the current market rate. Obviously, this is not a problem if the current rate in the market is worse, then the swap provides a better alternative. But where the underlying market has improved, the client will be unable to benefit, as he is obligated to deal at the original rate. As we have commented before, if you do not pay a premium you cannot expect to profit.

Once the maturity of the underlying loan or deposit extends beyond five years, the liquidity in risk management instruments begins to dry up. This is due partly to the Central Bank's reserve asset requirements, and partly to the prospect of a bank tying up its credit lines, to the client and to other banks when they hedge their swap position. The chapter on credit risk will explain this more fully, but generally each derivative product carries a risk. The longer the maturity of the product, the greater the risk. As clients do more business their credit lines become full up and no further business can be transacted.

The main risk management instrument for medium to long periods is the interest rate swap, although some long-term caps are used. Premium-based products become expensive as the maturity gets longer. An interest rate swap is similar but not identical to a series of sequential but linked FRAs, all at the same interest rate. The swap can fix the rate of interest for the whole maturity, but allows no profit potential.

Background

Swaps are probably the most flexible risk management tool around. They can cover exposures from six months to 25 years and recently one large bank transacted a 75-year interest rate swap. They are increasingly used by banks for their own risk management. They are often combined with bond issues to achieve favourable funding costs, and they can assist a borrower to find fixed rate funding if he is unable to access other lending markets. It must be borne in mind that swaps are not a method of raising finance, rather they are a way of managing an interest rate risk and possibly transform it from fixed interest rates into floating (LIBOR) interest rates or vice versa. In the last few years the market in long-dated currency and interest rate swaps has matured, and the volume of interest rate swaps has increased eight-fold in the last five years.

Table 4.1 shows how the notional volumes of major interest rate derivatives have grown from end March 1995 to end June 1998. Compare these figures with the outstanding nominal amount of

Reported amounts outstanding of OTC single-currency interest rate derivatives by instrument and counterparty at end March 1995 and end June 1998[1]

Table 4.1

In millions of US dollars

Category	End March 1995		End June 1998	
	National amounts outstanding	Gross market values	Notional amounts outstanding	Gross market values[2]
FORWARD RATE AGREEMENTS	4,597,453	18,308	6,601,502	38,671
with reporting dealers	3,371,429	14,748	3,258,151	9,259
with other financial institutions	905,419	2,329	2,779,551	24,589
with non-financial customers	320,608	725	563,799	4,823
SWAPS	18,283,530	562,633	32,942,460	1,186,407
with reporting dealers	10,803,557	308,404	15,581,491	485,611
with other financial institutions	4,358,662	136,725	13,247,744	514,224
with non-financial customers	3,121,130	115,598	4,113,224	186,572
OPTIONS SOLD	2,671,321	41,942	5,821,930	89,468
with reporting dealers	1,466,710	25,422	2,594,566	52,613
with other financial institutions	699,176	7,286	2,365,754	29,640
with non-financial customers	505,436	9,210	861,610	7,215
OPTIONS BOUGHT	2,342,703	43,642	5,319,784	89,279
with reporting dealers	1,465,776	26,302	2,633,263	46,612
with other financial institutions	525,960	8,305	2,058,274	29,417
with non-financial customers	350,967	9,013	628,249	13,251
TOTAL OPTIONS	3,547,781	60,162	8,527,800	126,134
OTHER PRODUCTS	216,437	7,257	52,279	2,344[3]
TOTAL CONTRACTS	26,645,022	648,360	48,124,040	1,353,556

[1] Data adjusted for inter-dealer double-counting. While data on 'total options' are shown on a net basis, separate data on 'options sold' and 'options bought' are recorded on a gross basis, i.e. not adjusted for inter-dealer double-counting.

[2] Counterparty breakdown partly estimated.

[3] Adjustment for inter-dealer double-counting based on the results of the 1995 triennial central bank survey·

interest rate swaps in 1993, which was $6,177 million. Interest rate swap growth has been exceptionally fast. As with all tables, care must be taken when using the information. It takes many months to compile the information, and as a result it is historic before publication, but it is still the most recent available.

All swaps have one common feature: one party is exchanging a benefit it has in one financial market for a corresponding benefit available to another party in another market. This is known as comparative advantage. For example, there may be two different clients, one with an advantage in the bond market, who has access to comparatively cheap long-term fixed rate money. A second client may be able to borrow on a floating rate basis (LIBOR) from his bankers at what he considers to be a very competitive rate. Each participant in the swap market uses his most advantageous market to borrow the physical money, and then through the swap, manages to 'swap' the interest basis on which his loan is based. For example, a client may wish to borrow based on a fixed rate, but the only way he can achieve it, is to borrow from the money markets on a LIBOR-based loan, a 'floating rate', and then to 'swap' into a fixed rate. A swap will allow the client to borrow wherever he likes, at the cheapest rates, and then to enter into an interest rate swap separately, to achieve the interest basis that best suits him, with the bank that has the most competitive swap prices.

There are five basic types of swap:

- **Single currency interest rate swap**
- **Basis swap**
- **Currency swap**
- **Currency basis swap**
- **Cross-currency interest rate swap.**

Currency swaps will be discussed in Chapter 5.

The market in swaps is made up of the world's major banks (central, commercial and investment), as well as supranationals, multinational and national corporates. Although swaps can be used for any period, the bulk of transactions are in the two- to seven-year maturity, with the longest dated swaps being placed against capital market issues for anything up to 75 years. The simplest type of swap is the single currency interest rate swap, which is also the most common. Volume increased world-wide by approximately US$2.5 trillion every half year in the period 1995–1998.

Definition

> *An* **interest rate swap** *is an agreement to exchange interest-related payments in the same currency from fixed rate into floating rate (or vice versa), or from one type of floating rate to another. New or existing debt can be swapped.*

Definition discussed

A swap is a legally binding agreement, where an absolute rate of interest will be guaranteed. One party will agree to pay the 'fixed rate'; the other, to receive this fixed rate and pay the 'floating rate', usually LIBOR. The underlying loan or investment is untouched, and may well be with another bank. The only movement of funds is a net transfer of interest rate payments between the two parties on pre-specified dates. The interest payments are calculated on an agreed principal amount which is not exchanged. Both interest payments are 'netted off' to help minimize credit exposure.

Single currency interest rate swaps

Key features

Insurance protection
Through a swap a client can guarantee the rate of interest he will pay or receive on an underlying loan or deposit. No premium is required, and the swap can be tailored to match exact underlying requirements.

Cash settlement
It is only the interest payments that are swapped, the principal sums are not exchanged.

Funding optimization
As the underlying loan or deposit may be with another bank, the client can deal where he gets the best borrowing and investment rates. The swap will be negotiated separately.

Credit risk
The credit risk of the counterparty must be carefully evaluated, although if a bank is acting as intermediary, it will normally guarantee the creditworthiness of each party to the other.

New or existing obligations
It is possible to swap new or existing debt.

Premium
Swaps are zero-premium instruments and a credit line will be required.

Interest rate swap

IRS	Interest rate swap, sometimes called interest rate insurance.
Fixed payer	The party wishing to pay the fixed rate on the swap (receiving LIBOR).
Fixed receiver	The party wishing to receive the fixed rate on the swap (paying LIBOR).
Swap rate, fixed rate, guaranteed rate	The swap rate agreed between the parties at the outset of the transaction.
Rollovers/ resets	The frequency of the LIBOR settlements, e.g., a two-year swap against 6-month LIBOR. The dates when the 11 a.m. LIBOR fix, and the fixed rate on the swap are net cash settled. Settlement is in arrears.

For example, if on one reset date the fixed rate is 6.5 per cent, and LIBOR is 6.0 per cent, there will be a net payment of 0.5 per cent from the fixed rate payer.

Comparative advantage

The literature on swaps seem to imply that you cannot enter into a swap agreement unless there is 'comparative advantage' present. This is not entirely true.

The easiest way to understand the term 'comparative advantage' is to recall that the word 'swap' is not a financial term. It has come from the playground. Imagine two little boys: one has two red cars, one has two blue cars. One little boy says to the other, 'I'll swap you one of my red cars for one of your blue cars'. If the cars are identical except for colour, the swap may proceed, the key element is that both boys should be better off afterwards, each has a blue car and a red car. But if the little boy with the blue cars has very special blue cars, maybe bigger with more chrome, then he may not wish to proceed with the swap, as he may see himself as being worse off after the swap. However, in this example, one boy has a comparative advantage in the red car market and one in the blue car market.

This seems to suggest that both of the swap participants need to have an advantage somewhere. In fact, if a client simply wishes to hedge an interest rate risk, he will deal directly with a bank who will then become his counterparty, and at the same time an intermediary between the client and maybe another financial institution when the bank hedges his position. Swap banks make money from acting as intermediaries. A swap has no premium payable, so the client, once he has concluded the transaction, will be unable to improve the rate on his hedge, but will be obligated to transact at the swap rate, whatever the current rates are in the market.

There are two distinct types of single currency interest rate swap:

- fixed/floating single currency interest rate swap (also known as a 'vanilla' or 'coupon' swap)
- floating/floating single currency interest rate swap (also known as a basis swap).

Fixed/floating interest rate swaps

A fixed/floating swap is so called because one party pays the fixed rate and the other pays the floating rate. To many in these markets, the term used is 'vanilla' swap. This is the simplest type of swap available, named after the simplest type of ice cream. Capital markets practitioners may call these swaps 'coupon' swaps, to highlight the fact that they are linked to an underlying bond issue, where the interest coupon is being swapped.

For a swap to be known as a vanilla swap it must have the following characteristics:

- a constant notional principal amount (NPA)
- an exchange of fixed against floating interest (coupon swap)
- a constant fixed interest rate
- a flat floating interest rate (e.g. LIBOR flat)
- regular/not necessarily simultaneous payments of fixed/ floating interest
- an immediate or spot start
- no special risk features such as embedded options.

Hedging with a fixed/floating US dollar interest rate swap

Example

A UK company has agreed to purchase and equip a new hotel in the US. Funds of $10 million are required for a period of five years, and the treasurer would ideally prefer a fixed rate of interest for the period. The only fixed rate funds available to her she considers too expensive. Her alternative is to borrow the $10 million on a floating rate basis from the money markets, and rollover the funds every six months. This would, however, leave the company exposed to rising rates. The company has been quoted 6-month LIBOR plus 0.5 per cent for the floating rate loan.

Strategy

The company can take out an interest rate swap which would fix the rate of interest and remove the threat of rising rates. It is important for the swap to match the underlying transaction in all respects.

In our example, the company wishes to 'pay the fixed and receive the floating' (rate). The treasurer has put up one of the brokers' screens to get an indication of current levels in the market (see Figure 4.7).

Our client wishes to pay fixed, so she is on the high side of the price, i.e., at or around 7.04 per cent. This is an inter-bank screen and our client is not a bank. Her price will be higher to allow for the fact that her company credit rating is not as good as that of the banks. Let us assume that the swap trader has quoted her a rate of 7.06 per cent. This is the rate that she will pay semi-annually (this is the norm but other payment frequencies are available). In return she will receive 6-month LIBOR, which will be reset every six months in line with market rates.

The dates on the swap and the underlying loan must be matched, so that the LIBOR payment received under the swap can be paid straight through to the underlying loan.

Outcome

On each of the rollover dates which are specified in advance, the two interest payments will be calculated and offset. For example, if on the first six-month date, the LIBOR was 8.25 per cent at the 11 a.m. fixing, we would not have one payment of the fixed rate at 7.06 per cent and another in the opposite direction of 8.25 per cent. In fact, the difference of 1.19 per cent will flow from the bank to the client. This helps in reducing the amount of credit line required.

Summary

(i)   The client obtains fixed rate funding at 7.56 per cent (including the 0.5 per cent margin), which is better than the original five-year fixed rate quoted.

(ii) On each rollover date, the two interest payments are 'netted off' and the balance transferred to the appropriate party.

(iii) The underlying transaction is untouched.

The example illustrates the hedging nature of swaps, without going into the complications of comparative advantage. As long as the treasurer can achieve cheaper funding via the swap, rather than direct with the bank, it will be the preferred route.

Our next example will focus more on the concept of advantages and disadvantages, and using comparative advantage.

Indication of dollar swap prices

Fig 4.7

Tullett and Tokyo Global | **USD Derivatives**

Forward Rate Agreements

1 × 4	6.28	6.31	14:15		1 × 7	6.54	6.57	14:16
2 × 5	6.36	6.38	14:08		2 × 8	6.64	6.67	14:23
3 × 6	6.50	6.53	14:09		3 × 9	6.75	6.78	14:39
4 × 7	6.63	6.66	14:23		4 × 10	6.85	6.80	14:33
5 × 8	6.76	6.79	14:39		5 × 11	6.95	6.98	14:39
6 × 9	6.87	6.90	14:39		6 × 12	7.05	7.08	14:39
7 × 10	6.95	6.98	14:39		12 × 18	7.34	7.39	14:38
8 × 11	7.02	7.05	14:39		18 × 24	7.41	7.46	14:38
9 × 12	7.13	7.10	14:39		12 × 24	7.51	7.56	14:38

Int Rate Caps Vols

1 YR	15.00	16.00	12:17		1 YR	15.00	16.00	12:24
2 YR	17.85	18.85	12:18		2 YR	17.85	18.85	12:24
3 YR	19.65	20.65	12:18		3 YR	19.65	20.65	12:24
4 YR	20.70	21.80	12:18		4 YR	20.70	21.70	12:24
5 YR	21.40	22.60	12:18		5 YR	21.40	22.40	12:24
7 YR	21.90	23.20	12:18		7 YR	21.90	22.90	12:25
10 YR	21.90	23.20	12:18					

Basis Swap vs USD Flat

2 YR	-6.50	-4.50	13:59
3 YR	-6.75	-4.75	13:59
4 YR	-7.25	-5.25	13:59
5 YR	-7.50	-5.50	13:59
7 YR	-8.00	-6.00	13:58
10 YR	-10.00	-8.00	13:59

Interest Rate Swaps Semi Annual

2 YR	7.04	7.07	14:38
3 YR	7.12	7.15	14:38
4 YR	7.07	7.11	14:44
5 YR	7.00	7.04	14:44
6 YR	6.93	6.97	14:44
7 YR	6.86	6.90	14:44
8 YR	6.79	6.83	14:44
9 YR	6.72	6.76	14:44
10 YR	6.65	6.69	14:44

07-Jan-00 14:44 LDN (c) BRIDGE

Source: Tullett and Tokyo Liberty plc (courtesy: Bridge Information Systems)

Fig 4.8

Swap – interest rate flows

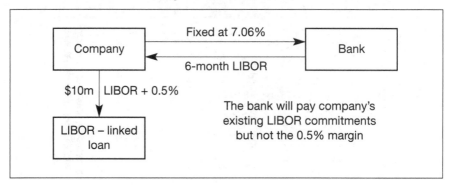

Example

A top-rated multinational, Grady Co. can raise fixed rate sterling through a bond issue for five years at 10 per cent, but it requires floating rate funds (it wishes to borrow on a LIBOR basis). The bank has quoted a rate of LIBOR + 0.5 per cent for the funds.

Blythe Co. want to borrow for five years on a fixed basis, but their investment bankers have advised them against a bond issue at this time as their name is not presently well rated. A floating rate loan can however be arranged for five years at LIBOR + 0.75 per cent, but Blythe want fixed rate funds. An assumption has been made that if Blythe were offered fixed rate funds at 10.5 per cent they would take them.

Summarizing the information

Grady Co. could borrow fixed at 10 per cent, but wants to pay floating at less than LIBOR + 0.5 per cent. Blythe Co. want fixed rate funding at 10.5 per cent or less, but could borrow at LIBOR + 0.75 per cent. These rates are summarized in Table 4.2. Why are these parties considering a swap at all? Grady Co. believes it has an advantage in the bond market and that the borrowing rate will reflect that. But when it asks for a quote for LIBOR-based funds, the bank wishes to charge a margin of 0.5 per cent over LIBOR which it considers does not accurately reflect their credit standing in the market. They believe that if they can borrow in the bond market at favourable rates,

Table 4.2

Example: Summary of interest rates

	Fixed rates	*Floating rates*
Grady Co.	10%	LIBOR + 0.5%
Blythe Co.	10.5%	LIBOR + 0.75%
Comparative advantage	0.5%	0.25%

they can then 'swap' its advantage into the floating rate market, and achieve a lower all-in rate (i.e., lower than LIBOR + 0.5%).

Question: In which market does **Grady Co.** have the most advantage, and **Blythe Co.** the least advantage?

Answer: Grady Co. has a cost advantage in both markets, as it is the better credit, but a greater advantage in the fixed rate (0.5 per cent against 0.25 per cent).

This first step will be to allow the participants to choose which underlying market they will borrow in. The swap will transform only their interest rate obligations. Grady Co. raises funds where it has the most advantage, the fixed rate bond market at 10 per cent, and Blythe Co. uses traditional funding and borrows floating rate from its bankers at LIBOR + 0.75 per cent, where it has least disadvantage.

Absolute advantage

This will show us if there is a likelihood of an interest rate swap working. There is a 0.5 per cent advantage in the fixed rate market and a 0.25 per cent advantage in the floating rate market, making an absolute advantage of 0.25 per cent, (0.5% − 0.25% = 0.25%), these basis points are available to be shared among the three parties, **Grady Co., Blythe Co.**, and the intermediary bank.

If we look at Figure 4.9(a), we can see the position before the swap, showing only the underlying cash flows.

Arrows coming out of the boxes represent interest paid, arrows coming in represent interest received.

Outcome

The two participants will then swap the interest flows with an intermediary bank, as shown in Figure 4.9(b).

Grady Co. requires the bank to pay the fixed rate, which it will then pay onwards to the bond holders; whereas Blythe Co. requires the bank to pay the 6-month LIBOR (exclusive of margin), which it will pay onwards to the lending bank. Let's assume the swap trader has quoted a rate of 9.65 per cent to 9.60 per cent. This shows how the bank receives the fixed rate, and how the bank pays the fixed rate. If you are ever unsure which side of the price you will be dealing on, remember, the bank is going to take the profit out of the dealing spread. The bank will always want to receive on the high side of the swap, and pay on the lower side.

It is now necessary to see whether both parties are better off after the swap (see Figure 4.10).

The 25 basis points are divided between the parties. The LIBOR payment is six-monthly unless specified otherwise. The 25 points will be included in the fixed rate payment, not the LIBOR. In most cases it will be useful to draw up mini-balance sheets representing receipts and payments of interest (see Table 4.3).

Fig 4.9

Swapping the interest flows with the intermediary bank

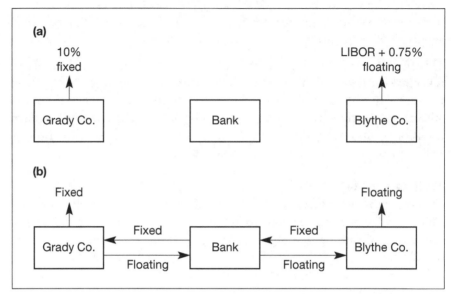

Fig 4.10

Actual swap – interest rate flows

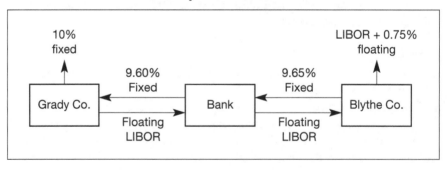

Table 4.3

Example: Receipts and payments of interest

Grady Co.		Blythe Co.	
Receipts	Payments	Payments	Receipts
9.60%	10% LIBOR	LIBOR	LIBOR + 0.75% 9.65%

Net cost: LIBOR + 0.40%   Net cost: 10.40%

Grady Co. will pay 10 per cent to the bond holders but receive 9.6 per cent towards it, making a net cost of LIBOR + 0.40 per cent, a saving of 10bp.

Blythe Co. will pay and receive LIBOR so these payments will cancel out, leaving it to pay the 9.65 per cent swap rate plus its margin, a net rate of 10.40 per cent, a saving of 10 bp, but it got fixed rate funds where there were none previously available.

The bank takes a 5 bp fee for the credit risk and acting as intermediary.

Single currency basis swaps

Banks and financial institutions which commonly engage in transactions between assets and liabilities will from time to time experience an interest rate 'gap'. This is where there may be differing interest bases for different maturities. There are many financial institutions which borrow from the money markets and on-lend to commercial clients on a different interest basis at higher rates. There are also building societies who receive mortgage interest on a monthly basis, yet have funded themselves on a 3-month LIBOR basis in the wholesale inter-bank market. In this case both the receipt and payment are based on a floating rate but there is a mis-match. A basis swap can go some way to correcting the balance. With a basis swap both parties will be paying a floating rate of interest, of which one is often LIBOR and sometimes both. For example one party may wish to pay LIBOR and the other a commercial paper rate; alternatively both parties may wish to pay LIBOR: one may pay 3-month LIBOR and the other 6-month LIBOR.

Hedging with a sterling basis swap

Example

A major US bank has lent £10 million to one of its clients for 12 months. Under the terms of the facility the loan is rolled over monthly, based on 1-month LIBOR + 75 bp. The US bank's funding for this facility forms part of a much larger arrangement with one of the large inter-bank players, but the funding is based on 3-month LIBOR flat. The sterling desk manager wishes to even out the cash flow and the basis by entering into a basis swap.

Strategy
The swap bank have been asked to quote for a 1s against 3s, 12-month basis swap. The client, in this case the US bank, wishes to pay 1s (1-month LIBOR) and receive 3s (3-month LIBOR) to set off against his money market funding. Basis swaps are quite sought after, consequently they are fairly expensive, which is why the swap bank may only quote a

rate for the US bank to pay 1-month LIBOR + 45 basis points against 3-month LIBOR flat (see Figure 4.11).

FIG 4.11

Basis swap – interest rate flows

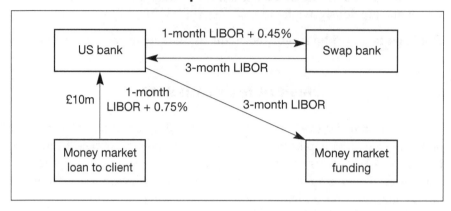

The net return to the US bank, after taking into account the interest rate movements on the swap, is 0.30 per cent; this does not take into account the cost of capital or balance sheet costs.

Generally, basis swaps can involve different combinations of fixed and floating rates.

- **Different maturities in the same index, 3-month LIBOR vs 1-month LIBOR.**
- **Same maturity and the same index, but one carries a margin: 6-month LIBOR vs 6-month LIBOR + 60 bp.**
- **Same or different maturities within the same index: US$CP rate (US dollar commercial paper rate) vs prime, or 3-month $ LIBOR vs three-month bill rate.**

Swap pricing

In countries where the swap market is not so well established, swap prices are quoted on an all-in basis in absolute terms (the full percentage annual yield, e.g. 7.1 per cent). This includes countries such as Australia and New Zealand.

Where the swap markets are well developed, such as the USA and the UK, the price is quoted in two parts: a swap spread and a benchmark rate, (usually a government bond such as a UK gilt, or a US treasury bond), e.g. 60 basis points over the gilt. The benchmark rate will be the yield, on the most liquid bond closest to the maturity date of the swap. For example, at the time of writing, the reference gilt for the five-year swap is currently the 6¾% of 2004 (the '6T04' for short). Quoting this way allows both parties to agree the 'spread' over the gilt, while allowing the gilt to move separately.

The benefits of this occur when there is a fast-moving market and the underlying gilt or treasury bond may be quite volatile with the price swinging all over the place. This makes it nearly impossible for the swap trader to keep the price firm even when he is just checking the availability on the client's credit line. At least by agreeing the 'spread' over the bond yield in advance, all that is left is to determine where the gilt or bond is trading at the final moment in time, then add the dealer's spread.

The figures shown in Table 4.4 are compiled by one of the brokers, and are indication levels of where the business can expect to be done, although the broker will not be a counterparty, simply a facilitator, putting together willing payers and willing receivers on the swaps. The first column shows the maturity, the second column the all-in prices on the swap. The third column shows the benchmark gilt, and the fourth shows the 'spread' over the gilt. The prices quoted are two-way prices. The five-year rate shows that the dealer is prepared to receive at 76 basis points over the gilt, and pay at 71 basis points over the gilt. The underlying gilt which is the 6¾ of 2004 must have been trading at a yield of 6.28 per cent, to equate to the 7.04–6.99 per cent rates shown in the table.

Sterling swap quotations

Table 4.4

01/07	09:33 NYC	[GARBAN - INTERCAPITAL LONDON]		4902
SEE 4914 FOR SHORT SWAPS		GBP/IEP SWAPS 020 7256 9292		07/01 14:32 GMT

GBP				IEP	
2 YRS	7.06–7.02	1 YR/A3	6.84–6.81	1 YRS	4.00–3.97
3 YRS	7.15–7.11	MAR/MAR	7.10–7.07	2 YRS	4.50–4.46
4 YRS	7.12–7.07	JUN/JUN	7.33–7.30	3 YRS	4.83–4.79
5 YRS	7.04–6.99	6T 04	+76/+71	4 YRS	5.08–5.04
6 YRS	6.97–6.92	8H 05	+76/+71	5 YRS	5.25–5.21
7 YRS	6.90–6.85	7H 06	+76/+71	6 YRS	5.40–5.36
8 YRS	6.83–6.78	7Q 07	+79/+74	7 YRS	5.55–5.51
9 YRS	6.76–6.71	9 08	+76/+71	8 YRS	5.68–5.64
10 YRS	6.68–6.63	5T 09	+98/+93	9 YRS	5.78–5.74
12 YRS	6.57–6.50	8 13	+123/+115	10 YRS	5.86–5.82
15 YRS	6.39–6.31	8 15	+131/+123	12 YRS	5.99–5.95
20 YRS	6.12–6.02	8 21	+128/+118	15 YRS	6.14–6.10
25 YRS	5.97–5.86	8 21	+114/+104	20 YRS	6.22–6.18
30 YRS	5.84–5.72	6 28	+122/+110	25 YRS	6.24–6.20
40 YRS	5.70–5.53	6 28	+107/+93	30 YRS	6.24–6.20

Source: Garban–Intercapital plc (courtesy: Bridge Information Systems)

Negotiating the deal

The most important component in a swap is the level of the swap's fixed interest rate. If the swap is quoted as a 'spread over', then the spread will be agreed first, as this is the most volatile component. A trader will then need to check that they have room on their credit lines for the counter-party, once this is cleared, then the trader will agree with the client the level of the benchmark gilt or bond, which will then be added to the spread to ascertain the all-in price. Figure 4.12 illustrates the stages in negotiating the swap transaction.

FIG 4.12

Flow chart for negotiating the swap transaction

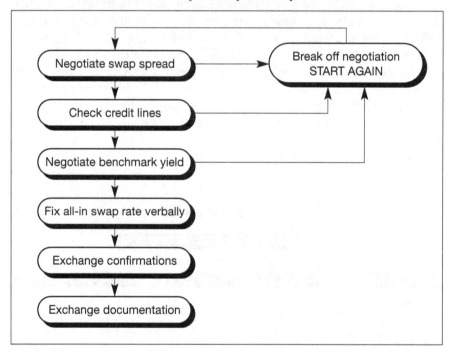

Swap documentation

Once the swap transaction is agreed on the telephone, the legal obligation is in place. However, it is a courtesy for both sides to confirm the details within 24 hours to check, for example, that all the dates match, and the structure is as agreed. The final copies of the exchange documentation are sent later. These are called 'execution documents' and will contain authorized signatories, etc. For some years it has been market practice for regular users of the swap market to deal with each other using a standard set of documents. There are two providers of swap documentation, essentially:

- ISDA (the International Swaps and Derivatives Association)
- BBA (the British Bankers' Association).

The ISDA master document is the most popular among the banking fraternity and is divided into two sections: first, the basic terms and conditions, and second, a schedule that includes all swaps transacted between the particular counterparty and the bank. The schedule will also contain any agreed modifications to the basic terms and conditions. Once an ISDA 'master' is in place between the two counterparties, it then covers all further swaps. Each time a new swap is added, a new contract is created assuming all outstanding deals; this process is known as 'novation'. Of necessity, an ISDA agreement needs to be in place for each of the bank's counterparties, and should be negotiated before dealing commences.

The BBAIRS (British Bankers' Association – Interest Rate Swaps) documentation is really designed to cover short-term swaps in major currencies, and is less comprehensive than ISDA, but most swaps under two years long can be covered. Nearly all swap participants now use ISDA documentation, when they can.

Availability

Single currency interest rate swaps are available in all major currencies for minimum amounts of U$1 million or £1 million, with no maximum amount. Periods of one to ten years are usually available, and sometimes up to 40 years.

Practical considerations

Anyone can deal in an interest rate swap, subject to credit considerations. This means that the credit department of the bank(s) with whom you wish to deal need to assess their counterparty risk with you. They will need to consider the maturity and amount of any swaps you may wish to do with them, and may even specify, for example, no swaps over five years. Dealing lines and credit lines must be set up in advance.

Within the swap itself, the rollover frequency can be monthly, quarterly, semi-annual or annual. It is not necessary for the fixed payment and the LIBOR to be paid on the same day, but you must specify the frequency of all interest payments at the time of dealing. For example, a 12-month swap could be:

- **Semi/semi:** both payments at six-monthly intervals.
- **Annual/semi:** the fixed payment annually and the LIBOR every six months.
- **Annual/quarterly:** the fixed payment annually and the LIBOR every three months.
- **Annual/1s:** the fixed payment is annual and the LIBOR is monthly.
- **Quarterly/quarterly:** both payments at three-monthly intervals.

Each swap price will factor in the payment frequency, and the swap rates will be different to reflect this.

There are a number of swap providers in the market, but not all of them make a market in all currencies and all periods. It is worth shopping around. Some of the smaller banks provide a very good service in niche markets.

Further reading

Most large commercial banks will have literature specifically written for clients on FRAs and interest rate options (or guarantees), and interest caps, collars and floors.

Interest Rate Swaps, Self-Study Workbooks, published by IFR, 1994.
   View the following websites:

www.liffe.com
www.bis.org
www.eurexchange.com

'. . . the products used to risk manage a position are the very same products that can be used to speculate.'

Currency Derivatives

INTRODUCTION

There are many different types of derivatives that can cover an exposure in currency. Both short- and long-term exposures can be hedged; in this context a short-term exposure can be a few days. A long-term exposure may be linked to a foreign currency bond issue that could have a ten- or 20-year term. It almost goes without saying that the products used to risk manage a position are the same products that can be used to speculate. Most trading or speculative positions, as opposed to hedging positions, are likely to be of short duration, usually within the year and mostly within a few months or weeks. A hedger wants to remove or manage his currency risk. A trader wants to take currency risk in the hope of making a profit.

What is currency risk? The risk to a hedger is of either receiving a smaller amount of the base currency than expected, or paying out more of the base currency to purchase a required amount of foreign currency. For example, a UK company may have sold some goods to the USA; their base currency is sterling, but they have agreed to receive payment in US dollars. If their sterling price (including profit margin) to the buyer was £250,000, they would need to convert this amount to US dollars for invoice purposes. Let us assume that they choose the current exchange rate on the day, which is £1 = US$1.60.

This means that when they send their invoice to the US buyer it will state that US$400,000 is due, say in three months' time. If the company does not hedge its currency exposure on this invoice, it could make a profit or a loss on the transaction. A profit is unlikely to cause a problem (but in some companies it may), but a loss will certainly not be wanted. If the company decides not to hedge its position on the foreign exchanges, it is running a risk.

It is impossible to predict the direction of an exchange rate with confidence, so we must assume one of two things can happen. The rate can increase or decrease against the base currency, which in this case is sterling. In three months it is not impossible for the currency rate to move five cents in either direction. The spot rate of exchange (the rate quoted today for value two business days later) could have moved as follows by the end of three months:

US$ increases (strengthens) to £1 = US$1.5500
US$ decreases (weakens) to £1 = US$1.6500

The company needs to receive £250,000 for the transaction. If it does not hedge its position, it will be compelled to accept the exchange rate on the day the dollars arrive.

- **If the dollar has strengthened to US$1.5500, the company will receive £258,064.**

- If the dollar has weakened to US$1.6500, the company will receive £242,424.

In the first instance the company has made a windfall profit, in the second case it has not received what it needed for this transaction. They may end up selling the goods at a loss. Yet, the client has paid what he was asked to, and the company quoted the dollar equivalent on the day. No one is to blame, but world-wide events have changed either the value of sterling or the value of the US dollar. This is why currency risk must be accepted as a way of life for companies who both export and import goods. In the case of an importer, he may need to buy Euro to pay a supplier and budgets on the piece of equipment costing say, £175,000. But, when it comes to payment date, and the company buy the Euro on the foreign exchanges, they cost £195,000.

Different companies view foreign exchange risk in different ways. There are two extreme views: first, the company whose view is that, 'we make widgets, we do not speculate on the foreign exchanges'. In that case they would hedge every single transaction denominated in foreign currency, either by using forward foreign exchange contracts, or by using currency options. Forward foreign exchange has been around for years: it involves the bank guaranteeing a rate of exchange for the client, at no cost. However, the client is then obligated to deal at that rate, whatever the spot rate of exchange is at maturity, and as we have seen, the spot rate could have moved into a profit position. A client who sells all his currency against forward transactions will have guaranteed rates, but be unable to profit from market moves.

> 'A hedger wants to remove or manage his currency risk. A trader wants to take currency risk in the hope of making a profit.'

The currency option provides an alternative method of hedging that allows the client not only to hedge his risk and guarantee a rate of exchange, but also to make a profit if the market moves in his favour. But a fee, or premium, is payable for the product, whereas a foreign exchange forward transaction costs nothing.

Second, there is the company who wish to profit from their currency transactions, and may deliberately not hedge any of their currency exposures. They may in some cases actively seek foreign exchange risk as a means of enhancing income. The danger here is that the commercial side of the business which may be profitable in its own right could be overshadowed by foreign exchange losses if some bad decisions on the currency are taken.

In a bank, a foreign exchange trader wishes to take risk by buying and selling currency for a profit. He may have a short-term view on the direction of the US dollar, or a long-term view on some other currency. He will then position himself accordingly, by either buying or selling the currency now, in order to reverse out of the deal later, hopefully making money in the process. The trader can use the traditional foreign exchanges and deal in either the spot or forward markets, or he can use derivative products to support his view.

Table 5.1 shows a range of currency derivatives.

Table 5.1

Range of currency derivatives

	Exchange traded	OTC
Currency futures	✓	
Currency options	✓	✓
Currrency swaps		✓

Most liquidity in currency derivatives is present in the over the counter market (OTC). The main reason for this is historic. For many years the major banks that were active in foreign exchange, both for their own hedging and trading purposes, and for client business, had only the global FX market to operate in. Spot and forward foreign exchange is technically OTC, and the volumes are enormous. It has been estimated that the average daily volume of foreign exchange transacted through London is in the region of £300 billion. When the derivatives market started to become popular, the idea of buying and selling currency derivatives on an organized exchange was anathema to most traders. As a result, the liquidity in currency derivatives traded on organized exchanges was never that good, and in some cases has dried up completely. This book will concentrate on the OTC market, as this is where the major volumes are traded today. This limits the section to:

- OTC currency options (traditional and reduced premium strategies)
- OTC currency swaps.

OVER THE COUNTER CURRENCY OPTIONS

Introduction

Risk management with regard to foreign exchange revolves around one concept; that the actual out-turn amount of a foreign currency transaction needs to be known in advance. Quite simply, how much sterling have I generated with this foreign currency, or how much sterling must I pay for this foreign currency? Until 1971, estimating sterling proceeds was not too much of a problem. Most currencies were linked officially or unofficially to the US dollar, which, in turn, was tied to the gold price. This meant that trying to forecast a foreign exchange rate was not too difficult, as there was little or no movement. After 1973, things got considerably more arduous as the major currency relationships finally disintegrated with the OPEC Oil Crisis. Forecasting exchange rates is now something which is reserved for bank economists and end-of-year competitions.

The two main reasons why it is hard to forecast a rate are:

- **Currencies tend to deviate away from anticipated trend paths.**

- **Continuing short-term volatility affects the currency values.**

Post-1973, and certainly after 1979, when the UK Exchange Controls were abolished, the ability to protect a currency against fluctuations was vital. It was no longer possible to predict with any certainty what the prevailing rate of exchange for currencies would be in the future. Currencies were also becoming increasingly volatile. The concept of hedging or mitigating risk is well known now, but in the mid- to late 1970s it was a comparatively new discipline.

The simplest way for a client with a currency exposure to hedge against foreign exchange risk is to sell or buy forward the currency using a foreign currency forward contract. This entails the client calling the bank for a forward foreign exchange rate which would be guaranteed by the bank, but where the client would have no flexibility. Whatever the rate of exchange was, when the dollars arrived or the yen were paid away, the client would transact at the pre-determined forward rate, even if the exchange rate in the market offered him a better alternative. The forward contract is an obligation, but it costs nothing except perhaps a lost opportunity should the foreign exchange rate improve. The currency option is an alternative hedging mechanism. It allows both risk management and the chance for the holder of the option to take a profit if the underlying foreign exchange rate moves favourably.

An option is one of the three derivative tools used for both risk management and speculation (options, swaps, futures). The basic option concepts and terminology have already been covered in Chapter 3 in the section on *basic option concepts*, and if readers are unfamiliar with options, then they may find it advantageous to look through that section first. This section will focus on over the counter (OTC) currency options.

Options as a product have been around for years, with the first recorded option being on a tulip bulb hundreds of years ago. It is only comparatively recently, in the early 1970s, that options in the financial sense have come about. Both the corporate market and the banks claim the glory for inventing the currency option. Nevertheless, the original research in 1972 by two Americans, Fisher Black and Myron Scholes, into a reliable option-pricing model is probably the one single thing that made options commercially available.

> A **currency option** gives the buyer, the right but not the obligation, to buy or sell a specific amount of currency at a specific exchange rate, on or before a specific future date. A premium is due.

Definition discussed

This option gives the client the chance to fix the rate of exchange that will apply to a forthcoming transaction. The client need not proceed with the option if he can find a more advantageous exchange rate elsewhere. The option instrument will let the client choose his guaranteed rate of exchange (the strike) and then the writing or selling bank will guarantee that rate if or when required. Because this option provides a sort of insurance or guarantee that is optional, the client is not obligated to take the cover, so a premium or fee is required. This is normally paid within two business days, in either of the currencies of the option. Some banks may take the premium payment in a third currency, but it is at their discretion.

In these circumstances, the customer or client is the buyer of the option and must pay the premium, and the bank is the seller or writer of the option. It is the bank who must have the 'underlying' foreign exchange ready in case the client requires it. The bank will also need to hedge any risks on the option position. The underlying in this case is the receipt or payment of one currency against another currency. Options can be cash settled at expiry or they can be sold back at any time during the life of the transaction for residual or 'fair value' (see Glossary). Alternatively, the currency can be physically delivered or paid to the writing bank and the client will receive the countercurrency at the strike rate previously agreed under the option. It should be noted that there may not always be a positive benefit on the option, and some options will expire worthless. The currency option is more flexible than the traditional forward foreign exchange contract, and gives the buyer (holder) of the option four alternatives, the choice of:

- **when** to exercise
- **whether** to exercise
- **how much** to exercise
- the exercise price (strike).

When?

There are two types of "vanilla" currency option; an American option and a European option. Under an American-style currency option a greater flexibility is offered. Consider an American-style US$ put option against sterling: on exercise, the dollars can be delivered by the option holder to the bank, on any business day until expiry, for value two business days later. By comparison, under a European-style option, the holder can deliver the dollars against exercise *only* on the actual expiry date (for value two business days later), as specified in the option contract. A European-style option operates in a similar way to a forward contract.

But with the forward contract, the currency must be delivered on the maturity date. If a client has sold forward some dollars for sterling against a two-month forward contract, and the dollars do not arrive in time, the forward contract must still be honoured, even at the expense of buying the required amount of currency from the market – possibly at a worst rate, and then delivering it under the forward contract. With the European-style currency option, if the dollars do not arrive, the option is simply abandoned, or if there is value remaining it can be sold back to the writing bank and the residual (fair) value realized.

Occasionally, the underlying exposure that the option is covering may be shortened, or for some reason the option is no longer required; then, the option can be sold back to the writing bank for fair value. If the underlying exposure is lengthened, it is not possible to extend the option at the same strike, or to roll it over into a new deal, as these practices are open to fraud. If the option maturity needs to be extended, the most effective way to do this is to sell the original option back to the bank for fair value, and take out a new transaction covering the fresh maturity date at the current prevailing market conditions.

Whether?

An option will be exercised by the holder only if it is profitable for him/her to do so. Where the spot exchange rate on maturity remains more favourable than the option strike price, the option will be allowed to lapse, and the underlying transaction will be effected in the spot market. This is known as 'abandoning the option'.

How much?

When the currency option is originally established, it is for a specific amount of a reference currency, and it is upon this figure that the premium is based. This is a notional maximum amount of currency. If the resulting currency receipt/payment turns out to be for a lesser figure, it may be possible (in some cases) for the excess cover to be sold back for fair value to the writing bank. Should an excess amount of currency arrive there is no provision for additional cover under the original option.

Strike

The strike of the option is chosen by the client at the outset. The premium that is due for the option will be a function of how the strike relates to the current market price and various other inputs (see *premium determinants*).

Currency options

Insurance protection

A premium is paid by the buyer of the option to the writing bank, which in turn guarantees a fixed rate of exchange if/when required by the holder.

Profit potential

The option eliminates any chance of currency loss: the only outflow of funds relates to the premium payment. If the underlying market movement is in the holder's favour, then upside potential is available. An option profile exhibits 'asymmetry of risk'. The most that a holder can lose is the option premium; the most he can profit is limited only by how far the market moves.

Sell-back

The option can be sold back in whole or in part, for fair value to the writing bank. This is not a negotiable piece of paper and cannot be on-sold to a third party.

Premium

A premium is due, based on a series of variables that are input into an option pricing model, derived from the original Black and Scholes model.

Premium determinants

There are a number of major factors that affect the premium due on a currency option:

- strike price
- underlying price
- maturity

- put or call
- expected currency volatility
- interest rate differentials
- american or European.

(a) Strike price vs underlying price

The underlying benchmark against which the strike on the currency option is measured is the appropriate forward foreign exchange rate, known in the market as the 'outright forward'. Occasionally, a client will ask for at the money spot options, but they don't really exist. A client can have an option struck at the spot rate, but it will be either slightly ITM or slightly OTM. Table 5.2 illustrates the concept of 'in/at/out of the money'.

Strike prices are referred to as follows:

At the money (ATM)	Where the strike is equal to the current outright forward rate.	**Terminology**
In the money (ITM)	Where the strike is more favourable than the outright forward rate, and the option premium is higher than that for an ATM option.	
Out of the money (OTM)	Where the strike is worse than the outright forward rate and the option premium is lower than that for an ATM option.	

Illustration of the concept 'in/at/out of the money'   **Table 5.2**

Client purchases option to sell dollars against sterling		Client purchases option to buy dollars against sterling
$1.40 -----------------	IN THE MONEY	----------------- $1.60
$1.50 -----------------	AT THE MONEY	----------------- $1.50
$1.60 -----------------	OUT OF THE MONEY	------------- $1.40

Note: Assume the current forward rate of dollars against sterling is £1 = US$1.50.

(b)Maturity

The longer the time to expiry or maturity, the higher the probability of large exchange rate movements, and the higher the chance of profitable exercise by the buyer. The buyer should be prepared to pay a higher premium for a longer dated option than a short-dated option. The relationship between the premium due on an option and the maturity of the transaction is not a linear relationship as Figure 3.17 showed: the premium due for a six-month option is not double that of a three-month option, and is never likely to be (see page 68).

(c) Put or call

This will relate back to whether the currencies are at a premium or a discount to each other (see section on *interest rate differentials*).

(d)Volatility

It is the volatility element that differentiates one bank's price from another. All other premium determinants are matters of fact that are available to market participants simultaneously. If a client purchases an option with high volatility, he has purchased an asset with a high possibility of profitable exercise. See *basic option concepts* in Chapter 3 for a fuller discussion of volatility.

Implied volatility

This is the current volatility level implicit in today's option prices. It can be derived from both exchange-traded options and OTC options. It is often published by the infomation providers. An example is shown in the Telerate page on Figure 5.1 from Garban-Intercapital plc.

Historical volatility

It is possible to analyze the spread of movements of the underlying commodity by recording, for example, the closing prices of US$/JPY. If these prices were plotted on a graph a type of scatter pattern would emerge. Volatility is in effect the definition of this scatter, 'the normalized, annualized, standard deviation of the underlying price'.

While this type of analysis allows historical data to be examined, it can only ever indicate future prices, it will not be able to predict them, but rather give an idea of where they should be, taking into account how the commodity has moved in the past.

When an option trader has to price an option, he will need to input a level for volatility in percentage terms. This can be quite difficult, as in effect he is being asked to guess the way a currency pair will perform in the future. We earlier saw that the premium/maturity profile was non-linear: but the profile of premium/volatility is linear, as shown in

Indication of OTC option volatility

Fig 5.1

01/10   06:57   NYC

[GARBAN - INTERCAPITAL]
[CURRENCY OPTIONS]

01/10   06:40   4720
10/01/00   11:40   GMT

	GBP/USD	EUR/USD	CHF/EUR	USD/JPY	EUR/JPY	AUD/USD
R.R	0.0 - 0.25	0.4 - 0.65	0.0 - 1.0	1.75 - 2.1		0.1 - 0.3
1 WK	6.5 - 8.0				14.0 - 15.25	8.1 - 8.75
2 WK						
1M	7.2 - 7.6	11.2 - 11.35	0.1 - 0.15	12.3 - 12.7	14.05 - 14.55	8.9 - 9.15
2M	7.45 - 7.9	11.05 - 11.3	0.0 - 0.25	12.6 - 13.0		8.95 - 9.15
3M	7.6 - 8.0	11.0 - 11.2	0.2 - 0.35	12.85 - 13.05		8.95 - 9.15
6M	8.25 - 8.6	10.9 - 11.1	0.25 - 0.5		14.1 - 14.6	8.9 - 9.15
1 YR	8.35 - 8.7	10.75 - 11.0	0.4 - 0.6		14.1 - 14.6	8.85 - 9.1

Source: Garban-Intercapital plc (*courtesy*: Bridge Information Systems)

Figure 3.20, i.e., the higher the perceived volatility, the higher the premium. Higher volatility implies a greater possible dispersion of prices at expiry.

(e) Interest rate differentials

Forward foreign exchange rates are calculated using the interest rate differentials of the two currencies concerned. Currencies are said to be at a premium or discount to each other, reflecting whether the forward points are added or subtracted from the spot rate. This differential will affect the premium due on an option.

Interest rates affect option pricing in two ways:

(a) By affecting the forward price of the asset and hence the intrinsic value.

(b) By affecting the present value calculations within the option-pricing model, and ultimately the present value of the option premium.

(f) American or European

Generally, an American-style option gives the holder greater flexibility. If the client wishes to call a currency with a higher interest rate (discount currency), the American-style option will be more expensive. If the client wants to call a premium currency the price of the American and the European option will be the same.

Terminology	Currency options	
Call option	The right (not the obligation) to buy foreign currency.	
Put option	The right (not the obligation) to sell foreign currency. *It is always necessary to specify the two currencies in order to avoid confusion.*	
Exercise	Conversion of the option into the underlying transaction.	
Strike price	Exchange rate chosen by the holder. Prices can be described as: – at the money (ATM) – in the money (ITM) – out of the money (OTM).	
Expiry date	Last day on which the option may be exercised, up to 10 a.m. New York time, two business days before the value date.	
Value date	The day on which the currency is delivered.	

Premium	The price of the option.
American option	An option which can be exercised on any business day, up to and including the expiry date.
European option	An option which can be exercised on the expiry date only.
Intrinsic value	Difference between the strike price and the current market exchange rate.
Time value	Difference between the option premium and intrinsic value; including the time left until expiry, volatility, forward points and including market expectations.
Fair value	Combination of intrinsic value and time value, as calculated by the option-pricing model.
Volatility	Normalized, annualized standard deviation of the daily SPOT rate for the exchange rate concerned.

Terminology

Terminology discussed

It is very important to specify whether you are the buyer or seller of the option and whether you are selling or buying the underlying currencies. Potentially, there could be a four-way price, which is why we need the added terms of puts and calls. There are also a number of different ways in which people describe options. Some talk about 'calling' or 'putting' the foreign currency, others about calling or putting the dollar. There is added confusion when you consider cross-currencies, for example, if the currencies are Euro/yen, which one is foreign? It is always safer to specify both sides, not just to call the Euro, but to call the Euro and put the yen; then there is no possibility of confusion. The option premium calculated by the pricing model can be divided into two parts, intrinsic value and time value. The intrinsic value is measured by the present value of the amount by which it is in the money.

Example:
A European-style US dollar put, sterling call, is used to cover a dollar receivable against sterling in three months' time:

Forward outright rate for three months is $1.47

Option strike rate is $1.44

Intrinsic value is present value (PV) of $1.47 – $1.44 = PV of 3 cents.

Intrinsic value provides the *minimum* price at which the option will trade.

The time value component of the option expresses the risk premium in the option and is a function of several variables:

- the relationship between the strike price and the spot rate
- the time to maturity
- the interest rate differential between the two currencies
- the volatility of the currency pair.

To the option writer, this risk premium is highest when the option is 'at the money', because at this point there is the greatest uncertainty over whether the option will expire worthless or have some value at maturity.

If the option moves 'into the money', the writer can be more sure the option will be exercised, if it moves 'out of the money' the opposite applies. The more deeply 'in' or 'out' of the money the option moves, the greater the confidence of the option writer in the final outcome, for example, will it or won't it be exercised?

In simple terms, the longer the time to expiry the more an option is worth. As time passes, the option writer can define the risk more accurately, and in the last few days before expiry the time value diminishes rapidly. The time value of an option decays as expiry approaches. Time value decay follows a particular pattern and the rate of time value decay is called **Theta**, which is one of the option Greeks, to be discussed later.

Comparisons of currency options against forward foreign exchange

Table 5.3 summarizes the main differences between OTC currency options and traditional forward foreign exchange. A forward contract is perfectly acceptable as a hedging product if you have complete information at your disposal; you know the amount, the currencies, and when – to the day – the currency will be paid/received: 'the end of the month' is not acceptable, it is too vague. In everyday business, the luxury of complete information is not always available, dates and amounts have to be estimated, and some clients simply pay late. In those circumstances an option is the perfect alternative. It is not zero cost like a forward, but it is immensely flexible, and some options can be designed to have very low premiums.

Comparison between currency options and forward contracts

Table 5.3

Currency options	Forward contracts
Right to buy or sell	Obligation to buy or sell
No obligation to deliver	Must deliver on/before maturity
No loss possible – excluding premium	Unlimited opportunity loss possible
Eliminates downside risk and retains unlimited upside potential	Eliminates downside risk – but no upside potential
Perfect hedge for variable exposures	Imperfect hedge for variable exposures

Using a currency option to hedge a currency receivable

2 April

A major British company has won an export order in Thailand. Delivery and payment will be in three months' time and will be in dollars. The treasurer is not sure on which exact day the money will be available in his account, and is worried that the value of the dollar may fall (depreciate) before he receives his invoice amount of US$1,250,000. If he does nothing and the value of the dollar falls, he will not realize sufficient sterling from the resulting foreign exchange conversion, but if the value of the dollar increases he will be very happy. He is not sure in which direction the dollar will move, but he is not allowed to do nothing. If he transacts a forward contract with one of his bankers, he must give up any windfall profits, but if he transacts an option, he has insurance if things go wrong and profit opportunities if things go right.

Action – 2 April

The Treasurer will ask for an indication level on a dollar put, sterling call option, American style, strike = at the money, and an expiry date in three months' time (2 July) for value two business days later.

The current financial information is available:

£/US$
Spot rate: 1.5500
Outright forward rate: 1.5450.

The strike on the option will be at the money forward (ATMF), at $1.5450. The premium due for this option is, say, 1.20 per cent of the dollar amount. The total premium is 1.2 per cent of $1,250,000 which is US$15,000, and must be paid to the bank two business days after the deal is struck. The option can now be filed or put in a drawer for three months until expiry, or until the dollars arrive, whichever is earlier.

Action – 2 July

The dollars arrive on time. The treasurer will call his bank to check the current level of the spot exchange rate. If the dollar has strengthened (appreciated) to, say, US$1.4950, then the option will be worthless and will be abandoned, and the transaction will be affected in the spot market. If the dollar has depreciated to, say, US$1.5950, the client will exercise the option at the agreed rate of $1.5450. The treasurer will need to call the bank and confirm that he wishes to exercise his option, as exercise is not automatic. Under the option, the treasurer will deliver $1,250,000 and receive sterling at US$1.5450, giving a sterling out-turn of £809,061.49. Technically the option premium should be deducted to work out the breakeven rate (to be absolutely correct, the net present value (NPV) of the premium). This would give a net sterling out-turn of £809,061.49 less the amount of the option premium in sterling (for premium conversion purposes, the spot rate is always used: US$15,000 divided by £/$1.5500 = £9,677.42) – a total figure of £799,384.07.

Under the terms of this currency option, it does not matter when the dollars arrive, as the treasurer has purchased an American-style option, allowing him to deliver his currency on any business day in the period (for value two business days later). If, originally, the company had bought a European-style option, then there would be a restriction and the dollars would need to be placed on deposit until the expiry date, when they could be delivered under the option.

As Figure 5.2 shows, there is always a best and worst case, indeed the nature of FX means that no one knows how far or how fast a currency will move. A 5-cent move in the three-month period has been used for the purposes of illustration.

If the client had chosen a traditional forward contract and been lucky with the receipt of the dollars on the correct date, he would have achieved at best (or worst) a rate of $1.5450, and an out-turn of £809,061.49.

The option will always be the second best alternative in hindsight. If the client knew with 100 per cent certainty that the dollar was going to depreciate, he would sell forward, a hedging alternative that would cost nothing and allow no profit. But if you are not expecting to profit, you have given

Currency options – best and worst case

Fig 5.2

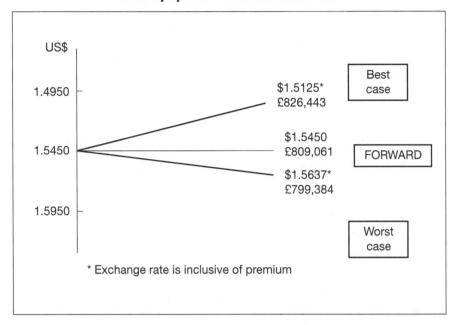

* Exchange rate is inclusive of premium

up nothing. If the client knew with 100 per cent certainty that the dollar would appreciate, he would do nothing and simply sell the dollars at the better rate when they arrived in three months' time. The option allows the client to get the best possible outcome, the 'insured' rate when required, or the profit when the market moves favourably, but a premium is required.

Option mechanics

So far we have looked at options in the very simplest terms. They are, however, quite complex and each type of option has a particular 'signature'. The most straightforward way to go about understanding the way options work is to draw the profit and loss profile (P/L) of the transaction. Forget options for a moment: consider the currency pair US dollar/CHF. If a trader bought cash CHF today in the expectation of the Swiss Franc strengthening, the P/L profile would look like that shown in Figure 5.3.

If a trader had bought the CHF at US$/CHF 1.50, then as the Swiss Franc appreciates, and the dollar weakens (towards $1.40), the position will start moving into profit. Likewise if the CHF depreciates, and the dollar strengthens, the same position would move into loss. This is an unhedged position, with an equal probability of profit or loss.

Alternatively, instead of running a spot risk, an option could be purchased, with a strike of US$/CHF 1.5000, which would allow the same 1:1 profit opportunity, but where the only potential downside would be the loss

Fig 5.3

Profit and loss profile – cash position

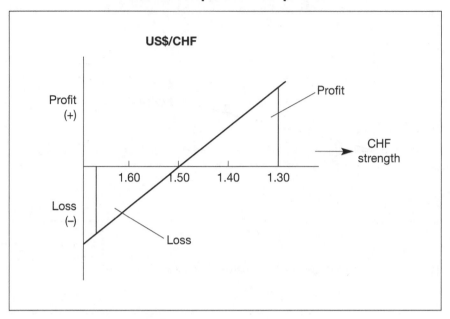

of the premium paid. This would be a Swiss Franc call, put on US dollars. The option has been bought, so the trader is 'long' the call (see Figure 5.4).

Fig 5.4

Profit and loss profile – CHF call option – long call

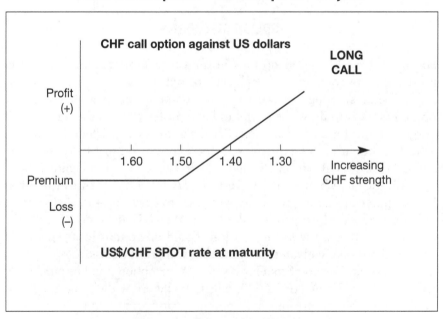

The profile of the option mirrors that of the unhedged position, except that it starts from a negative position reflecting the premium paid. It is important to take into account the premium on the option and any associated interest rate costs. An option purchaser may need to fund (borrow) the option premium, and an option writer must deposit the premium, so the deposit interest rate that the trader obtains must be factored into the final option premium. There are also associated opportunity costs that should not be overlooked.

The bank writing the Swiss Franc call option shown in Figure 5.4 would have a mirror image position, where they had received the premium: this is shown in Figure 5.5.

With this position the bank that has written the option is 'short' the call option. All they have taken in is the premium, yet their potential for loss is comparatively high.

Let us now assume that the trader has changed his mind about the direction of the Swiss Franc. He now feels that it is about to weaken, so with his new trade he needs to buy a CHF put, US dollar call option (see Figure 5.6).

The profit and loss profile shows again that the holder of this option can lose only his premium, but can profit as long as the market moves in his favour. In comparison, the writer of option shown in Figure 5.7, who is 'short' the Swiss Franc put option, could lose a considerable amount, if no hedging is undertaken.

Profit and loss profile – CHF call option – short call

Fig 5.5

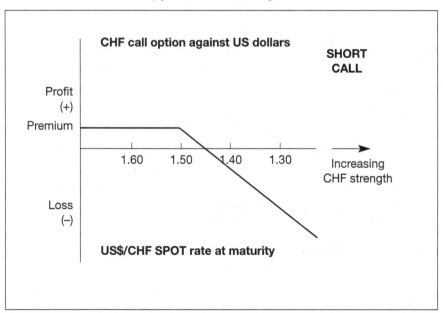

Fig 5.6

Profit and loss profile – CHF put option – long put

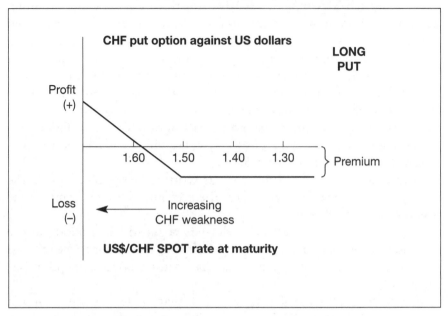

In all, there are four basic building blocks in options: calls and puts, bought and sold.

The four strategies, long call, short call, long put, short put are shown in Figures 5.4, 5.5, 5.6 and 5.7.

Fig 5.7

Profit and loss profile – CHF call option – short put

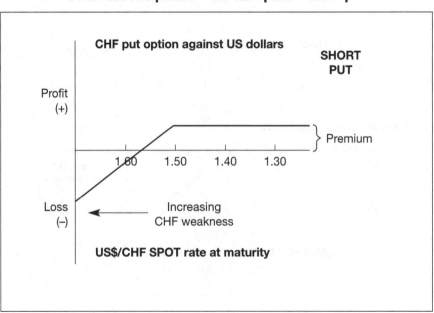

Basic workings of currency options

The following rules apply:

(1) The option is exercised only when it is advantageous for the holder.

(2) If the ruling spot rate is more favourable, the option will be abandoned.

(3) The downside risk is protected, with a 1:1 gain, if the market moves favourably.

(4) The writer of the option is obliged to deliver the 'underlying' if the option is exercised.

Put/call parity

The profit and loss profile of a forward contract is similar to the profile of the unhedged position.

Figure 5.8 superimposes the profiles of a European-style long call and European-style short put upon the forward. You can see that once the premiums are netted off, then the combined strategy of buy a call and sell a put at the same strike price equal buying forward. Similarly, buying a put and selling a call at the same strike price equal selling forward. These are known as synthetic forward positions.

Profit and loss profile – put-call parity

Fig 5.8

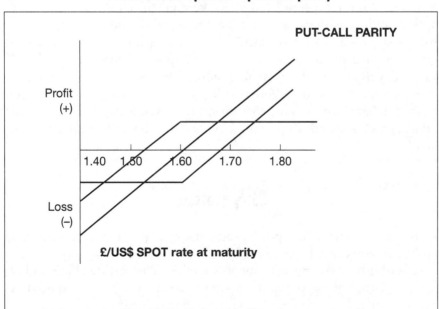

PUT-CALL PARITY

Profit (+)

1.40 1.50 1.60 1.70 1.80

Loss (−)

£/US$ SPOT rate at maturity

Using currency options to speculate

A private client believes that the yen will appreciate against the dollar over the next month. He is prepared to put on a position equivalent to US$10 million. He has no desire to hold either currency physically and no requirement for flexibility on the date, so he will purchase a one-month European-style option that he can sell back, but will not need to exercise. When the option is sold back to the option writer, the currency gain, if there is one, will be factored into the sell-back price. This obviates the need for physical foreign exchange transactions.

Current financial information:

US$/yen
Spot rate   115.00
Outright forward rate   114.00

Strategy

The client will purchase a European-style yen call, US dollar put in US$10 million for expiry in one month's time. Option premium is calculated at 0.8 per cent, which is US$80,000 or JPY 9.20 million, payable within two business days of the transaction date. This option has one calendar month to run. The client must decide when he believes he has the maximum profit on the deal. Let us assume that three weeks after inception, the option trade is showing a healthy profit. The strike on the ATM option was originally set at $/JPY 114.00, the spot rate is now 111.50 and the client does not think there will be much more movement, so wants to close out his position and take a profit. As this is a European option, all he has to do is to call the writing bank and ask them to 'buy back' the option. They will calculate the buy-back premium through the option-pricing model. The buy-back premium will incorporate the FX gain and will also incorporate any residual time value.

Figure 5.9 shows the different risk profiles. The long yen call option against dollars, with limited loss illustrating asymmetry of risk, and the unhedged or spot position, with a potential unlimited profit or unlimited loss.

Early exercise

If the private client had purchased a more expensive American-style option, he could still have sold it back at any time, but why pay for exercise flexibility if you never want to exercise? The private client had no need for either of the physical currencies, so exercise is not required; he simply wanted to profit from his view on exchange rates.

Using options to speculate – profit/loss profile of US$/yen position

Fig 5.9

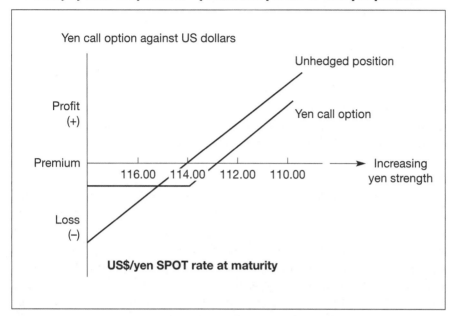

The other problem with exercising an option early is that all the client or trader would receive is the intrinsic value; that is, the amount by which the option is in the money, the amount by which the option is better than the underlying market rate. If there had been any time value left, this would be lost. Instead of early exercise, it is always better to sell back an option. This ensures that the time value component is always included in the sell-back premium.

Another consideration for using European options and selling them back, is that if the client chose to exercise the option, it would be necessary for him to take delivery of the physical yen and pay for them with physical dollars, simultaneously needing to sell the yen back into the market to crystallize the profit. In that case the transaction costs on the foreign exchange deals may be significant on their own.

Option Greeks

The option-pricing model needs a number of inputs so that it can calculate the option premium. Only the strike will remain fixed; all the other variables will change with the market or with the passage of time. Each variable changes in a distinct way and the way each variable changes has its own name. Collectively these names are known as the option Greeks. They define how the particular variable changes while all the others remain the same These variables measure the sensitivity of the option. The four most important option Greeks are:

- delta
- gamma
- theta
- vega

Those of you with a classical education may not recognize vega as a Greek letter. It probably came from 'Star Trek'!

Delta

The definition of delta is: 'The change in the option premium for a unit change in the underlying exchange rate'. This is an important measure as it shows how the price of the option will change as the underlying market moves. The values of delta ranges from zero to one. An option which is deeply out of the money (OTM), with no chance of profitable exercise, will have a delta of 0.00. An option which is deeply in the money (ITM) will behave like the underlying cash market because there is a 100 per cent certainty that the option will be exercised, in this case the delta will be 1.00. An option which is at the money (ATM) will have a delta of 0.5. The deltas of ITM options increase as expiry nears and exercise becomes more certain. Deltas of OTM options decrease as expiry nears and the option looks like being abandoned.

Delta is also known as the 'hedge ratio'. This means that the delta on a particular option can meaningfully help hedge the position. Consider a trader who has bought an ATM Swiss Franc call, US dollar put option in CHF 10 million, with a one-month expiry. As the underlying spot rate moves, so the option will become worth more or less, it will not stay ATM. If the option goes into the money, the trader will exercise the option, and the writing bank must have the CHF10 million ready for him. If the option at expiry is OTM he will not exercise it and the writing bank needs to hold zero CHF. On the day of purchase, when the option is still ATM, the chance of profitable exercise is deemed to be 50 per cent, the delta is 0.5. The option writer therefore needs to hold 50 per cent of the underlying CHF ready for the buyer, should he require it at expiry. The option writer will buy in 50 per cent × CHF 10 million. A week later, assume the spot market has moved and the delta is now 60 per cent, or 0.6: the option writer needs to buy in another 10 per cent of cover. The next day the market moves back to 55 per cent, or 0.55: the option writer needs to sell 5 per cent of the cover, and so on. Every time the position is re-hedged the trader must pay away the bid–offer spread.

This procedure is known as delta hedging: it is time consuming and costly. If the position is delta neutral, or delta hedged, the volatility has been locked in. Option portfolios that are not exposed to small movements in the underlying exchange rate are said to be delta hedged or delta neutral (see Figure 5.10).

Gamma

The definition of gamma is: 'The rate of change of delta for a unit change in the underlying exchange rate'. The more frequently an option portfolio needs to be re-hedged the higher will be the gamma. It reflects how much and how fast the hedge ratio changes. Options with a small gamma are easy to hedge, because the hedge ratio will not change much as the spot rate moves. Options with a high gamma, such as short-dated ATM options, can be treacherous to manage and very costly. Imagine the last day of an option's maturity: it is still ATM, a very small move in the underlying spot rate, say +0.0005, may swing the option ITM. In which case the option writer needs to have 100 per cent of the underlying ready for the option holder not if, but *when* he exercises. Twenty minutes later the spot rate has moved back – 0.0007, the option is now OTM. The option writer now needs to hold 0 per cent cover. Every time the market moves, even in very small amounts, the delta may swing from zero to one, with nothing in between: this is the classical high gamma position. Figure 5.11 illustrates the gamma of a call option.

Delta of a call option at various points

Fig 5.10

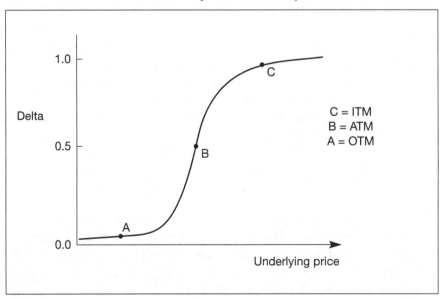

C = ITM
B = ATM
A = OTM

Fig 5.11

Gamma of a call option

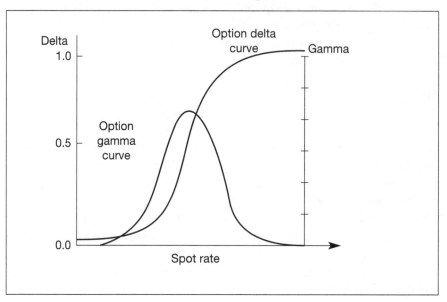

Theta

The definition of theta is: 'The change in the option premium for a given change in the period to expiry (usually the passage of a day)'.

Long-dated options have more time value than short-dated options, because as an option ages, so its inherent time value will decay. Theta describes exactly how much time value is lost from day to day, and is a precise measure of time decay. At inception an option will have 100 per cent of its time value. Consider a 90-day ATM option. How much time value has been lost after one day? Answer: $\frac{1}{90}$. The next day, the option loses $\frac{1}{89}$, and so on. So in the early part of an option's maturity, it retains most of its time value. Time decay is almost constant for about two-thirds of the option's life. The decay increases in the last third of the option's life, and in the last week it loses progressively one-seventh, then one-sixth, then one-fifth, etc., of the time value that is left. Theta is highest in ATM options close to expiry.

The graph of time value decay is best illustrated with ATM options, as in Figure 5.12.

Vega

The definition of vega is: 'The change in the option premium for a 1 per cent change in volatility'. This is a straight-line relationship. As volatility increases, so does uncertainty, and so does the premium. An option with a high volatility gives the holder a greater chance of profitable exercise than an option with low volatility (see Figure 5.13).

Graph of time value decay

Fig 5.12

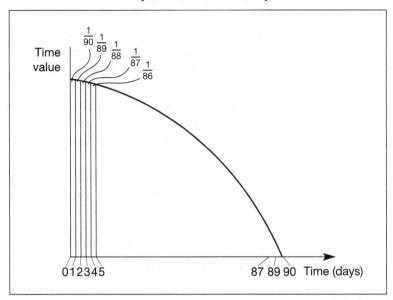

Volatility of an ATM call option

Fig 5.13

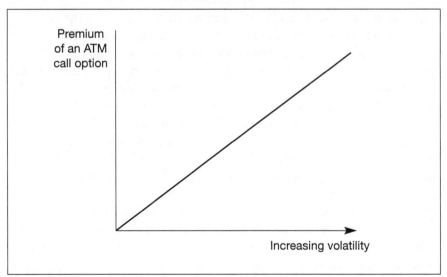

Trading volatility

Options are the only product, derivative or otherwise, where volatility is an input. We have discussed volatility at some length, and we have looked at how a hedger and a trader may use options, either to risk manage a currency position or to speculate on the direction of a currency. It is also possible to trade or speculate on volatility. This does not mean we are trying to forecast the direction on an exchange rate, rather, we are trying to forecast a 'slowdown' or a 'speed up', or an increase or decrease in uncertainty.

Mostly it is banks who trade volatility, and corporates would need very clear mandates from their board of directors to allow them to trade in this way.

Volatility strategies

The long straddle

A trader takes the view that volatility will increase; it often does at the beginning of a new financial year when everyone is back in the market, 'bright-eyed and bushy-tailed'. The direction of the market is unknown, but the trader feels definitely that it will move. If he thought the currency would strengthen, he would buy a call option; if he thought it was going to weaken, he would buy a put option. In fact, he will buy both the call option and the put option. This will entail paying two premiums. But if the market moves far enough, one of the options will be heavily in the money, and when it is sold back, will more than cover the cost of the two original option premiums, and allow for some profit.

If the market strengthens, the call option goes ITM. If the market weakens, the put option goes ITM (see Figure 5.14). Whichever option goes in to the money you sell it back, hoping that the profit on the one option will cover the cost of the two premiums. As long as the market moves, you make profit with this strategy. You will make most money if there is a big swing in one direction quickly, then when you sell the option back, you can recover some time value. You will lose most money – both your premiums – if the market does not move at all.

The short straddle

It is early December. In the run-up to Christmas and New Year many banks' trading operations tend to quieten down, staff go on holiday, and it is rare for big positions to be put on at this time. If a speculative position goes wrong, it may be hard to trade out of as liquidity will be lower.

Profit and loss profile – long straddle

Fig 5.14

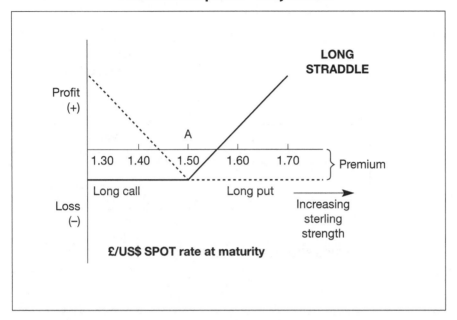

A bad position may affect the dealer's bonus, that he has earned that year, and which is paid annually, based on profits up to 31 December; the last thing he wants to do is something risky that may lose him money. Bearing this in mind, you would expect volatility to decrease; fewer players in the market and smaller positions. But should you buy a call or a put? The call would be the right option if you thought the currency was going to strengthen, the put option if you thought the currency would weaken. But your view on volatility will not give you a guide as to the direction of the currency.

The answer is that you sell both the call and the put, ATM, receiving two option premiums (see Figure 5.15). This is a high-risk strategy. In this example, you have taken in two expensive premiums, but if the view on the market is wrong and volatility increases, not decreases, then there is a possibility of serious loss. In effect you will have sold options at, say, a volatility of 9 per cent and have to buy them back to close out the positions at 12 per cent, making a loss. You will make most profit if the volatility decreases or remains the same, and you will lose if the market exchange rate moves by even a small amount in either direction. The extent of the loss will be realized only at expiry or sell-back: potentially, it could be very big indeed; it will be limited only by how far the market moves (in *either* direction).

Each of the volatility trades described can be used in any of underlying markets, interest rates, equity, commodity and, of course, currency.

Fig 5.15

Profit and loss profile – short straddle

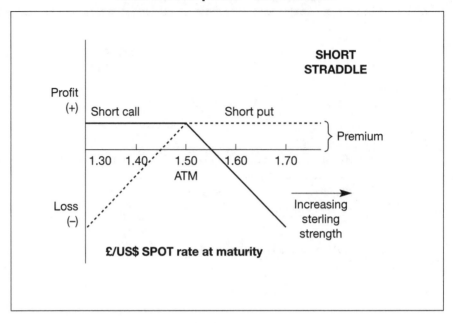

Availability

The OTC currency option is very liquid and most commercial banks will have an option service that they offer to clients. The large international banks will offer a service in many currencies, while some smaller banks will concentrate on niche markets. The minimum transaction size for a currency option will vary from bank to bank, but is likely to be in the region of US$250,000 or equivalent. To be assured of a competitive price the size of the transaction will ideally be in excess of US$250,000.

Practical considerations

What does a potential user of OTC currency options need to do before he can pick up the telephone and deal?

A client will need to set up credit lines with one of his banks. If he always wishes to purchase options, his only responsibility will be to pay the premium, in that case the credit risk to the bank is minimal. If sometimes he may want to sell options, the risk assessment is more complicated, but is generally regarded as being similar to the risk on forward foreign exchange. A good rule of thumb is that if you have a forward line with the bank, they will almost certainly let you sell options to them. If you are able to trade only in the spot market with them, they might specify they will only sell options to you, not buy them from you.

Not all banks will offer a service in every possible pair of currencies, so shop around and ensure that the banks with which you deal will be able to cater for all your requirements. If, from time to time, you need to cover an exotic pair of currencies, see if they will be able to help.

There are many banks making prices in the market, so make sure you are getting competitive quotes; either ask two banks to quote for the business, or check with brokers or information screens.

Realistically, the minimum deal size for a good price is about US$500,000 or equivalent; anything smaller than this, and the banks may charge an extra premium.

Make sure that you understand the documentation; if not, ask the bank to send someone to explain it to you.

Once the option facility is established, and there are deals on the book, be careful of exercising early. If a client buys an American-style option, he has the possibility of exercising the option early, and physically delivering or paying the currency early. If he does this he will lose any remaining time value, *but* will gain the intrinsic value. If the option is sold back, the sell-back premium will include intrinsic value and any remaining time value.

CURRENCY OPTIONS: REDUCED PREMIUM STRATEGIES

INTRODUCTION

In the previous section we looked at how to cover or 'insure' the exchange rate on a currency deal by using option-based products. Then the client would need to purchase a call or a put, depending upon whether he wished to sell or buy the underlying currency. In any event, a premium is due, and as volatility in the currency option market is quite high, the premium can sometimes be quite large. Some currency pairs are especially volatile and expensive to cover. Even if the premium is accurate, and all of the banks in the market are making the same price, it may still be too high for the client, based on his own perceptions of where the currency may move during the transaction period. In these cases another alternative is needed to make the strategy economically viable for the client. We need to consider some way of reducing the premium. In fact there are a number of ways, but we shall examine only three of them:

- out of the money options
- currency collar options
- participating forwards.

Premium reduction strategies – out of the money options

There are a number of ways that the client can reduce the premium payable on a currency option. The immediate choice is usually to 'go out of the money'. Instead of the client having insurance at today's spot or forward rates, he may take his option cover, at say, 2 cents away, this would make the option 2 cents out of the money. The foreign exchange market will then have to move a little further against the holder before the option becomes valuable. Calls and puts are often transacted out of the money, but it is never possible to go so far out of the money that the option cover costs nothing! For a dollar receiver, even if the option is only 0.5 cents out of the money, the premium will be lower than that for an at the money option. However, in some cases the client may be looking for a greater premium reduction than he can attain solely by going out of the money, or perhaps he is not prepared to go sufficiently out of the money to achieve the reduction he is looking for. Then we need to investigate other methods of premium reduction; in other words still pay the premium, but not with money. That begs the question, how else can the client pay the premium? The only available alternative is for the client to agree to give up some of his potential profit under the option, should the exchange rates move in his favour. But it must be stressed that exchange rates may not move in the client's favour; it is only a *potential* profit that the client is giving up. If rates do not move in the client's favour, he has given up nothing, and he still has his insurance cover, although he will have achieved it at a reduced cost.

Currency collar options

A currency collar will involve the client buying the call or put option cover he requires to guarantee his insured rate, and simultaneously selling the opposite option back to the bank. This second option will have a strike rate exactly at the point where the client has agreed to give up any further profit. On the first option the premium is paid to the bank, but this will be offset by the second option with the premium that is received from the bank. The resulting net premiums can be positive, negative or zero, depending on exactly how much profit potential the client is willing to give up. The collar option exhibits put/call parity.

> A **collar option** *gives the client the right, but not the obligation, to sell or buy his currency at a particular exchange rate on or before a specific future date. Should he be able to transact at a rate which is better than a second pre-determined level, the client agrees to give up any further profit. Premiums can be positive, negative or zero. The collar option involves a combination of two options: one bought and one sold. Both transactions are simultaneous, and tailored to fit the exact currency profile.*

Definition

Definition discussed

Let us take the case of a client who wishes to sell US$1 million and buy sterling three months forward. The current forward rate is £/US$1.60. The client is familiar with the concept of options, yet feels they are too expensive, given his outlook on the currency.

First, the client needs to confirm with the bank the strike on the option that he wishes to buy (although he considers it too expensive at the moment). He will need to buy a US dollar put, sterling call option, and let us assume that option is already 3 cents out of the money, but the premium quote of 1.1 per cent of the dollar amount is still too expensive for him. He does not wish to go further out of the money, but still wants a cheaper alternative. In that case the bank will need to examine other ways in which he can pay the premium. Let us assume that over the three months the client believes that the dollar/sterling exchange rate may fall – the dollar strengthens (he can profit), but only by 3 cents. The client can then put that in writing, in effect guaranteeing to the bank that should rates fall below this second rate (3 cents lower than the current forward rate) he will take no further profit. The way he does this is to sell the opposite option – a US dollar call, sterling put option to the bank at strike of £/US$1.5700. The bank will price the option at this strike price and pay him, say, 0.9 per cent of the dollar amount. This can go to offset the original premium that he paid on his option. The resulting net premium has now fallen, from a level of 1.1 per cent, to 1.1% – 0.9% = 0.2%.

Multiple product
A collar option consists of two options which offset each other, transacted simultaneously. On one the premium is paid, on the other the premium is received.

Insurance
The client pays a premium to insure against currency risk. The premium is lower as he accepts part of the risk himself, he also agrees to share part of the profit with the bank.

Profit potential
A currency collar reduces the risk of adverse currency movements while retaining the client's ability to benefit from part of any favourable movement.

Cost
A cheaper hedge than a standard option. The client selects the degree of risk he is prepared to take and the level of profit he is prepared to give up and the final net premium may be, positive, negative or zero, depending upon exactly how the two premiums offset.

Example

22 October
A UK exporter has sold some goods abroad and will receive US$1.5 million in three months' time. He wishes to use an option to protect his profit potential should the dollar rise (appreciate). The current forward rate is $1.55, and the exporter wishes to hedge his budget rate of $1.60. The exporter has telephoned his bank, and they advise that the premium for a standard option with a strike of $1.60 is 1.3 per cent (of the dollar amount), which the exporter considers too expensive.

Action – 22 October
The exporter **buys** an OTM option for three months to sell dollars and buy sterling at $1.60 – *client buys a dollar put, sterling call option*. Simultaneously, the client **sells** an OTM option to the bank for three months to sell them dollars and receive sterling – *client sells a dollar call, sterling put option*. The strike price of the option written by the client is dependent on the size of the premium he wishes to pay. Our exporter has requested a series of different strikes for the option he will sell to the bank. He could sell any one of them but is looking for a zero-premium strategy. In which case (see Table 5.4 for the figures), the zero-cost line will involve the bought dollar put at $1.60 and the dollar call sold at $1.51. It is at this point that premiums net exactly to zero.

Example: figures

Table 5.4

Client buys option with strike at	Premium payable (%)	Client sells option with strike at	Premium earned (%)	Net cost/ benefit (%)
$1.60	1.3	$1.40	0.3	Client pays 1.0
$1.60	1.3	$1.45	0.75	Client pays 0.55
$1.60	1.3	$1.47	1.10	Client pays 0.20
$1.60	1.3	$1.51	1.30	Zero cost

Outcome

By executing a transaction (at $1.60 and $1.51), the exporter has insured against an adverse currency fluctuation for nil cost, while still allowing himself any profitable movement up to a limit of $1.51 but not beyond.

There are a number of possible outcomes as shown in Figure 5.16.

- No exercise takes place if the spot rate at maturity is within the collar bands (between $1.51 and $1.60).
- If the dollar depreciates above the cap rate, the exporter will exercise his option (anything over $1.60).

Structure of zero-cost collar option

Fig 5.16

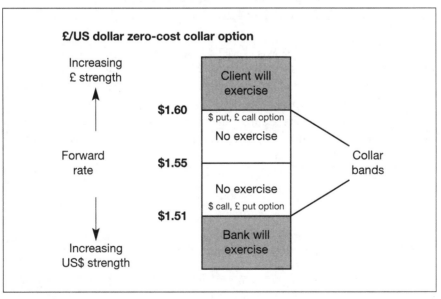

£/US dollar zero-cost collar option

Increasing £ strength

Forward rate

Increasing US$ strength

$1.60

$1.55

$1.51

Client will exercise

$ put, £ call option

No exercise

No exercise

$ call, £ put option

Bank will exercise

Collar bands

- If the dollar appreciates below the floor rate, the bank will exercise the dollar call option they have bought from the client (anything below $1.51).

Put/call parity

The notion of paying for one option by selling another illustrates the very important concept of put/call parity. As we saw earlier, a synthetic forward contract can be created by buying a call, and selling a put option – or vice versa, if they have the same strike price which is ATMF (at the money forward). The two premiums will be exactly equal and will offset. A forward contract is also zero cost. If we extend the theory a little, examine what will happen if the option bought by the client and the option sold by the client move equally out of the money: if both the put and the call are 1 cent OTM, then technically their cost will again equate to zero, so this will be another zero-cost structure. There are an almost infinite number of possibilities, for zero-cost collars, as long as each option is equally OTM, and the volatility is not different. The theory breaks down a little when you start to realize that the option trader will have a bid–offer spread between buying and selling options, this and his profit margin mitigate against a zero-cost collar being exactly equally distant either side of the current forward rate.

Participating forwards

These can also generate a zero-cost structure for a client, and also involves buying one option and selling the other. In this case, however, the option strike rates are the same, but the principal amounts on each option are different.

Consider a client who wishes to hedge the receipt of US$5 million against sterling in six months' time. He wishes to achieve a zero- or reduced cost strategy, but his expectation on exchange rates is that they may well come a substantial way in his favour – the dollar will strengthen. If he transacts a collar structure he would of necessity give up all further profit beyond a certain level, and he has already checked with the bank where that level is.

Current financial information shows:

£/US$
Spot rate   1.6000
Forward rate   1.5900
Zero-cost collar strikes 1.6200 and 1.5700

The client is certain the dollar will strengthen below 1.5700 and he still wants to profit beyond this level.

Strategy

The client will buy the option he requires in the normal way. He will purchase a US dollar put in $5 million, sterling call option, strike 1.6200 (OTM), expiry six months, the premium for this option is 1.9 per cent of the dollar amount. He still needs to pay the premium. To pay it, he will sell an option to the bank as before. But the option he sells will be a US dollar call option, sterling put option, expiry six months. The option written by the customer will have the *same* strike as the first option – $1.6200. It is therefore 3 cents in the money (ITM), and as such the bank will pay a high premium. Let us assume they will pay 3 per cent for this. This is more than enough to pay the original premium of 1.9 per cent.

The principal amount on the second option needs to be adjusted to reflect this, and we want to match the dollar amount of the premium as closely as possible.

Option 1
US dollar put, sterling call   Premium paid 1.9% = $95,000

Option 2
US dollar call, sterling put   Premium received 3% = $150,000

Principal amount required:
1.9% ÷ 3% = 0.6333
0.6333 × US$5,000,000 = US$3,166,666

The principal amount on the second option needs to be only US$3.167 million, for the premium receivable to be $95,000 (at a rate of 3 per cent). The amount of participation will increase the further OTM the option strike is pitched.

There will be a range of possible outcomes (see Figure 5.17).

(1) If the dollar weakens above the cap rate, the client exercises his option (anything over $1.62), to sell the full amount of $5 million.

(2) If the dollar strengthens to anywhere below the 1.6200 cap rate, the bank will exercise the option they have bought from the customer, also at 1.6200. This option has a principal amount of $3.167 million which leaves the client a balance of $1.833 million which needs to be sold spot. In practical terms 63 per cent of the transaction amount is locked in at $1.62, while the rest can be sold spot at whatever is the best rate in the market.

Fig 5.17

Structure of participating forward

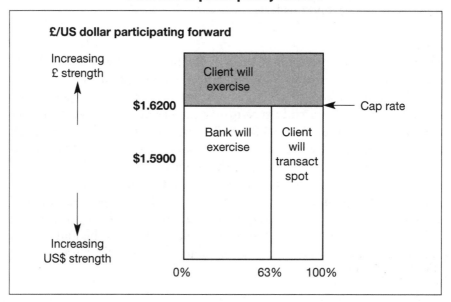

£/US dollar participating forward

Increasing £ strength

Client will exercise

$1.6200 ← Cap rate

Bank will exercise

Client will transact spot

$1.5900

Increasing US$ strength

0%   63%   100%

A zero-cost structure of this type allows the client more flexibility, especially where he believes there is likely to be a large movement of the currency, as part of the principal amount will always need to be sold spot.

Practical considerations

The most effective collar options are written when the option purchased by the client has a strike price OTM compared to the outright forward, and where both the options are European style. This is because the customer must be absolutely sure that he has the underlying currency, should the bank exercise the option they have bought from him. At least if both options are European there is no danger of the customer exercising, and then the bank asks to exercise their option some days later when the dollars in this example have already been converted into sterling at an earlier date. This structure is not advisable for uncertain or seasonal cash flows.

As this strategy involves the client writing an option to the bank, the risk is similar to that of a forward foreign exchange deal, and a forward line or treasury derivatives credit line will be required.

Minimum amounts on these zero-cost structures will vary; with collars the minimum amount is likely to be around US$100,000 or equivalent. For participating forwards, the amounts are higher, as the second option is only a proportion of the underlying principal. The minimum is likely to be about US$500,000, but check with the banks. It is not necessary for both options to be transacted by the same bank. It is perfectly feasible to buy one option from one bank, and sell the other to another bank. Care must be taken with lines and internal dealing mandates.

It is an interesting discussion point whether companies who are not allowed to sell 'naked' options outright to a bank (as a speculator) will be allowed to transact a collar structure which is a hedge with a lower all-in cost. Both positions involve selling options – one to speculate, the other for reduced cost risk management.

As with the interest rate derivatives, where options are concerned, there are a wealth of different names for the same thing. Reduced premium structures can also be known as:

- zero- (or reduced) cost collars
- zero- (or reduced) cost cylinders
- range forwards.

CURRENCY SWAPS

Introduction

The currency swap market developed in the early 1960s in the UK, and was originally used as a means of avoiding exchange controls. When the Exchange Control Act was abolished in 1979, it did little to affect the growth in these instruments. The currency swap that we are familiar with today has grown out of the two techniques known as parallel loans and back-to-back loans.

Parallel and back-to-back loans
A US multinational company might need sterling for its UK subsidiary, and a large UK company may have surplus sterling but need dollars for its US operations. With the parallel loan, each company would lend the other equivalent amounts in each currency for the same maturity. Figure 5.18 shows that in the UK, the UK company will lend £10 million to the US company and receive in return 9 per cent interest per annum. In contrast, in the USA, the US company will lend US$16 million to the UK company and receive 7 per cent fixed per annum. The rate of exchange used is £/US$1.60.

> 'The currency swap that we are familiar with has grown out of the two techniques known as parallel loans and back-to-back loans.'

There were a number of problems with this arrangement, mostly concerned with securing an adequate right of set-off in the event of default by one of the parties, and the complex documentation involved. The

Fig 5.18

Parallel loan

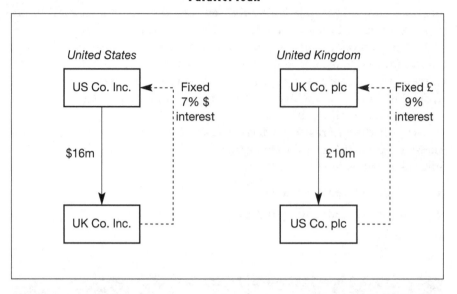

back-to-back loan (see Figure 5.19) was then introduced to try and over-come some of the obstacles and to simplify the structure. This newer structure was only partly successful, but it was some time before the cur-rency swap was developed in the 1970s, incorporating the best features of both parallel and back-to-back loans (see Figure 5.20). In 1981 the World Bank did a highly publicized currency swap with IBM which

Fig 5.19

Back-to-back loan

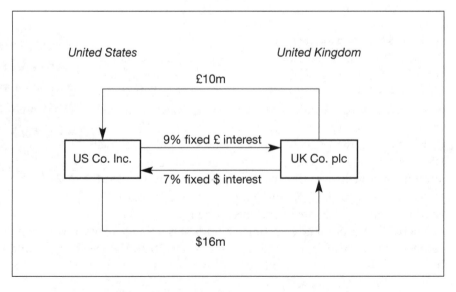

Currency swap

Fig 5.20

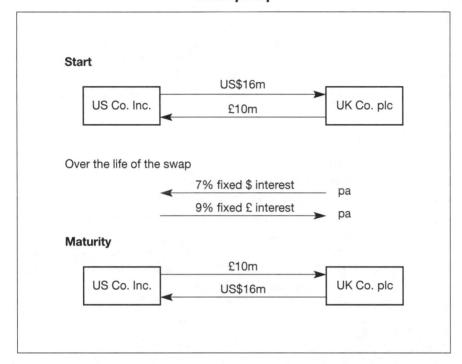

ensured that the currency swap became respectable. Since then the market has grown, although it is still considerably smaller than that for single currency interest rate swaps. As at June 1998, the outstanding amounts were US$2,324 million, for currency swaps, against US$32,942 million, for interest rate swaps (*Source: Bank for International Settlements*). The reasons why the growth of the currency swap market has been much slower centre upon the following points:

- Currency swaps involve an exchange of 100 per cent of principal, resulting in a much higher credit risk weighting. Their uses are very much confined to currency hedging, rather than speculation.
- Higher capital requirements have been imposed on currency swaps than interest rate swaps.
- There is less liquidity in the currency swap market so a bank would find it harder to hedge its positions.

Definition

> *A **currency swap** is an agreement between two or more parties to exchange interest obligations/receipts, for an agreed period, between two different currencies, and at the end of the period to re-exchange the corresponding principal amounts, at an exchange rate agreed at the beginning of the transaction.*

Definition discussed

Currency swaps differ from interest rate swaps in that they involve an exchange of interest in two currencies, and also involve an exchange of principal amounts. They therefore impinge on the balance sheets of each counterparty. As a result, currency swaps are used almost exclusively to hedge a risk, rather than to trade a speculative position.

Like an interest rate swap, a currency swap is a legal obligation, and at the outset each party has to agree what its role will be, and on what interest basis it will pay and receive. There are three types of currency swap:

- fixed/fixed
- fixed/floating
- floating/floating.

The interest rates are determined in advance, either as a fixed rate, e.g., 10 per cent per annum, or a specified floating rate such as six-month dollar LIBOR. At maturity the two counterparties will exchange the principal amounts. The exchange rate used is set at the beginning of the transaction.

Example

Dragon Bank, a UK bank, wishes to enter into a commitment to exchange US$80 million for sterling in three years' time. This deal is rather large for a traditional forward contract, and so Dragon Bank is looking at using currency swaps. Bank Georgia is prepared to take the other side of the swap.

The sequence of activities will be:

(1) Over a period of three years Dragon Bank to pay Bank Georgia (a US Bank – the swap counterparty) a stream of US dollar interest on US$80 million. The interest payments will be at a rate agreed at the outset.

(2) Also over three years, Bank Georgia pays to Dragon Bank a stream of sterling interest on £50 million, at an interest rate agreed at the outset.

(3) Dragon Bank and Bank Georgia to exchange at the end of the period the principal amounts of US$80 million and £50 million on which interest payments are being made. Exchange rate also agreed at the outset as £/US$1.60.

Principal and interest obligations

Example: principal and interest obligations

Fig 5.21

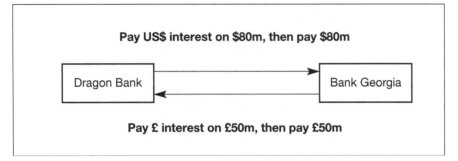

Pay US$ interest on $80m, then pay $80m

Dragon Bank   Bank Georgia

Pay £ interest on £50m, then pay £50m

Cash flows on the swap with no initial exchange

If there had been an initial exchange, each counterparty would borrow their home currency and then enter into a spot deal with the other party to convert it into the counter currency (see Figure 5.22).

Maturity
A currency swap provides a simpler, more liquid solution to long-term FX exposure than can be provided through conventional foreign exchange markets.

Size
Large amounts can be accommodated within one transaction avoiding the need for repeated recourse to the markets.

Confidentiality
Identities of swap participants need not be revealed in the market.

Bypass mechanism
Currency swaps can be used to bypass exchange controls (where they still exist) and help clients gain access to restricted markets.

New or existing obligations
It is possible to swap new or existing commitments.

Initial/final exchange of principal
Principal amounts can be exchanged at the start of a currency swap. This is normally where the swap is associated with a new borrowing, or where one of the counterparties needs the principal amount of one

Fig 5.22

Cash flows on a currency swap

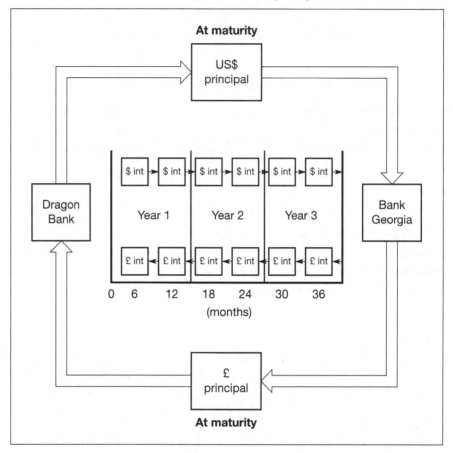

At maturity

US$ principal

Dragon Bank

| $ int | $ int | $ int | $ int | $ int | $ int |

Year 1   Year 2   Year 3

| £ int | £ int | £ int | £ int | £ int | £ int |

Bank Georgia

0   6   12   18   24   30   36
(months)

£ principal

At maturity

of the currencies being swapped. A swap with an initial exchange, using the previous example, would need Dragon Bank to sell the sterling spot for dollars to Bank Georgia. The exchange rate does not need to be exactly the spot rate and is often rounded to the nearest 'big figure' (e.g., $1.5997 becomes $1.60). The sterling sold spot by Dragon Bank initially would be borrowed by them specifically for swapping into the dollars, and vice versa. At maturity there would be a re-exchange of currencies at the original exchange rate.

The sterling principal repaid to Dragon Bank by Bank Georgia would be used to repay the sterling borrowing, and the sterling interest received during the swap will be used to service the debt repayments on the loan. The borrowings which are taken out to fund the initial exchange are separate from the swap itself. Where a swap has initial as well as final exchange, the credit risk is substantially reduced.

True derivatives?

A currency swap is not a true derivative as it will always involve a final exchange of principal. Market convention, however, deems that it should be treated as one.

Currency swap

Payer The party wishing to pay the agreed currency.

Receiver The party wishing to receive the agreed currency.

Swap rate, guaranteed rate The swap interest rate agreed between the parties at the outset of the transaction.

Rollovers/ resets The frequency of the LIBOR settlements, e.g., a two-year Euro swap against 6-month $ LIBOR. Dates when the swap rates are net cash settled. Settlement is in arrears.

Different types of currency swap

- A traditional *currency swap* would keep the fixed interest rates constant and simply swap into a different currency (fixed US$ vs fixed yen).
- A *cross-currency swap* will swap fixed for floating as well as crossing the currency (fixed US$ vs floating sterling). These are also known as cross currency coupon swaps.
- A *currency basis swap*, will swap two different floating rates in two different currencies (floating sterling vs floating Euro).

Occasionally the terms asset and liability swaps are used. These terms merely denote whether the interest flows at the start come from an asset or a liability.

Liquidity considerations

There is less liquidity in currency swaps than in interest rate swaps, and because of this, it is sometimes necessary to go through a third intervening swap, usually a fixed/floating US dollar swap, to end up at the interest and currency basis required by both parties. These multilegged swaps are sometimes known as cocktail swaps, or tripartite swaps.

In Figure 5.23, the bank is trying to hedge a swap in yen and dollars that it has just undertaken with client A. The only way it can protect itself is to use another yen/dollar swap for the correct maturity from the inter-bank market, but this is matched only on the yen side not on the dollar side. So an intervening fixed/floating dollar swap is installed with another swap bank in the inter-bank market.

Fig 5.23

Cocktail swap or tripartite swap

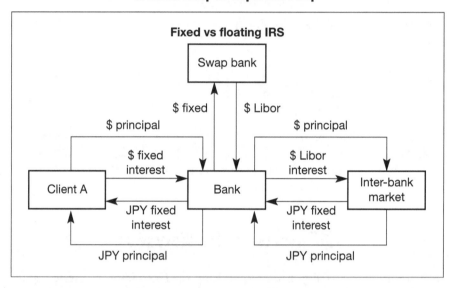

Currency swap quotations

It is banking practice for the 6-month US$ LIBOR to be the standard index for the floating rate, in both cross-currency coupon swaps, and cross-currency basis swaps. Given the complexity of currency swaps with their interest payments in various bases in one currency and their principal repayments in another, care must be taken when asking for prices. It is a good idea to specify both sides of the deal, for example: 'I wish to pay 6-month yen LIBOR against five-year fixed dollars'. Then there can be no confusion.

Currency swaps are generally quoted as inclusive prices, e.g., 5.18 to 5.28 per cent: on one side the client is a payer, and on the other side he receives, but what exactly?

- Cross-currency coupon swaps – paying and receiving refer to the fixed rate, the floating rate is assumed to be 6-month dollar LIBOR.

- Currency basis swaps – both sides of the swap need to be identified.

- Fixed vs fixed currency swaps – both sides of the swap must be specified.

Hedging with a fixed/floating currency swap

A UK communications company with mostly sterling revenues has bor-rowed fixed rate dollars to finance the purchase of plant and machinery from the USA. It expects the dollar to appreciate, owing to sustained interest rate rises. But an increase in the value of the dollar would increase the amount of sterling required to repay the original loan. The sterling equivalent cost of interest payments may also increase. A cur-rency swap is being considered. The swap would fix the rate at maturity where the UK company could exchange sterling revenues for the dollars needed to repay the borrowings. This would hedge the exchange risk. The communications company also believe that sterling interest rates may fall, but not by very much. Consequently they could, through the swap, take a view on their own domestic interest rates as well as hedge their currency risk. They could swap from the fixed rate dollars needed to repay the dollar loan into floating rate sterling. This would be described as a cross-currency coupon swap. It does, however, open the company up to an interest rate risk, an element of speculation. The simplest structure will not involve an initial exchange of principal and in any case the origi-nal borrowing was taken out years ago. The UK communications company will contact their swap bank and they will:

- Fix the currency rate at which the principal will be exchanged at matu-rity (probably the spot rate).
- Agree the interest rates for the swap.

The UK communications company will pay a stream of sterling floating rate interest and receive a stream of fixed dollars from the swap counter-party. The dollar interest received will be used to service the underlying dollar borrowings. The sterling interest paid on the swap will come from UK earnings, and will reduce if LIBOR rates fall.

At maturity, the UK company will pay a sterling principal amount through the swap and receive in return a dollar principal amount. The exchange rate used for the conversion will be the one both parties agreed to at the outset. The UK company will fund the payment of sterling prin-cipal from accumulated sterling earnings, and will use the dollars it receives to repay the original dollar borrowings (see Figure 5.24).

Both currency swaps and forward foreign exchange allow a hedger to protect himself against future movements in exchange rates. The instru-ments are similar, and both take account of interest rate differentials, but do so in different ways.

Fig 5.24

Example: currency swap cash flows

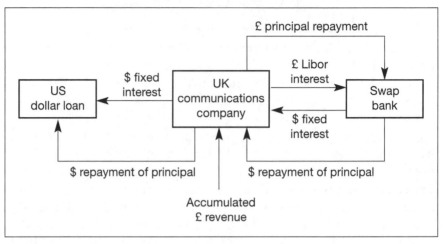

Comparison of currency swaps and forward foreign exchange

Consider a company, Corporate X, which wishes to sell forward US$16 million for sterling. A currency swap will involve throughout its maturity an exchange of streams of dollar and sterling interest, and then finally at maturity, the exchange of principal of, say, $16 million and £10 million, corresponding to an exchange rate of $1.60. Under the currency swap treatment we would see the flows illustrated in Figure 5.25.

Fig 5.25

Currency swap cash flows

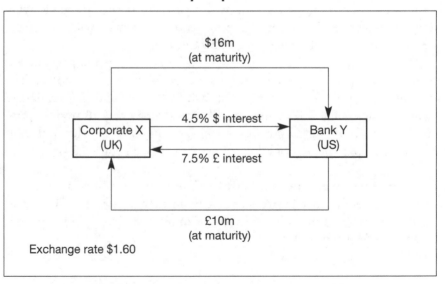

The swap

- Involves exchange of interest and principal.
- The exchange of principal takes place at a rate agreed at the start of the swap, usually (but not always) the spot rate.

Outright forwards

With an outright forward deal the interest rate differential is accounted for in a different way, by including the difference in the currency conversion rate.

- No interest amounts are exchanged, only principal.
- The exchange of principal amounts takes place at maturity, *but* at a rate different from the spot rate.

In our example the forward rate of $1.4749 would mean that at maturity, the principal amounts would be £10 million and $14.751 million. This would compensate for the lack of interest flows during the life of the deal (see Figure 5.26). The implied forward points for the deal are:

$$\$1.6000 - \$1.4749 = 0.1251$$

If the cash flows were to be compared between the swap and the outright forward, they would equate to the same thing. The two instruments have equal net present values. A normal yield to maturity rate is used to discount the cash flows on the swap, but a zero-coupon interest rate is used for the outright forward. In summary, outright forward deals reflect the interest differential in the FX rate, whereas with currency swaps there is an exchange of interest cash flows and the FX rate is untouched. For further information on the valuation of swaps see *Further reading* at the end of the chapter.

Outright forward FX deal cash flow

Fig 5.26

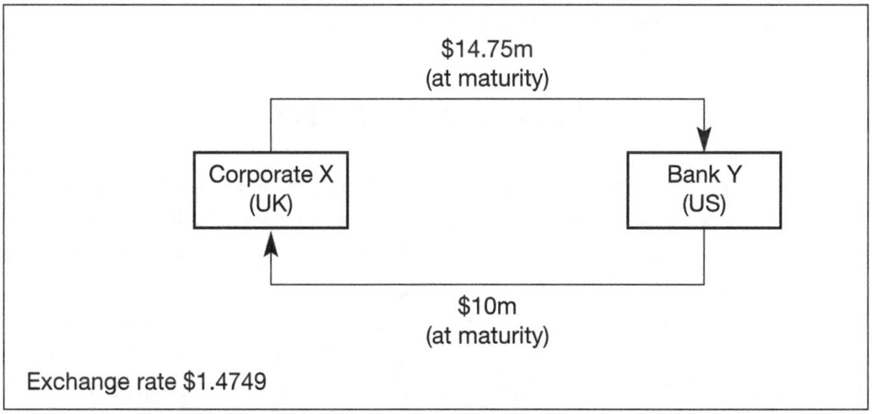

Exchange rate $1.4749

When to use currency swaps

Currency swaps can be used to hedge foreign exchange risk, and on occasions allow the client to take a view on the strength or weakness of his own domestic currency. However, as we have already seen, the overriding rule of when to use swaps is that both counterparties (and the bank) should be in a better position after the swap. It follows, then, that there are circumstances when a currency swap should not be contemplated. These are:

- When the existing currency of a *foreign currency liability* is expected to *depreciate*. This would reduce the amount of domestic currency required to repay the liability, which is a good thing.

- When the existing currency of a *foreign currency asset* is expected to *appreciate*. This would increase the domestic currency value of the asset, also good.

- When the currency into which the *liability is to be swapped* is expected to *appreciate*. This would increase the amount of domestic currency required to repay the liability, which is to be avoided.

- The currency into which an *asset is to be swapped* is expected to *depreciate*. This would reduce the domestic currency value of the asset, also to be avoided.

Availability

Currency swaps are available in most major currencies and some cross-currencies, in minimum amounts of £5 million or US$5 million (or equivalent). Smaller amounts may be available on request, but there will be a price to pay included in the swap rate. Periods of up to 15 years are possible, but due to the heavy nature of the credit risk, the majority of deals are transacted for seven years and under.

Practical considerations

Any counterparty can deal in a currency swap, subject to credit considerations. Unfortunately, the credit risk on these deals includes not only the possible interest rate movements, as in interest rate swaps, but also the potential movement between the two currency exchange rates for entire maturity. The risk to the counterparty bank is therefore very much higher. The credit department of the swap bank will need to assess its counterparty risk with the client. They will need to consider the maturity and amount of any swaps the client may wish to execute, and may even specify a terminal maturity, say, nothing longer than seven years. Dealing lines and credit lines must be set up in advance.

In addition to credit lines, the documentation is quite onerous for those dealing with swaps for the first time. The market has adopted the International Swaps and Derivatives Association CISDA document, which is a master agreement that must be set up in advance of the first deal. This is not a precondition as such, but the documentation is quite long, and company lawyers and solicitors may need to spend some time examining the main document. All swap deals are dealt 'subject to docs': if the documentation cannot be agreed within a fairly short period, the swap will be cancelled.

Within the swap itself, the rollover frequency can be monthly, quarterly, semi-annual or annual. It is not necessary for the fixed and floating payments to be paid on the same day, but the client must specify the frequency of all interest payments at the time of dealing. Each swap price will factor in the payment frequency, and the swap rates will be different to reflect this.

There are a number of currency swap providers in the market, but not nearly as many as in the interest rate swap market. As a consequence, swap counterparties may be harder to find, and the product is certainly less liquid.

Further reading

For further reading on products mentioned in Chapter 5:

Currency Swaps – Self-Study Workbooks, published by IFR, 1994.

For further reading on currency options contact the main banks for their customer literature. This is the best source of information.

For technical aspects of options:

Financial Engineering by L. Galitz, published by FT/Prentice Hall, 1995.

'Mastering Foreign Exchange and Currency Options', by Francesca Taylor, published by FT/Prentice Hall, 1997.

'The growth in equity derivatives is phenomenal. . . . the BIS survey shows turnover has increased from US$475 billion to US$1,442 billion in the last three years.'

Equity Derivatives

INTRODUCTION

The derivatives that are used to hedge against equity risk or to speculate upon it are the same as the derivatives that we have studied in previous chapters. There are only three classifications of derivatives: futures, options and swaps. When we apply these techniques to equity the results are:

- **stock index futures**
- **options on stock index futures or options on single stocks**
- **equity swaps.**

Equity derivatives can be exchange traded or OTC, with exchange traded futures and options making up the majority of transactions. OTC equity swaps are a very important part of this market, gaining in popularity all the time. However, the aspect of credit risk is very different with OTC equity products such as equity swaps and options, as we shall see later. Many equity deals are proprietary. The only gauge we have of the scope of general equity derivative activity is from the BIS survey, which shows turnover has increased from US$475 billion to US$1,442 billion in three years.

BACKGROUND

When people discuss equity, they generally mean stocks and shares. In the UK, we talk about owning shares in a company, and in the USA, we refer to common stock. An equity investor is participating more fully in the risks of that business than any other type of investor in the same company. This is because a rate of return is not guaranteed to the equity investor, neither is there a maturity date for the investment or a fixed redemption amount. Should the company experience difficult trading conditions and not make the expected profit, there will be no share of the profits for the investor. The income that the equity investor receives is known as the dividend, and it can be as high or as low as company fortunes permit. Some years there may be no payment at all. To counter these perceived disadvantages, the investor is allowed to vote at company meetings on matters of policy and also to have a say in electing the board of directors. Never forget that the owners of the business are the shareholders, but the controllers of the business are the board of directors. It is this conflict that can sometimes cause problems, especially when a large block of shares is owned by one person who wants a say in his investment. Really, what he wants is a say in running the company, but unfortunately the board of directors running the company may disagree with him.

When an investor wishes to liquidate his holdings in a company he must sell his shares in the secondary market, as there is no redemption date. At the time of the sale, the market share price can be anywhere, and will react to supply and demand in the market. The efficiency of the secondary market is paramount, as investors must be confident that they can sell or buy shares at any time.

There is another important difference between equity and the other underlying primary markets that we have examined so far. With equity the cash market is a lot less liquid. Consider the global equity market; it is estimated to be roughly equivalent to US$20 trillion. This is split into equity in different countries, denominated in different currencies. Within each country there are different sectors, with many different companies in each sector. If an investor is trying to hedge against a movement in a stock with equity options, the bank writing the option could have problems in hedging its own position, especially if the transaction size is large. They may need to buy or sell quantities of stock for the hedge position, at times when the market may be very tight and illiquid. Contrast this with say dollar/yen currency options; the inter-bank market world-wide will make prices in spot dollar/yen, liquidity will never be a problem. But how many market makers are there in an individual share, in a particular country? The answer must be a lot less.

SINGLE STOCKS OR EQUITY INDICES?

When you examine equity risk further, it can be subdivided into two sections. First, how does 'the market' move? Second, how do the individual shares that make up the market move? As we have already discussed, an individual company may be in distress and its share price may fall, but the stock market as a whole may be increasing in value. This is an important point. Are we looking to hedge or speculate on the 'market' or on an individual equity? The answer lies in the different motivations of the user.

Case 1

A portfolio manager holds a number of different stocks and will generally be more concerned about the performance of them as a group, than about how a single one of them performs – although he would always hope that the individual share prices will increase too. To counteract the effect of a single share performing badly, the portfolio manager will need to have a diversified portfolio of different stocks that are unrelated. If one stock goes down another may go up. Generally about 60 per cent of the risk that affects individual shares relative to the index can be eliminated with about ten reasonably uncorrelated stocks. If the number of stocks in the portfolio is raised to 20, all but 10 per cent of this risk can be removed (see Figure 6.1).

Fig 6.1

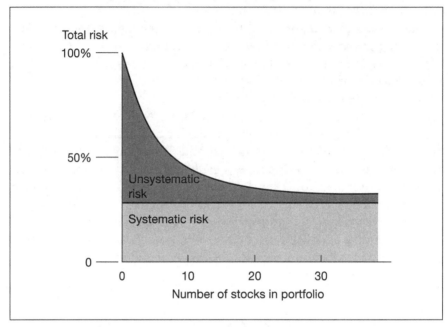

Systematic and unsystematic portfolio risk

Source: LIFFE

This type of derivatives user will prefer to hedge or to speculate on the performance of an index which contains many shares.

Case 2 A private client may well hold substantial amounts of single stocks, and be concerned about how those stocks perform individually. He will then be looking to use derivatives on that particular stock, either using an exchange-traded option if available or by using OTC products.

Futures

A hedger looking to protect himself from a fall, or a trader looking to profit from a movement in the stock market can use futures on the appropriate index. However, a single stock hedger or trader may have problems. This is because single stock futures are available only on the Australian market, and only in a limited way, covering a very few shares.

Options

There are exchange-traded options on most of the indices (options on futures), and also options on some single stocks, although each exchange will offer a different selection. The OTC market is quite limited by comparison, due to hedging constraints and counterparty credit risk. But if a client needs an option on a company where there is no option quoted on the exchange, he will be compelled to go to one of the OTC providers in the market.

> 'There are only three classifications of derivatives: futures, options and swaps.'

Swaps

Equity swaps are by definition an OTC derivative, and can be completely tailored to the specific requirements of the client. Equity swaps are constructed with stock indices or LIBOR rather than individual equities.

Equity indices

A stock index tracks the changing price of a hypothetical portfolio of stocks. It is used to measure a stock market's performance. The price of each stock is weighted by the stock's market capitalization. This 'value weighted' approach means that movements in stocks with large market capitalizations can have a disproportionately large impact on the index. This is important for two reasons. First, movements in the index will mirror changes in the market portfolio. Second, a portfolio can be constructed to match the index and 'index track' it.

There are four main market indices used in the UK:

1. FT Ordinary Share Index (or FT 30)
Based on 30 actively and highly capitalized companies representing British industry. It is calculated on a real-time basis while the market is open.

2. FT Actuaries All Share Index (FTA)
A weighted arithmetic index of 720 stocks. Used to create a benchmark for measuring the performance of a market portfolio.

3. FT-SE 100 (Footsie)
Used to support the FT-SE 100 future. A weighted arithmetic index based on the top 100 UK companies by market capitalization. The component shares are reviewed quarterly. This index covers about 65 per cent of the FT Actuaries All Share Index.

4. FT-SE 250 (the Mid-Cap)

Introduced to support the FT-SE 250 future, comprising the next largest 250 companies by market capitalization.

In the USA there is a range of market indices but the three main ones are as follows.

1. The Dow Jones Index

Equivalent to the FT 30 index, it is unweighted but calculated arithmetically.

2. The S&P 500

Equivalent to the FTA, based on the 500 major stocks listed on the New York Stock Exchange (NYSE). It includes 400 industrials, 40 utilities, 20 transportation companies and 40 financial institutions. This index accounts for nearly 80 per cent of the total market capitalization on the NYSE.

3. The NASDAQ 100 Index

Mostly technology and non-financial shares; the 100-share index was launched in 1985, with a base of 250.

Each index has its own characteristics; some assume that stock dividends are reinvested and the value of the index is adjusted accordingly; others do not. For example, the DAX index, which is the German market index, covering 30 stocks, assumes that dividends are re-invested, but in neither the FT-SE 100 nor the American indices does this occur. Table 6.1 lists the major equity indices.

Table 6.1

Major equity indices

Australia	All-Ords	All-Ordinaries Index: prices weighted by market capitalization over 250 mainly industrial shares
Canada	TSE 35	Toronto Stock Exchange 35 Index: prices weighted by market capitalization of 35 shares
France	CAC 40	Compagnie des Agents de Change 40 Index: prices weighted by market capitalization of 40 of the 100 companies with the highest market capitalization listed on the 'forward' section of the Paris Bourse
Germany	DAX	Deutsche Aktien Index: prices weighted by market capitalization of the shares of 30 top blue-chip companies

Continued

Table 6.1

Hong Kong	Hang Seng	Index of prices weighted by market capitalization of the shares of 33 shares
Japan	Nikkei 225	Index of unweighted prices of the shares of 225 blue-chip Japanese companies listed on the Tokyo Stock Exchange
	TOPIX	Tokyo Price Index: prices weighted by market capitalization of all shares listed on the 'first section' of the Tokyo Stock Exchange
UK	FT-SE 100	Financial Times-Stock Exchange 100 Index: prices weighted by market capitalization of the shares of the 100 companies with the highest market capitalizations
	FT 30	Financial Times Ordinary Share Index: prices weighted by market capitalization of the shares of the 750 companies with the highest market capitalizations
USA	DJIA	Dow Jones Industrial Average: prices weighted by market capitalization of the shares of 30 blue-chip companies listed on the New York Stock Exchange
	NYSE	New York Stock Exchange Composite Index: prices weighted by market capitalization of the shares of all companies listed on the New York Stock Exchange
	S&P 500	Standard & Poor's 500 Index: prices weighted by market capitalization of the shares of the 500 companies with the highest market capitalizations
	NASDAQ 100	NASDAQ 100 Index: market value-weighted index based on the top 100 companies listed on NASDAQ stock market; typically technology stocks
Europe	EUROTOP 100	EUROTOP 100 Index: prices from 100 most activity traded stocks in nine European countries (Belgium, France, Germany, Holland, Italy, Spain, Sweden, Switzerland,UK)

Other equity products

Some instruments are unique in having multiple characteristics. The general name given to these types of products is hybrids. For example a convertible bond starts life as a bond, but when certain pre-determined conditions are satisfied, it can convert into equity. This gives the owner of the bond the chance to move into equity if he so desires at a later date. A preference share pays a level of guaranteed dividend, resembling a bond structure. It is also easy to embed equity derivatives into, for example, Eurobonds, providing an 'equity kicker'. These products, together with warrants, rights issues and convertibles, fall outside the scope of this book.

STOCK INDEX FUTURES

Introduction

Stock index futures started to trade in the early 1980s. The underlying commodity is the basket of shares that make up the index. The index itself conveys information about stock market movements, but says nothing about the relative level of the index. This is because the initial value of the index was chosen arbitrarily.

For the index to be used correctly as a hedging mechanism, it needs to be assigned a monetary value for each point of movement. With the FTSE 100, this value is £10 per full index point or £5.00 per tick (half-point), and with American S&P 500 index, it is US$250 per full index point. This monetary value is also known as the index multiplier. If the value of the FT-SE 100 on a particular day is 6120, then the 'cash value' of the index is £10 × 6120 which equals £61,200. In simple terms, if you hold a portfolio of shares which exactly matches the FT-SE 100 basket of shares, you will need one future to cover each £61,200 of portfolio. Tomorrow the cash value of the index may have changed, and more or less futures will be required. Consider a fund manager who is managing a portfolio worth £5 million. He will need the following number of futures if he wishes to hedge his position.

$$\frac{5,000,000}{61,200} = 81.70 \text{ futures contracts (round up to 82)}$$

As with all futures contracts it is not possible to trade in a fraction of a contract, so the figure will need to be rounded up or down. On any particular day the formula used to calculate the number of futures for hedging purposes is:

$$\frac{\text{Total value of portfolio}}{\text{FT-SE 100 Index level} \times \text{Index multiplier}}$$

It is not too difficult to choose a basket of shares that corresponds to the FT-SE 100 Index without resorting to having to purchase the exact 100 shares in the index, although there may be an element of 'tracking error'. This occurs when the make up of the index is different, and may not exactly match the movement of the FT-SE 100. For example, assume that the FT-SE 100 is standing today at 6110: if a portfolio manager exactly replicated the FT-SE 100 Index by purchasing the individual shares in the correct weightings, it would cost him £61,100, (excluding transaction costs). The behaviour of this basket of shares would exactly match the performance of the index. If the index moved from 6110 to 6160, the arbitrary cash value of the index would increase from £61,100 to £61,600, and the value of the basket of shares would increase by the same amount. If, on the other hand, the portfolio manager had a basket of shares where most of them matched fairly closely those stocks of the FT-SE, but also included some highly volatile, say, pharmaceutical stocks, then this portfolio will be more volatile than the FT-SE 100. It will outperform the FT-SE 100 on the way up, it will reach a higher figure or make a greater incremental profit. It will also outperform the index on the way down – it will fall further and lose more money.

> A **stock index future** is an agreement between two parties to compensate each other for movements in the value of a stock index over the contract period. The value of the stock index is defined as being the value of the index multiplied by a specific monetary amount (the index multiplier).

Definition

Definition discussed

As with all futures contracts traded on a regulated exchange, there is a contract specification that determines the role of each person in the transaction. Stock index futures do not have the specific contract sizes that are common in other futures contracts. The value of a stock index future will vary from day to day as the FT-SE 100 Index rises and falls.

Example

Index level 6000 – value of one futures contract is £60,000 (6000 × £10)

Index level 6250 – value of one futures contract is £62,500 (6250 × £10).

The future can either be bought or sold; if you believe that the index will fall, you sell the future, if you think the index will rise, you will buy the future. Profits or losses are determined by how many ticks profit made or lost between the buying and selling prices, and contracts are settled, not with the delivery of a basket of shares, but with cash settlement. Only about 2 per cent of futures contracts ever reach delivery or contract expiry, the rest of them are closed out well before.

Index futures contracts

Market
Futures are traded on a regulated exchange with contract sizes based on market levels and specific delivery dates. Trades are executed by a member firm or broker, physically on the floor of the relevant exchange.

Contracts
In the UK, available to cover the top 100 companies by market capitalization – FT-SE 100, and the smaller companies through the Mid-Cap 250 that covers the next 250 companies down the list, by market capitalization. In the US, there are various indices, the S&P 500, the Dow Jones, etc. In Japan there is the Nikkei, and in Europe, there is the EUROTOP, and almost every country has its own index (see Table 6.1).

Pricing
This is a competitive auction-based market, and prices are generally quoted as a bid–offer spread in index points. Once a trade has been executed, the price is then widely disseminated through various information networks, providing world reference levels.

Market operations
Both buyers and sellers must put up minimum levels of collateral for each open contract that they hold. This is known as initial margin. The actual level is calculated by the relevant exchange and can change if market volatility changes. Initial margin will be returned with interest when the position is closed out. Positions are 'marked-to-market', and profits or losses are crystallized daily. If the position loses money during the day, the losses must be paid that day. If the position is in profit, a payment will be received that day. These daily payments are known as variation margin.

Availability

There are many index futures contracts world-wide, each primarily designed for its own domestic market, for further details, contact the exchange direct.

Cash settlement

At maturity or 'delivery' there will be a cash settlement of the differences, based on the exchange delivery settlement price (EDSP) and the level of the futures contracts. The EDSP is based on the average level of the FT-SE between 10.10 a.m. and 10.30 a.m. on the last trading day of the particular contract. There is no requirement to deliver or take delivery of the underlying physical securities.

Using index futures

To illustrate more clearly how this works, the contract specification of the FT-SE 100 future is shown in Table 6.2.

FT-SE 100 Index future – contract specification

Table 6.2

Unit of trading	Value at £10 per index point (e.g., value £65,000 at 6500)
Delivery months	March, June, September, December
Delivery day	First business day after the expiry date
Last trading day	10.30 (London time) third Friday of the delivery month
Quotation	Index points (e.g. 6500)
Minimum price movement	0.5
Tick value	£5.00 per half-tick
Trading hours	08.00 – 17.30 (London time) LIFFE CONNECT

Source: LIFFE

What exactly are we trading?

Traders, hedgers and arbitrageurs will buy or sell these futures contracts depending on whether they believe the level of FT-SE 100 Index will rise or fall. Although the contract specification indicates that index futures contracts can be traded up to a year forward, it is only the nearest three contracts (representing nine months of cover) that are available for trading; in practice most volume is in the nearest contract.

Example

An index futures trading transaction

It is mid-March, and all the recent economic data suggests that the stock market is about to rally. Today the June FT-SE 100 Index future is quoted at 6555, and the equity trader believes that the market will advance further. She wishes to make a profit from predicting this upward movement in share prices. Her trading amount is a notional £5 million.

Action – 10 March

Buy the required amount of futures based on the following formula:

$$\frac{\text{Total value of portfolio}}{\text{FT-SE 100 Index level} \times \text{index multiplier}}$$

substituting in the numbers:

$$\frac{£5,000,000}{6555 \times £10} = 76.27 \text{ futures contracts (round down to 76)}$$

Outcome

On the third Friday in June, the exchange delivery settlement price (EDSP) on the June FT-SE future is 6735. The position 'will go to delivery', so her position will be marked against the EDSP at 6735.

Profit or loss?

The view on the market was correct and the FT-SE rose. Our trader has made a profit.

Opening FT-SE 100 futures level	6555 (bought)
Closing FT-SE 100 futures level	6735 (sold)
Profit	**180 points**

What is this profit worth in real money?
The trader has made a profit of
76 contracts × 180 index points × £10.00 each full point
a total of £136,800.

If our trader had put on the same trade, but her view on the market direction was wrong, and the stock market had fallen instead of rallied, she would have lost on the position, as she would have originally bought the futures at the same level of 6555, but she would have then sold them lower down, resulting in a loss.

Market structure and operations

The operation of the equity futures market is identical to other futures markets – the only difference being that the underlying commodity upon which the future is based is different. The transactions take place in a regulated exchange such as LIFFE, where the market participants are able to buy or sell the futures contracts as required. Each contract is subject to a contract specification which details the responsibilities of the buyer and the seller. The transactions must be executed through a broker or through a member firm, either on the floor of the exchange or via an electronic platform, such as LIFFE CONNECT™. Once the contracts have been sold/bought, the trade is registered into a trade registration system (TRS), and then the contracts will be 'cleared'. At this stage, the clearing house becomes counterparty to both buyer and seller. The different underlying commodity will not prove to be a problem, as these contracts will be 'cash settled'. In effect, the parties will compensate each other for movements of the index. These contracts can also be known as contracts for differences or CFDs. Trading is executed through open outcry, or through PC-based trading. Market practitioners who use equity futures tend to be fund managers, portfolio managers, unit and investment trusts managers, as well as pension fund managers and other holders of equity. For further information on futures market structure and operations, see *financial futures contracts* in Chapter 3.

Initial and variation margins

As with all futures contracts, initial and variation margins must be paid according to the specific regulations of the exchange. With the LIFFE FT-SE 100 Index future, the initial margin at the time of writing is £3,000 per contract for both buyers and sellers. This initial margin must be maintained throughout the open contract position, but is repaid on maturity or close out plus a small level of interest. This initial margin is placed first of all with the broker who is executing the business, and then placed by him with the clearing house on behalf of particular client trades. Most exchanges world-wide operate a type of 'netting' system, where a client's complete portfolio is evaluated with some contracts offsetting each other.

The overall margin requirement is then notified to the client. In London the system used is the standard portfolio analysis of risk (SPAN) system. This was originally developed by the Chicago Mercantile Exchange to monitor how risky a client's position becomes.

Example

	Margin account (£)	
Day 1		
Buy 40 DEC FT-SE 100 contracts at 6430		
Initial margin paid @ £3,000 per contract	120,000	
Futures settlement price is 6410		
Trading loss = 20 index points (6430 – 6410) × 40 contracts × £10 per point		
= (£8,000)	112,000	(Original £120,000 balance less the £8,000 daily loss)
Margin call £8,000 from the clearing house	120,000	Balance back-up to £120,000 the minimum required to support 40 contracts
Day 2		
Futures settlement price is 6470		
Trading profit = 60 index points (6470 – 6410) × 40 contracts × £10 per point		
= £24,000	144,000	Profit of £24,000 added to the balance on the margin account
		This profit can be withdrawn, as long as the balance does not fall below that required to support 40 contracts

Margin account (£)
b/f
144,000

Day 3

Futures rally further to 6510

Trading profit = 40 index points (6510 – 6470)
× 40 contracts x £10 per point

= £16,000	160,000	Profit of £16,000 added to margin account
Sell 40 contracts at 6510 to close out	160,000	Balance returned to client on close out

In the last example, the trade was profitable. It is possible to ascertain the final profit/loss on a futures position only at close out, when all the variation margin payments can be added together to give an overall figure. On days where the position makes a profit, the balance on the margin account will be credited with the profit. Technically, the extra monies on the margin account can be debited by the trader as long as the balance on the margin account equates to £3,000 per contract of open position. If not, the clearing house will call for extra margin to support the open position: this is known as a 'margin call'. If the extra margin monies are not forthcoming, the exchange will close out the extra futures contracts that are unsupported by margin.

Hedging with FT-SE 100 Index futures

Example

23 June

A pension fund manager has made some respectable gains over the spring and summer months on his £20 million portfolio of shares. His portfolio matches the FT-SE 100 Index almost exactly although he only has 40 shares in it. His target for the year is to increase the value of the portfolio by 20 per cent, and so far he has managed 12 per cent with careful stock selection and a general increase in the value of the stock market. Now, market intelligence suggests that the index may be in for a sharp reversal, and he wishes to hold on to his 12 per cent gain so far. He is considering using index futures to protect his profit, and immunize him from further moves in the market up until the end of September.

His market information comes from yesterday's copy of the *Financial Times*. The current level of the FTSE is 6300 and the Sep and Dec futures

Table 6.3

Extract from the *Financial Times* showing index futures levels

	Open	Sett price	Change	High	Low	Est. vol	Open int.
■ **FT-SE 100 INDEX FUTURES** (LIFFE) £10 per full index point							
Sep	6235.0	6343.0	+141.0	6373.0	6231.5	25762	177471
Dec	6325.0	6402.0	+141.0	6404.0	6325.0	522	8093
Mar		6452.0	+141.0			0	1976
■ **FT-SE MID 250 INDEX FUTURES** (LIFFE) £10 per full index point							
Sep		6033.0	+1.0			0	6047
Dec		6073.5	+3.5			0	0

Source: LIFFE

closed the previous day at 6343 and 6402 respectively (see Table 6.3). He carries out a desk exercise on the deal, assuming a possible 100-point movement in either direction.

23 June – Action

Pension fund manager sells SEP FT-SE 100 futures at 6343, according to the following formula:

$$\frac{\text{Total value of portfolio}}{\text{FT-SE 100 current index level} \times \text{index multiplier}}$$

substituting the numbers:

$$\frac{£20,000,000}{6300 \times £10} = 317.46 \text{ futures contracts (round to 317)}$$

The position will require initial margin of £951,000 as collateral. The fund manager expects to hold the position for three months, so should consider the opportunity loss on the interest of his margin money: for example, could he get a better rate of interest on his deposit elsewhere?
   Almost certainly.

I. Assuming a 100-point fall in the index

From the current cash level of 6300, giving an EDSP of 6200.

Action – 23 June

Sell 317 SEP futures at 6343

Action – 20 September

Buy 317 SEP futures at EDSP of 6200

Profit = 143 index points (6343 – 6200) × 317 contracts × £10 per point
       = £453,310, plus the return of the initial margin.

Normally the profit/loss on the position is paid daily. For clarity, these figures assume that the monies are paid in one block on contract delivery.

But is this enough profit on the futures transaction to offset the fall in the value of the physical stocks?

A 100-point move down to 6200 represents a move of 1.613 per cent on the portfolio, a reduction in value from £20,000,000 to £19,682.532; a fall of £317,468. The futures profit more than offsets the loss. This is because the SEP future is already trading away from the cash level at a premium of 6343. This does not mean that the market believes that the FT-SE is going to rally, but reflects the cost of carry on the position – essentially the cost of funding the position less the dividend income from the shares.

II. Assuming a 100-point rise in the index
From the current cash level of 6300, giving an EDSP of 6400.

Action – 23 June
Sell 317 SEP futures at 6343

Action – 20 September
Buy 317 SEP futures at EDSP of 6400

Normally the profit/loss on the position is paid daily. For clarity, these figures assume that the monies are paid in one block on contract delivery.

Loss = 57 index points (6343 – 6400) × 317 contracts × £10 per point
    = £180,690 plus the initial margin will be returned

The underlying portfolio will increase in value by 100 points or 1.59 per cent, from £20,000,000 to £20,318,000 – a profit of £318,000 – and the futures hedge will lose £180,690. Not such a bad outcome.

Given the overriding concern to protect the 12 per cent increase so far (and his bonus), and given his view that there is a greater probability that the index will fall rather than rise, the pension fund manager decides to hedge using the futures market.

This example illustrates how it is possible to be 'long of the cash market' and 'short of the futures market'. This fund manager cannot sell the stocks in advance of a stock market fall, as then he will have no portfolio to manage. Even if he has the mandate to sell the stocks, he will have to sell them individually, and take into account the transaction costs of selling the physical stock, and selling stock in a falling market is never a good idea. Using futures is especially good where there is expected to be a sharp movement. Why sell the shares today to buy them back two weeks later? In that case, transaction costs will need to be paid twice.

Cash futures relationship

The futures in the example are trading at a premium to the cash market, but are they trading significantly higher or lower than we would expect from ruling market conditions? It is possible to calculate a theoretical or fair futures price (FFP).

Fair futures price = cash index level + net cost of carry
The net cost of carry can be ascertained by:

$$r \times n/365 - (d \times p)$$

where r = funding rate
        n = number of days
        d = expected annual dividend yield on the FT-SE
        p = proportion of the annual dividend paid out during the maturity period of the futures hedge

Using these data, we can infer the following relationship, giving a theoretical value for the futures:

Fair futures price = spot index + cost of funding – dividend income
Assume 3-month LIBOR is 5 per cent and that the futures hedge is going to run from 23 June to 20 September – a total of 89 days. Assume also that the historic yield on the FT-SE 100 is about 3.75 per cent with dividends paid equally throughout the year.

Fair value of the SEP future
Fair futures price = spot index + cost of funding – dividend income
    = 6300 + (6300/365 x 0.05 × 89) – (6300 × 0.0375/4)
    = 6300 + (76.81 – 59.06)
    = 6300 + (17.75)
    = 6317.75

It is normally the case that dividend yields on the FT-SE 100 are below money market rates. In this case you would expect the future to trade at a premium relative to the cash market. If the premium is significant, then arbitrageurs will come in and try to profit from the discrepancy. They will buy the stock and short (sell) the futures, rather like our pension fund manager, but he was already long of the stock to start with. In this case, the current futures price of 6343 is trading at a premium of just over 25 points to the theoretical value, making it expensive to buy, but quite a good proposition if you wished to sell. Calculations are based on a 365-day year for FT-SE 100 transactions and a 360-day year for most other indices.

Stock betas

In the example, the portfolio was similar to that of the FT-SE 100 Index and had a close correlation. But consider a portfolio with many volatile recovery stocks. This will almost certainly react differently to changes in market sentiment from a traditional FT-SE portfolio. It will be more volatile, it may be twice or three times as volatile, needing twice or three times the amount of futures to cover it. In these circumstances the stock betas need to be examined to achieve a realistic hedge. These are similar but not identical to a measure of volatility, and indicate how much riskier a stock is compared to the FT-SE 100.

The FT-SE 100 Index has an overall beta of one, and individual shares have their own betas, which can be found through Bridge, Bloomberg and other information providers. Each portfolio needs to have the betas of the individual shares weighted by the amount of the holding and added up to establish the beta of the portfolio. The futures hedge should then be 'beta weighted' to reflect the different volatility inherent in the non-market portfolios.

A fund manager has a portfolio of four shares, with individual betas as shown in Table 6.4.

Example

Example: fund manager's portfolio

Table 6.4

Company	Beta	Amount of holding
Company A	0.96	£2,000,000
Company B	0.63	£1,500,000
Company C	1.4	£750,000
Company D	1.95	£2,250,000
Total value of portfolio		**£6,500,000**

To calculate the beta of the portfolio:

$$\frac{(0.96 \times 2,000,000) + (0.63 \times 1,500,000) + (1.4 \times 750,000) + (1.95 \times 2,250,000)}{6,500,000}$$

$$= \frac{(1,920,000 + 945,000 + 1,050,000 + 4,387,500)}{6,500,000}$$

$$= 1.27731 \text{ (round to 1.28)}$$

A beta of 1.28 suggests the portfolio is 1.28 times more volatile than the FT-SE 100 Index. To calculate the number of futures required to hedge the position accurately, we need to amend the original formula.

Original formula:

$$\frac{\text{Total value of portfolio}}{\text{FT-SE 100 Index level} \times \text{index multiplier}}$$

Amended formula:

$$\frac{\text{Total value of portfolio} \times \text{portfolio beta}}{\text{FT-SE 100 Index level} \times \text{index multiplier}}$$

(A) Assuming the FT-SE Index still stands at 6300, and using the figures above, if we do not *beta weight* the hedge, then the number of futures contracts we need are:

Original formula:

$$\frac{\text{Total value of portfolio}}{\text{FT-SE 100 Index level} \times \text{index multiplier}}$$

$$= \frac{6,500,000}{6300 \times 10}$$

$$= 103.17 \text{ futures contracts (round to 103)}$$

(B) If we do weight the futures hedge we shall need:

Amended formula:

$$\frac{\text{Total value of portfolio} \times \text{portfolio beta}}{\text{FT-SE 100 Index level} \times \text{index multiplier}}$$

$$= \frac{6,500,000 \times 1.28}{6300 \times 10}$$

$$= 132.06 \text{ futures contracts (round to 132)}$$

Nearly 30 more futures contracts are required to 'weight the hedge'. This will incur extra initial and variation margin costs, but will offer a tighter hedge. The extra contracts are not taken out for speculative purposes but rather to reflect the increased volatility in the underlying portfolio.

Trading with S&P 500 futures

Example

10 January

A US fund manager is holding a portfolio matching almost exactly the makeup of the S&P 500. He wishes to execute an additional trade to enhance the performance of his portfolio. The present level of the index is, say, 1386, and the index multiplier is US$250 per full index point. The Chicago Mercantile Exchange web page gives historical and live data and shows that the March future closed yesterday at 1460.50 (see Table 6.5).

CME S & P 500
settlement prices

Table 6.5

01/07/00 07:00 PM										
MTH/		---- DAILY ----				PT	EST	---- PRIOR		DAY
STRIKE	OPEN	HIGH	LOW	LAST	SETT	CHGE	VOL	SETT	VOL	I
MAR00	1403.00	1461.00	1397.50	1460.90	1460.50	+5650	100K	1404.00	97293	35
JUN00	1442.50	1480.00B	1442.50	1480.00B	1479.30	+5720	343	1422.10	278	
SEP00	1466.30	1497.30B	1465.30A	1497.30B	1498.90	+5760	370	1441.30	111	
DEC00	1512.00	1517.60B	1512.00	1517.60B	1519.40	+5780	12	1461.60	112	
MAR01	1518.20	1540.60B	1513.60A	1540.60B	1542.40	+5780	2	1484.60	2	
JUN01	1552.00	1563.60B	1552.00	1563.60B	1565.40	+5780	2	1507.60		
SEP01	----	1586.60B	----	1586.60B	1588.40	+5780		1530.60		
DEC01	-----	1609.60B	----	1609.60B	1611.40	+5780		1553.60		
TOTAL							EST.VOL		VOL OPEN INT	
TOTAL							101291		97796	36

Source: Chicago Mercantile Exchange web page

The fund manager believes that the index could rise as far as 1600 over the next few months, and he wishes for additional profit over and above his existing holding, which will also increase in value if he is right. He wishes to put on a trade in a notional amount of US$5 million. Assume that the initial and variation margins are paid and maintained as specified by the regulations on the exchange.

Action – 20 January

The fund manager needs to calculate how many futures to trade, by using the following formula:

$$\frac{\text{Total value of portfolio}}{\text{S\&P 500 Index level} \times \text{index multiplier}}$$

$$= \frac{5{,}000{,}000}{1386 \times \text{US\$250}}$$

$$= 14.43 \text{ futures contracts (round to 15)}$$

If the fund manager thinks the index will rally, he must buy the futures contracts and sell them later, when they are hopefully trading at a higher level. He will need to buy 15 March S&P 500 futures contracts: these are currently trading at 1403.

Action – 20 February

The fund manager has experienced a short-term rally with his position, but it looks like the index may now retrace, and the chances of further gains are limited. He decided to close out his position by selling the futures back at the current level of 1478.1.

How much profit has the fund manager made?

Opening level	1403 (buy)
Closing level	1478.1 (sell)
Total profit	**75.1 index points**

In cash terms a profit of 75.1 index points × 15 contracts × US$250 per point value = US$281,625.

This profit excludes costs due to funding the initial margin, brokerage, clearing and other transaction costs.

Availability

Index futures contracts are available world-wide, in many countries and in many currencies covering various domestic indices (different baskets of shares). Each exchange will offer a slightly different range of futures contracts. Should a client wish for an index future based, not on the FT-SE 100 or the S&P 500, but on the client's own specific combination of shares, it is possible to construct the customer's own index or basket of shares that will track his portfolio exactly. This would need to be effected in the OTC market.

Practical considerations

Any potential user of equity futures will need to set up documentation which is market specific and based on the particular exchange where he wishes to trade. For further details on general futures documentation, see Chapter 3 on *financial futures contracts*.

Initial and variation margins must be posted as required, and initial margins can get very expensive. Eventually the initial margin will be returned to the client plus interest, but the interest on the margin deposit is inferior to that obtained elsewhere in the money markets. In some cases it is possible to put up the collateral required in another form, such as shares that are already held or gilts/bonds.

Administration of a futures hedge needs competent people to manage the various daily transfers between accounts. Bank charges may also be significant on each transfer, and combined with the brokerage required for the trade to be executed in the pit, as well as clearing fees, may all erode possible profits.

When the FT-SE 100 Index does not mirror accurately the makeup of the particular portfolio, 'tracking error' will exist. This can be positive or negative, with the basket of shares either outperforming or underperforming the FT-SE 100 Index. Ideally all futures (and options) hedges should be beta weighted to reflect the variety within different types of portfolios.

STOCK INDEX OPTIONS

Introduction

Both stock index futures and options started to trade in the 1980s. In May 1984 both contracts commenced at LIFFE. The index options that we discuss in this chapter are exchange traded and based on an underlying stock index. In the UK the index is the FT-SE 100 basket of shares, in the US the most widely used index option is based on the S&P 500.

Readers who are unfamiliar with basic option concepts may find it useful to refer to the section on *basic options* in Chapter 3 for background information. As previously discussed, an option contract is the only derivative instrument that allows the buyer (holder) to 'walk away' from his obligations. One of the key principles behind stock index futures and options is cash settlement. This is the process used at expiry (or exercise), whereby a cash difference reflecting a price change passes hands, rather than a physical delivery of the underlying basket of shares. As with all option contracts, if the holder of the index option is a hedger with an underlying exposure to the market, he can be considered to have bought insurance against adverse market movements – without the obligation to deal. In contrast, a trader using options to speculate on an index move will have no underlying market exposure. For example, the holder of a call option will be hoping the market will rally so that he can exercise the option and make a profit. This is an important point; hedgers who have bought options can (but not always do) make a profit if they have not needed the option as insurance. As then the stock index must have moved to favour their underlying position. With a trader who has no underlying position, the option itself needs to become more valuable for him to make a profit.

Unfortunately, options do not come free of charge. A premium is due, usually paid upfront. The option allows a degree of flexibility, it does not completely take away all the risk, i.e., all the losses and *all the profit*. Instead it allows a degree of risk management which allows for risk control, not risk removal. Options exhibit 'asymmetry of risk'. The most that an option holder can lose is the original premium that he paid, whereas the amount he can profit is unlimited, being governed only by how far the market has moved in his favour. A seller of options, in contrast, can hope to keep only the premium, but the extent of his losses are potentially unlimited. Simplistically, buyers of options have rights, but no obligations, and writers of options have obligations, but no rights.

| Definition | *A* **stock index option** *gives the holder the right, but not the obligation, to buy or sell an agreed amount of an equity index at a specified price, on or before a specified date. A premium is due. The option will be cash settled, unless physical delivery is elected at expiry.* |

Definition discussed

An index option gives the client, who may be a portfolio manager or equity hedger, the chance to secure the level of the stock market in advance. The holder of the option chooses his own level for the index (the strike), from those specified by the exchange. As this transaction provides a level of insurance that is optional, a premium is required which must be paid upfront, to the seller on the business day following the trade. The premium is quoted in 'index points' per contract. With exchange-traded options the premium itself is margined.

Table 6.6 gives the contract specification for the FT-SE 100 Index option (American-style exercise).

FT-SE 100 Index option (American-style exercise) – contract specification
Table 6.6

Unit of trading	Valued at £10 per index point (e.g. £65,000 at 6500)
Expiry months	June and December plus such additional months that the nearest four months are available for trading
Exercise day	Exercise by 16.45 on any business day, extending to 18.00 for expiring series on the last trading day
Settlement	Settlement is the first business day after the expiry day
Last trading day	10.30 third Friday of the expiry month
Quotation	Index points
Minimum price movement	0.5
Tick value	£5.00 (per half-point)
Trading hours	08.00 – 16.30 (London time)

Source: LIFFE

Most open option positions will be closed out or exercised prior to expiry. Remaining open positions are automatically closed out at the exchange delivery settlement price (EDSP).

Example

The holder of 25 FT-SE 100 call options at a strike of 5950, wishes to hold his position until expiry. The calls were originally bought at a premium of 35 points, making a total cost of £8,750 (£10 × 25 × 35). The EDSP is calculated at 6024, when the holder will receive a profit of 74 points (6024 – 5950), on each of the 25 contracts at £10 per full point, a total of £18,500. This must be offset against the premium paid, resulting in an overall profit on the deal of £9,750.

Premiums on exchange traded options are 'margined', and are dealt with in a different manner to OTC option premiums.

The FT-SE 100 Index option can be American or European style and each contract has its own code. The American-style option which can be exercised on any business day has the code SEI, while the newer European option that can only be exercised on the expiry date has the code ESX.

Margined premium

(courtesy of LIFFE)

Day 1

A fund manager sells two FT-SE 100 Index call options at a premium of 144 index points, a total premium due to him of £2,880 (£10 × 144 × 2). At close of business the option premium is at 142 points.

Day 2

The fund manager will receive £2,880 from the original option sale into his LCH account. The clearing house will calculate the profits/losses on the day with the SPAN system. Under SPAN scenario 13, the maximum loss on the position is calculated at £270 per contract, a total of £540. The value of the position at close is worth £2,840 (2 × 142 × £10). This amount is known as the net liquidation value or NLV. The total margin liability is, therefore, £2,840 + £540, a sum of £3,380. The margin liability is offset against the premium received leaving a total of £500 to be paid to the clearing house. At close of business the option premium has risen to 148 index points.

Day 3

The fund manager is still short two FT-SE option contracts. The total margin liability due today (for yesterday's movements) will again be calculated by SPAN plus the NLV. SPAN calculates the maximum loss to be £285 per contract, and the NLV is £2,960 (2 × 148 × £10). Total margin liability at close of Day 2 and payable on Day 3 is £3,530 (£2,960 + (2 × £285)). But £500 was paid on Day 2 and LCH is still holding the premium payment of £2,880. The amount due is £3,530 – £500 – £2,880: a balance of £150.

The fund manager closes his position at a level of 142 index points.

Day 4

There will will be no margin liability, as LCH will pay the client £690: £2,880 premium less the £2,840 which is owed for purchasing the two contracts (2 × 142 × £10), plus the £650 the fund manager has lodged with the LCH (£150 + £500). A net profit of £40 (see Table 6.7).

Stock index options

Insurance protection

The client pays a premium to insure against adverse movements on the index. The clearing house agrees to guarantee the agreed rate if/when required by the client.

Profit potential

The risk of adverse stock market movements is eliminated, while at the same time, the buyer retains the potential to benefit from favourable movements. The option can be abandoned or exercised, or sold back into the market, dependent upon market movements.

Sell back

Open positions can be netted off via the clearing house.

Exercise

As the counterparty to each deal is the clearing house, if a client wishes to exercise the option, he is assigned a counterparty at random.

Cash settlement

Different index options are settled against different underlying prices. For example, options on the Chicago Board Options Exchange (CBOE) are settled against the corresponding index. Options on the Chicago Mercantile Exchange (CME) are settled against the S&P 500 future. Cash settlement allows participants to take profits from favourable movements without having to deal physically in the underlying stocks. Other types of settlement would be unsatisfactory in terms of :

- inconvenience
- time
- expense
- reduced contract efficiency
- potential market distortion.

Regulators in the US stipulate cash settlement as an essential criterion for an exchange-traded stock index contract.

Options traded in London may be settled physically if this is elected at expiry.

Table 6.7

Summary of margin flow on FT-SE 100 Index options

Action in the market

Day	Action	Position at close
1	open position	short 2 contracts at 142
2		short 2 contracts at 148
3	close position	long 2 contracts at 142 Net flat

Margin flow

Day	Premium due from LCH	SPAN	NLV	Total margin liability	Cash flow
2	£2,880 2×144×£10	£540 2×£270	£2,840 2×142×£10	£3,380 £540+£2,840	–£500 £3,380–£2,880
3		£570 2×£285	£2,960 2×148×£10	£3,530 £570+£2,960	–£150 £3,530–£3,380
4	£2,840 premium due to LCH				+£690 £3,530–£2,840
					+£40 £690–£650

Net profit of 2 index points on two contracts

Source: LIFFE

Premium determinants

The amount of premium payable by the purchaser of an index option is determined by the following factors:

- underlying price
- strike price
- maturity
- put or call
- dividends
- cost of carry of the position
- expected market volatility.

(a) Strike price

Different stock index options are marked against different underlying prices (see *cash settlement* earlier in this chapter). Strike prices are referred to as follows:

		Terminology
At the money (ATM)	Where the strike price is equal to the underlying price.	
In the money (ITM)	Where the strike rate is more favourable than the underlying price, and the option premium will be higher than that for an ATM option.	
Out of the money (OTM)	Where the strike rate is worse than the underlying price and the option premium will be lower than for an ATM option.	

(b) Maturity

The longer the time to expiry or maturity, the higher the probability of large index movements, and the higher the chance of profitable exercise by the buyer. The buyer should be prepared to pay a higher premium for a longer dated option than a short-dated option, although premium is not proportional to maturity.

(c) Put or call

This will affect whether the strike is in or out of the money, and also the final market price due to supply and demand swings.

(d) Dividends

The effect of dividends on option pricing can be difficult to factor in. Are they assumed to be continuous or non-continuous? The 1970s Black–Scholes option-pricing model assumes that dividends are spread evenly throughout the year, so many traders use a different binomial model that allows dividends to be explicitly built in.

(e) Cost of carry of the position

As this option is based on the underlying index future, the cost of carrying the position is a relevant factor. As shown in the previous chapter, a fair value can be calculated for the futures price. This is a function of the cost of borrowing the money to pay for the stocks that make up the index, for the exposure period.

(f) Expected market volatility

The higher the volatility the greater the possibility of profitable exercise by the customer. The option is more valuable to the client and the premium is higher.

Various market factors may lead to an increase in the option premium, these include events such as, corporate failures, new taxes, political stability, exchange controls, or general illiquidity in the market.

Terminology	Index options
Strike price	Specified index level rate where the client can exercise his right to cash settlement.
Call option	The right to buy the specified index.
Put option	The right to sell the specified index.
Exercise	The take up of the option at or before expiry.
Expiry date	The last date when the option may be exercised.
Value date	The date of payment (settlement) as determined by the exchange EDSP.
Premium	The price of the option, as determined by an option pricing model or the market.
Intrinsic value	Strike price minus the current market rate.
Time value	Option premium minus intrinsic value, reflecting the time until expiry, changes in volatility, and market expectations.

Hedging with a stock index option

10 September

It is the beginning of autumn, and an American fund manager is concerned about a possible fall in world stock markets. She has a number of portfolios, but the one that is causing her most concern moves fairly closely in line with the S&P 500 Index. If she were certain of the downward fall, she could use futures which would cost nothing in terms of an upfront cost, but could actually lose her money if her view of the market were wrong. However, there are certain factors in the market which lead her to believe that there may be major takeovers that could push index levels upwards. She decides to hedge her position using index options, and called up the CME page on the internet to get an idea of where prices were trading (see Table 6.8).

CME S & P 500 options settlement prices

Table 6.8

09/07/99 07:00 PM							
MPH/		----DAILY----				PT	EST
STRIKE	OPEN	HIGH	LOW	LAST	SETT	CHGE	VOL
OS OCT99 S & P 500 OPTIONS PUT							
1270	---	----	----	----	11.40	+140	
1275	11.00	12.00	11.00	12.00	12.00	+150	11
1280	11.50	11.70	11.50	11.70	12.70	+160	61
1290	----	13.50B	----	13.50B	14.20	+180	
1295	----	----	----	----	15.00	+190	
1300	14.50	16.50	14.50	16.50	15.90	+200	48
1305	----	----	----	----	16.80	+210	
1310	18.50	18.50	18.50	18.50	17.80	+220	5
1320	19.50	21.00	19.50	21.00	20.10	+250	12
1325	20.00	20.00	20.00	20.00	21.30	+270	5
1330	----	----	----	----	22.60	+290	
1335	----	----	----	----	24.00	+310	
1340	23.50	24.50	23.50	24.50	25.40	+330	12
1345	----	----	----	----	26.90	+350	
1350	26.70	27.50	25.50	25.50	28.50	+380	108
1355	----	----	----	----	30.20	+390	
1360	----	----	----	----	32.10	+410	
1365	----	----	----	----	34.10	+430	2
1370	36.00	36.00	36.00	36.00	36.20	+450	5
1375	----	35.00B	----	35.00B	38.40	+470	5

Source: Chicago Mercantile Exchange web page

The cash level of the S&P 500 Index is 1350, and the value of the portfolio is US$7.5 million.

Action – 10 September

First, she would need to calculate the number of options contracts for the hedge. Using the same formula for futures, as each option is based on a single index future, and, assuming a 1:1 correlation with the index (beta =1), she calculates the need for 27 option contracts.

Amended formula

$$\frac{\text{Total value of portfolio} \times \text{portfolio beta}}{\text{S\&P 500 Index level} \times \text{index multiplier}}$$

$$\frac{\$7,500,000 \times 1}{1350 \times \$250} = 22.2 \text{ contracts (round to 22)}$$

She needs to buy a put option. If she used the October put option at a strike of 1350, this would mean a cost of 25.50 index points in premium, making a total premium cost of US$140,250 (22 contracts × 25.5 index points × $250). This option is at the money and has the largest volumes traded. She decides to draw an expiry profile for the option strategy, and includes on the diagram the underlying portfolio where she was long of the stocks (see Figure 6.2).

From this she could see that her total exposure would be to the premium which would be lost if the option was not exercised, giving a possible down-

Fig 6.2

Profit and loss profile on the option strategy, all figures quoted in S&P Index points

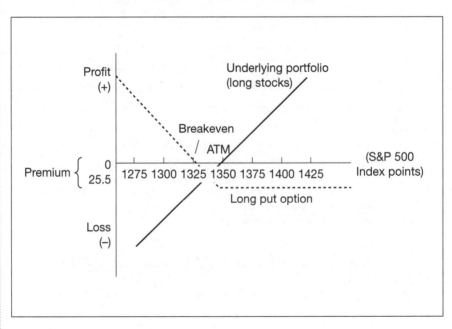

side on the option of US$140,250, but if that was the case, then the value of the underlying portfolio would have increased. By exactly how much would be unknown until the option expiry date. Alternatively, if she were right and the stock market did fall, then the loss in value of the portfolio would be offset by the increase in value of the option. In this case the breakeven level will be 1350 – 25.5 points = 1324.5. For this strategy to be worthwhile, she would need to assume a market move of at least of 25.5 index points. Given that she thought the index might swing by +/– 50 points, this was perfectly acceptable. She called her broker and transacted the hedge.

Availability

Each of the major exchanges world-wide has an index futures contract, and most have an option on the index. For precise details on all the options contracts, it would be necessary to contact the exchange or a broker for exact specifications.

Practical considerations

Any potential user of exchange-traded equity options will need to set up documentation which is market specific and based on the particular exchange where he wishes to trade. For further details on general documentation, see Chapter 3 on *financial futures contracts*.

A buyer of options has only one responsibility and that is to pay the premium. Buying options through an exchange can be expensive. Although the premium costs will be very competitive and the bid–offer spread tight, the cost of execution and the corresponding brokerage on the deal cannot be ignored.

With exchange-traded options the premium is margined. This is not so straightforward as the OTC market where a writer or seller of options receives single payment upfront, and may result in further minor receipts/payments as the underlying price moves.

Administration of the options hedge needs competent people to manage the various daily transfers between accounts. Bank charges may also be significant on each transfer, and combined with any brokerage required for the trade to be executed in the pit, as well as clearing fees may all erode possible profits.

Using options on the FT-SE 100 for short-term portfolio management should always be more cost effective than transacting in the underlying physical 100 stocks, as dealing costs and stamp duty may be significant.

When calculating how many option contracts to use on an index portfolio, it is always advisable to 'beta weight' the hedge, in just the same way as when calculating how many futures to use. This will assist in making the hedge more effective, and allow for the fact that most portfolios do not track an index exactly. When the FT-SE 100 Index option does not mirror accurately the makeup of the particular portfolio, 'tracking error' will exist. This can be positive or negative, with the basket of shares either outperforming or underperforming the FT-SE 100 Index.

Should a client need to hedge a different basket of shares to that of, say, the FT-SE, there are over the counter banks who specialize in designing customer-tailored baskets of shares, and then constructing OTC futures and OTC options to cover them.

SINGLE STOCK OPTIONS

Introduction

Exchange-traded options on specific equities add an extra dimension to equity risk management. These single stock options complement existing trading and hedging using futures and options on stock indices. Each stock exchange or futures exchange will have options on their own specific equities. From 1999, all equity option trading in the UK has been through electronic platforms at LIFFE (LIFFE CONNECT™) and the Stock Exchange (SETS) Table 6.9 lists the individual options currently available.

Table 6.9

LIFFE equity options

Company	LIFFE code	Expiry cycle	Company	LIFFE code	Expiry cycle
Abbey National plc	ANL	J	Imperial Tobacco Group plc	IMP	F
Alliance & Leicester plc	LEI	F	Invensys plc	BRT	F
Allied Domecq plc (package)	ALD	J	Kingfisher plc	KGF	F
			Land Securities plc	LS	J
Allied Domecq plc	ADQ	J	LASMO plc	LMO	F
Allied Zurich plc	AZ	J	Legal & General Group plc	LGE	F
Anglo American plc	AAM	F	Lloyds TSB Group plc	TSB	M
ASDA Group plc	ASD	J	Lonmin plc	LNR	M
AstraZeneca plc	ZCA	J	Marconi plc	MNI	F
BAA plc	APT	J	Marks & Spencer plc	M+S	J
Bank of Scotland (Governor & Co. of)	BSC	M	National Grid Group plc	NGG	J
			National Power plc	NPW	J
Barclays plc	BBL	J	National Westminster Bank plc	NWT	J

Continued

Table 6.9

Bass plc	BSS	J	Norwich Union plc	NU	M
BG plc	BG	M	Orange plc	ORA	M
Blue Circle Industries plc	CIR	F	Peninsular & Oriental Steam Navigation Co	P+O	F
Boots Co plc	BOT	J			
BP Amoco plc	BP	J	Prudential plc	PRU	F
British Aerospace plc	AER	F	Railtrack Group plc	TRK	M
British Airways plc	AWS	J	Reed International plc	REI	J
British American Tobacco plc	TAB	J	Rentokil Initial plc	RTO	F
British Biotech plc	BIO	M	Reuters Group plc	RUT	J
British Sky Broadcasting Group plc	BSK	M	Rio Tinto plc	RTZ	F
			Rolls-Royce plc	RR	F
British Telecommunications plc	BT	F	Royal & Sun Alliance Insurance Group plc	RYL	J
Cable & Wireless plc	C+W	J	Royal Bank of Scotland Group plc	RBS	J
Cadbury Schweppes plc	CAD	F			
Carlton Communication plc	CCM	F	Safeway plc	AYL	J
Centrica plc	CTR	M	Sainsbury (J) plc	SAN	J
CGU plc	CUA	J	Scottish Power plc	SPW	M
Corus Group plc	STL	J	Securicor plc	SCR	J
Diageo plc	GNS	F	Shell Transport & Trading Co plc	SHL	J
Dixons Group plc	DIX	M			
EMI Group plc	EMI	M	SmithKline Beecham plc	BHM	J
Freeserve plc	FRE	M	Standard Chartered plc	SCB	J
Gallaher Group plc	GAL	F	Tarmac plc (package)	TAR	M
General Electric Co plc	GEC	F	Telewest Communications plc	TWT	M
Glaxo Wellcome plc	GXO	J	Tesco plc	TCO	F
Granada Group plc	GDA	M	Thames Water plc	TW	J
Great Universal Stores	GUS	M	Tomkins plc	TMK	M
Halifax plc	HAX	J	Unilever plc	ULV	M
Hanson plc	HSN	F	United Biscuits (Holdings) plc	UBI	F
Hilton Group plc	LDB	F	Vodafone AirTouch plc	VOD	J
HSBC Holdings plc	HSB	J	Whitbread plc	WTB	M
Imperial Chemical Industries plc	ICI	J	Woolwich plc	WWH	J

The expiry months available for trading will normally be the nearest three expiry months. A new expiry month is available for trading the business day after the last trading day of an expiry month.

Source: LIFFE

In London, the standard contract size is 1,000 shares, and these options must be physically settled, through the Stock Exchange settlement system known as CREST. As with all exchange-traded products, a contract specification is used to ensure that all parties are aware of their commitments.

Table 6.10 gives the contract specification for equity options.

Table 6.10

Equity options – contract specification

Unit of trading	One option normally equals rights over 1,000 shares
Expiry months	**January cycle (J):** means the three nearest expiry months from Jan, Apr, Jul, Oct cycle **February cycle (F):** means the three nearest expiry months from Feb, May, Aug, Nov cycle **March cycle (M):** means the three nearest expiry months from Mar, Jun, Sep, Dec cycle
Exercise/ settlement day	Exercise by 17.20 on any business day, extending to 18.00 for all series on the last trading day. Settlement is six business days following the day of exercise/last trading day
Last trading day month	16.30 (London time) third Wednesday of the expiry
Quotation	pence per share
Minimum price movement (tick)	0.5 pence per share
Tick value	£10.00 per full point
Trading hours	08.00 – 16.30 (London time) LIFFE CONNECT

Source: LIFFE

A call option on Company XXX shares would give the holder the right to purchase 1,000 shares in that company. A seller of that option, on exercise, would be required to deliver 1,000 shares of XXX.

> A **single stock option** *gives the holder the right, but not the obligation, to buy or sell an agreed amount of a specific equity at a specified price, on or before a specified date. A premium is due. The option will be physically settled.*

Definition discussed

A single stock option gives the client, who may be a portfolio manager or equity hedger, the chance to guaranteee the exact level of a particular share price. The holder of the option chooses his own guaranteed price (the strike), from those available on the exchange, and a premium is due. This must be paid upfront, by the buyer, and credited to the option seller by 10.00 a.m. on the business day following the trade. The premium is quoted in pence per share, based on a 'parcel' of 1,000 shares. With exchange-traded options the premium itself is margined (earlier in this chapter for *stock index options*). The maximum duration of a traded option is nine months, and the expiry dates are arranged quarterly. These options are American style, and can be exercised on any business day, up to and including the expiry date. On exercise of an equity option, the exchange will randomly assign sellers to buyers, each of whom will receive an assignment notification. Writers are required to settle the underlying share transaction by the settlement date of the current account, as with any other share transaction.

Single stock options

Key features

Insurance protection
The client pays a premium to limit his risk to adverse movements on the particular stock. The writer and then, ultimately, the clearing house agrees to guarantee the agreed rate if/when required by the client. The premium is the maximum cost of this transaction to the client. If the market moves adversely, the option will be exercised.

Profit potential
The risk of adverse stock market movements is eliminated while, at the same time, the buyer retains the potential to benefit from favourable movements. Call options can be bought to profit from rising share prices and put options to profit from declining prices. Both calls and puts can be sold for a more aggressive strategy.

Key features ### Sell-back

Open positions can be netted off via the clearing house.

Exercise

As the counterparty to each deal is the clearing house, if a client wishes to exercise the option, he is assigned a counterparty at random.

Physical settlement

The option is physically settled, with each contract supporting 1,000 shares, or such other number as determined by the terms of the contract.

Flexibility

Changes in portfolios can happen very quickly. It may be more prudent to cover specific shares in particular circumstances rather than use the index derivative. It may be more judicious to buy put options on a share for a short period, than for a fund manager to sell the stock today, and then buy it back a week later.

Leverage (gearing)

Because of the low option premium needed to establish a market position in the underlying security, any given change in the share price can produce a much larger percentage change in the value of the option, than in the value of the shares.

Premium determinants

The amount of premium payable by the purchaser of an equity option is determined by the same factors as influence the stock index:

- underlying share price
- strike price
- maturity
- put or call
- dividends
- cost of carry of the position
- expected market volatility.

The only factor which needs highlighting concerns the payment of dividends. The holder of a stock option is not entitled to receive any payment of dividend declared on the underlying security unless the option is exercised before the stock was made ex-dividend.

Enhancing portfolio income using single stock options

It is January, the beginning of the year, and a UK fund manager wishes to start the year on a profitable note. Unfortunately, the stock market seems to be going nowhere and immediate gains look a little fanciful. The portfolio has within it a number of shares on which LIFFE-traded options can be transacted, and which are available in market amounts. The fund manager decides to use his holding of approximately £3.12 million of Cable & Wireless plc, equivalent to about 455,000 shares. He believes that the share price will not fluctuate much and decides to sell 'covered calls'. The option is covered as the fund manager already holds the underlying stock.

The current Cable & Wireless share price is £6.85, and the March call option with a strike of £7.00 is trading at 50 pence per share. The fund manager decides to sell 400 contracts, receiving in a premium of £200,000 (400 contracts × 50 pence per share × 1000 shares per contract). He draws himself a sketch to clarify the position, including the underlying asset holding, where he is long of the stocks (see Figure 6.3). He chooses to sell out of the money options to give himself some protection if there is a small upswing in the share price. Ideally, our fund manager does not want to part with the shares and certainly wants to keep the forthcoming dividend. He does not want these options to be exercised against him, but he does want to enhance his income, and is prepared to take the risk.

Profit and loss profile on the option strategy

Fig 6.3

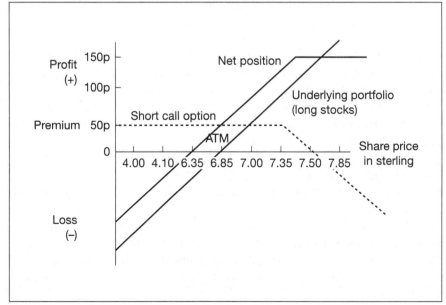

The fund manager draws up a list of potential outcomes:

(a) the market goes nowhere, he keeps the premium and the option is not exercised. Total income £200,000 + dividends.

(b) The share price swings above £7.00 and the option is exercised. He will lose the stocks, but at a much higher price where he is fairly happy. This strategy can be regarded as a 'target sell price'. Total income £200,000 + an increase in the value of the shares from £6.85 to £7.00, a profit of 65p per share (including the option premium), possibly plus dividends if these are received before exercise.

(c) The share price falls to £6.35. The option remains unexercised, and the underlying value of the shares drops by 50p, but this is offset by the premium received under the option. Dividends will also be received.

Availability

Not all exchanges offer single stock options. For precise details on availability it would be necessary to contact the exchange or a broker for exact specifications.

Practical considerations

A buyer of options has only one responsibility and that is to pay the premium. Buying options can be expensive. Although the premium costs will be very competitive and the bid–offer spread tight, the cost of execution and the corresponding brokerage on the deal cannot be ignored. If the manager of a large pension fund transacts hundreds of contracts a month, he will undoubtedly pay less brokerage per ticket than a smaller company.

Selling options on anything can be risky. The previous example of a covered call illustrates how to enhance performance of a portfolio, but in this case the fund manager is already holding the stock. As such he has no hedging to do, unlike a bank, which, if it sold the option 'naked', would need to delta hedge the resulting position.

Using options and indeed futures on the FT-SE 100 for short-term portfolio management should always be more cost effective than transacting in the underlying physical 100 stocks, as dealing costs and stamp duty may be significant.

A client may have the view that the stock market is going to fall, but at the same time believe that a particular share represents good value. On the one hand, he could buy the share and then either sell futures on the FT-SE, or, on the other, buy put options on the index while still purchasing the target share.

EQUITY INDEX SWAPS

Introduction

An equity index swap is similar to an interest rate swap and has evolved from it. Both transactions are obligations where each party swaps a cash flow. With an index swap, at least one of the cash flows is determined by reference to the performance of an equity index (with or without the inclusion of dividend payments). With an interest rate swap the cash flow is determined by reference to an interest rate. It is not necessary for both rates to be tied to the equity index, and it is quite common for one of the rates to be linked to a floating interest payment such as LIBOR. For example a US client may wish to receive the return on the S&P 500 (the US index), and pay away 6-month US dollar LIBOR. Alternatively, he may wish to pay or receive interest in a foreign currency, against the FT-SE 100. An equity index swap may involve only a single currency or may involve a second or cross-currency arrangement.

This market started to grow in the late 1980s. The existing technology was available without the requirement for too much alteration, and the equity market offered substantially higher returns to the major operators than, say, interest rate swaps, where nearly every bank had a swap capability. The market has seen explosive growth. It is possible to estimate that there are more equity deals than commodity deals, but equity deals are themselves far fewer than those for both currency and interest rate derivatives. It is certainly true to say that the market is still in its infancy, especially outside the USA.

The equity swap itself provides a mechanism whereby a client can hedge or take equity exposure at relatively low cost, for either a longer period than that available by using futures, or with lower administration costs. In some cases it is also possible to design transactions to offer tax advantages. Other types of transactions can synthesize exposure to other markets. For example, a 'vanilla' swap on the FT-SE 100 Index against LIBOR is an exact replication of an investor switching out of a sterling deposit account and into the constituent stocks of the FT-SE 100 Index, or vice versa. The underlying equity cash market is not as large or as liquid as, say, the interest rate or currency markets, so the big players in equity swaps will generally be the UK, US and Japanese securities houses that have a trading capability in the various stock indices and their components.

Definition

> An **equity index swap** *is an obligation between two parties to exchange cash flows based on the percentage change in one or more stock indices, for a specific period with previously agreed reset dates. The swap is cash settled and based on notional principal amounts. One side of an equity swap can involve a LIBOR reference rate.*

Definition discussed

The two parties to an equity swap are likely to be a bank and an investor who may be a fund manager or an insurance company. There is a substantive difference between equity swaps and interest rate swaps. Consider a swap transaction where the bank has agreed to pay the fund manager the percentage increase in the S&P 500 Index, based on an a notional amount of US$10 million. What happens if the S&P 500 falls over the period? Then the fund manager must pay the bank on the equity index leg (as the market has moved in the opposite direction), and, if the other side of the swap involved a LIBOR payment, the fund manager would also have to pay that. So instead of cash flows going in opposite directions, they both flow from the fund manager to the bank. Or a swap may have involved, a client receiving the percentage change in the FT-SE 100, against paying 3-month LIBOR minus 20 basis points. If the index level decreased the client would pay the negative percentage change in the FT-SE 100, and pay LIBOR less the 20-basis points. The 20 basis points spread is attached as an 'offset' to the LIBOR level and reduces funding costs, but realistically if the index fell 5 per cent, the 20bp is largely irrelevant and can help immunize the client from falls in the index. The swap is cash settled and payments are netted, as in interest rate swaps. Where one leg of the swap is linked to LIBOR, it is market practice to use 3-month LIBOR.

Example

A portfolio manager holds a selection of equities that trades very closely in correlation with the FT-SE 100 Index. He believes that the short-term returns from this portfolio are likely to disappoint him as he expects the stock market to decline. He is unwilling to sell the cash portfolio and buy the shares back later, due to the significant dealing costs he will incur. He does feel that UK interest rates will rise, and he decides to enter into an equity swap for one year where he pays the percentage change in the FT-SE 100 and receives 3-month LIBOR (see Figure 6.4).

Equity swap cash flows

Fig 6.4

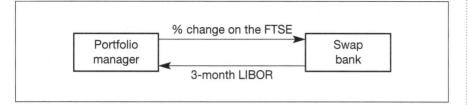

Equity index swaps

Cost effective

Through an equity swap, a client can invest directly in a stock market portfolio, and replicate cash investments without having to purchase/sell the underlying shares in the correct quantities. An equity swap avoids any requirement to pay stamp duty and other associated taxes and also negates the need for safe custody of certificates, etc.

Net cash settlement

It is only the cash flow payments that are swapped. The principal sum is not exchanged but is used as a reference point.

Index tracking

An equity swap has a 100 per cent correlation to the underlying index on which it is based. This is a great advantage for index-tracking fund managers. Through the swap they can maintain capital exposure and receive dividend income, but avoid the pitfalls of trying to achieve this through holding a basket of stocks. The more complex the underlying index, the harder it will be to track it, and therefore the greater the benefit of using the index swap.

Efficient portfolio management

An equity swap allows the portfolio manager to stabilize a portfolio without the need to change the makeup of the portfolio, to allow for changes in share prices or market capitalizations. The purchaser of an equity index swap transfers the responsibility of managing an index portfolio over to the issuer of the swap. For a passive fund that is seeking only to replicate or track the performance of a particular index, an equity swap is ideal since the objective is achieved without any of the administrative burden.

Income enhancement

An equity swap allows the fund manager to receive LIBOR if he believes that it will offer him a better return than the index portfolio he is holding, without the need to sell the stocks and invest in the money market. Alternatively, consider a two-year swap on the German DAX index, priced at LIBOR – 75 basis points. This is quoted with no dividend flow, as with the DAX the dividends are assumed to be re-invested. A buyer of this swap would receive the performance of the DAX over a two-year period while passing through interest income on the principal amount at 75 basis points less than money market rates.

Exposure to a foreign index

Allows the fund manager to exchange the return on the FT-SE 100 Index portfolio that he is physically holding, for, say, the return on the S&P 500, or any other foreign index, without the requirement to sell the stocks, and without worrying about local taxes and politics. He may choose to hedge the associated foreign currency risk or not.

Credit risk

The credit risk on an equity index swap is similar in some ways to that of an interest rate swap, in that principal amounts are not exchanged, and in some cases one of the 'legs' of the swap can be an interest rate. The other leg however can sometimes behave in such a way as to cause problems. The risk is significantly greater because:

- Swings in equity indices can be much larger than moves in interest rates.
- Equity index movements can be negative.

Collateral

Because of the volatile nature of the credit exposure to the client, some bank swap counterparties will call for collateral to be lodged as security for the swap transaction. Others will rely solely on a credit line as approved by the bank credit department.

Principal amounts

As the swap may involve the paying away and/or receiving the change in the relevant equity index, it is possible for the notional amount to change to reflect this. The client can either capitalize the profits and losses, thereby varying the notional amount, or he can keep the notional amount fixed and dispose of profits as income and losses as expenditure on the swap.

Resets

An equity swap is reset at various intervals throughout its maturity, and it is then that capital payments are exchanged between the parties. In reality the net payment is made up of three elements. There may be a capital appreciation of £500,000 on the underlying holding, plus dividend income of £100,000, and less interest payments of £175,000. In those circumstances, there would be a net payment of £600,000 less £175,000, an amount of £425,000 paid to the index receiver of the swap. The frequency of resets is usually every three or six months. With wholly sterling swaps, it is usual for the closing level of the index to be taken against that day's prevailing LIBOR 11 a.m. fixing rate. If the counter currency is non-sterling the LIBOR fix will be two business days earlier.

Equity index swap

EIS	Equity index swap, sometimes called portfolio insurance.
Index payer	The party wishing to pay the percentage change in the index.
Index receiver	The party wishing to receive the percentage change in the index.
Swap rate, fixed index rate, guaranteed rate	The swap rate agreed between the parties at the outset of the transaction, typically expressed as offset around the LIBOR rate.
Rollovers/ resets	The frequency of the LIBOR settlements, e.g., a one-year swap against 3-month LIBOR. Dates on which the payments flow between the counterparties.

A synthetic stock market investment

A UK fund manager is considering what action to take regarding the maturity of his £10 million fixed rate money market deposit. Should he roll it over for another year, or should he invest the money elsewhere, probably in equity? He could buy shares in major companies to create a portfolio which mirrors the FT-SE 100 Index, but he would need to pay all the relevant transaction costs. He believes that over the next year the FT-SE 100 Index will rally and offer a better rate of return than a simple money market deposit. He decides to investigate the use of equity index swaps, and summarizes the basic information received from his bankers:

Current FT-SE 100 level	6200
3-month LIBOR	5½ per cent
Spread to investor	10 basis points (10bp)
Payment frequency	Quarterly
Maturity	12 months
Underlying deposit	Linked to 3-month LIBOR

By using the swap illustrated in Figure 6.5, the total return/cost to the client will be the increase/decrease on the FT-SE 100 over the reference level of 6200. For simplicity he assumes a fixed notional amount of £10 million.

Fig 6.5

Single currency equity swap cash flows

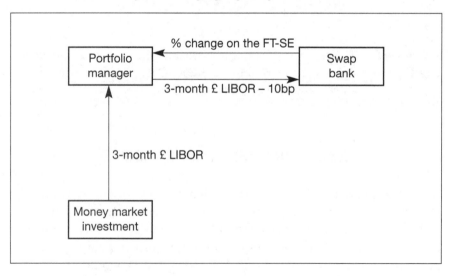

The fund manager decided to carry out a 'what-if' scenario:

(a) The market rises 400 points in the first quarter.

FT-SE 100 Index has risen from 6200 to 6600, a rise of 6.45 per cent. The bank must pay the fund manager this increase, an amount of:

$$(6.45\% \times £10,000,000) = £645,000.$$

The fund manager has also gained by 10bp on his funding, an amount of:

$$(0.10\% \times £10m \times \tfrac{91}{365}) = £2,493.$$

Making a total receipt of £647,493.

(b) The market falls by 300 points in the second quarter.

FT-SE 100 Index falls from 6600 to 6300, a fall of 4.545 per cent. The fund manager must pay this decrease to the bank, but will still gain the 10 bp spread on the funding. A total payment of:

$$(4.545\% \times £10,000,000) - (0.10\% \times £10m \times \tfrac{92}{365})$$
$$= £454,500 - £2,520 = £451,980.$$

(c) The market rises to 6775 in the third quarter.

FT-SE 100 Index has risen from 6300 to 6775, a rise of 7.54 per cent. The bank must pay the fund manager this increase, an amount of:
$$(7.54\% \times £10,000,000) = £754,000.$$

The fund manager has also gained by 10bp on his funding, an amount of:

$$(0.1\% \times £10m \times \tfrac{91}{365}) = £2,493.$$

Making a total receipt of £756,493.

(d) The market rises to 6900 in the last quarter.

FT-SE 100 Index rises from 6775 to 6900, an increase of 1.845 per cent. The bank will pay this to the fund manager, an amount of:

$$(1.845\% \times £10,000,000) = £184,500.$$

The fund manager has also gained by 10bp on his funding, an amount of:

$$(0.10\% \times £10m \times \tfrac{92}{365}) = £2,520.$$

Making a total receipt of £187,020.

If the fund manager had left his money on deposit, he would have achieved 3-month LIBOR over the period, assuming the LIBOR rates had moved as shown in Table 6.11.

Table 6.11

Example: LIBOR rates and day count

	LIBOR rate	Maturity
Commencement date	5.5%	91 days
Month 3	5.75%	92 days
Month 6	5.75%	91 days
Month 9	5.5%	92 days

The equivalent return using the LIBOR rate for each period is:

Quarter 1	£137,123
Quarter 2	£144,931
Quarter 3	£143,356
Quarter 4	£138,630

A total income of £564,040, equivalent to 5.64 per cent (ignores possible re-investment of interest income).

By using the equity index swap, the stock market move, in addition to the 10 bp spread on the funding represents a total return of:

$$+£647,493 - £451,980 + £756,493 + £187,020 = £1,139,026$$

This is equivalent to a straight interest rate of 11.39 per cent (ignores the possibility of re-investing the interest income).

The return through using the index swap is over twice as good.

Availability

Different banks each offer a different service in equity index swaps. This is very much a new and growing market with continual new developments.

Documentation

Documentation on all over the counter (OTC) deals is very comprehensive and is extremely rigorous for both parties. The industry standard document has been developed by ISDA, the International Swaps and Derivatives Association. This ISDA document is used where possible on equity swaps, and should reduce the time and effort required.

Practical considerations

Other index derivatives such as options and futures can also reduce administrative charges, but none of these instruments can exactly replicate the returns of the equity investment. The equity swap is the only instrument which provides the *actual* dividend flow: all other instruments factor in the *anticipated* dividend flow.

'The equity swap itself provides a mechanism whereby a client can hedge or take equity exposure at relatively low cost, for either a longer period than that available by using futures, or with lower administration costs.'

By purchasing an equity index swap, the investor transfers the responsibility of managing an index portfolio over to the issuer of the swap. For a passive fund that is only seeking to replicate or track the performance of a particular index, an equity swap is ideal since the objective is achieved without any of the administrative hassle.

Credit risk is a complex problem when dealing with equity index swaps. Each bank will look at this in a different fashion, some will require credit lines, some will require collateral, some will require both. If a bank requires collateral, it may take stocks of bonds and equities as well as cash. Try and avoid giving cash, the opportunity cost is very high.

Many of these swaps are tax driven and most of them will have tax implications. It would therefore be prudent to discuss those issues with a tax specialist in advance of executing the deal.

FT-SE 100 stocks are highly liquid with the ability to trade out of a cash position very quickly. This is not the case with equity index swaps. If a client wishes to terminate an index swap early, there is likely to be a substantial penalty possibly in the region of 2 to 3 per cent of the notional principal amount.

Equities are perpetual, and an investor holding them simply has to wait for his interest. The holder of an equity swap has a term instrument which on a future date will mature, possibly requiring a further swap.

As yet there is no market standard documentation, although many are trying to use their own with various ISDA 1991 amendments. Anyone considering transacting in equity swaps, would be advised to request the documentation in advance, and let the lawyers comment on it to see if alterations are required.

Further reading

For further reading on products mentioned in Chapter 6:

FT-SE Indices – Futures and Options, see www.liffe.com

Equity Options Workbook, published by LIFFE, 1999.

'The collapse of the oil price from US$ 25.60 in December 1996, to US$ 10.90 in December 1998, led many corporations to discontinue their oil hedging. Now, with prices much higher, the negative impact on the balance sheets will start to show.'

Commodity Derivatives

INTRODUCTION

The commodity markets are generally accepted to comprise energy (oil, gas and their related product derivatives as well as more recently electricity), bullion (gold, silver, platinum; and palladium), and base metals (copper, aluminum, zinc, lead, nickel and tin). In addition, there are the agricultural or soft commodities ('softs') which include grain, peanuts, orange juice, pork bellies, sugar, cocoa and coffee, etc. Each of these markets can potentially use derivative instruments for risk management and trading, but it is the energy and metals markets which are at present the most well developed, and where there are most parallels with other banking derivatives markets. This chapter will focus on the oil-based energy derivatives and their uses and applications, together with practical considerations.

The key question is, 'What determines the price of oil?' As with any other commodity, the supply and demand pulls will make the price cheaper or more expensive, but with oil there is another factor that cannot be ignored. This is simply that the oil price, or changes in the oil price, can make or break the economy of a country, and to many, oil is a cash equivalent. Consequently, politics and politicians are also integral factors.

Crude oil has no intrinsic value. It is valuable only in relation to the value of the products that can be made from it. What constitutes a 'best value' crude oil to a refiner will depend on its quality and availability, the location of the refinery and geographical and seasonal differences between the markets to be supplied. If absolute prices were stable, then these factors alone would be sufficient to determine confidently the prices of particular crude oils. However, in practice, oil prices are volatile (40 per cent volatility is not uncommon) and general market uncertainty can swamp the perceived value of a crude oil.

The value of any particular crude oil is compared to the 'benchmark' or marker crude for pricing in the final area of importation. The oil will then be sold at a premium or a discount, to the value on the day of the marker being used. The level of the premium or discount will relate to the crude oil itself, while the outright level of price is decided by the price level of the marker. In general, light crudes yield more gasoline and high-value products than heavy crudes.

As in all markets where derivatives are available, there is a choice of using exchange-traded products with their rigid contract specification, yet superb liquidity; or the over the counter (OTC) instruments which can be specifically tailored to the client's own requirements. OTC instruments are sometimes known as 'off-exchange' instruments. Most of the major oil companies have now consolidated their downstream activities, and markets have been created for independent brokers and traders. Price projections in the oil market are difficult, if not impossible, consequently the risk management of long and short positions is crucial to the long-term performance of the industry as a whole.

Background to the oil market

Oil has been seeping out of the ground literally for geological ages, usually without the local population being too concerned. If anything, an inconvenience, but occasionally oil could be used as a tar-based product for waterproofing. However, in the middle of the nineteenth century its usefulness as a fuel for light and heat came to people's attention. Edwin Drake is credited with the founding of the modern oil industry, when he made the first commercial discovery of crude oil in Pennsylvania in 1859.

More recently, in the 1950s and 1960s, the oil industry experienced a period of rapid growth. Investment in oil exploration and development led to a massive expansion in production activity. As a result, oil was abundant and relatively cheap, and fuelled the post-war economic recovery among the major industrial nations. In 1957 the US government imposed import controls; this meant that it was impossible for US companies and consumers to import foreign-produced oil. It also meant that the US oil companies were forced to market and sell all their non-American oil, notably that extracted from Middle Eastern, North African and other regions outside the USA, to Europe. By the time the US government oil controls were eventually lifted in 1971, the oil majors had established highly lucrative European markets.

During this period the oil business was dominated by the major international oil companies, through their ownership of both production and refining capabilities. From the production wellhead, oil was shipped in company-owned or chartered tankers to company-owned and operated refineries. The refined products were then distributed through company outlets. This left very little room for traders and speculators and the oil companies were usually involved in oil trading only as a means of managing their temporary surpluses or deficits.

To put all this into context: up until the early 1960s, the major oil companies were charging only US$1.80 a barrel, making their money by continually increasing their production levels. Their only worry seemed to be how long the oil would last before all the reserves had been exhausted.

Twelve years later the prices were between 10 to 15 times greater. This had come about partly because of the US insistence that only US oil could be used in the USA, and partly because the traditional US oil reserves had started to diminish and new supplies were not yet on-line. The USA had in fact changed from being a net producer of oil and had become a large oil importer.

Growing demand for oil in the USA and Western Europe, combined with oil supplies that were increasingly concentrated in the Middle East, meant that the governments of the oil-exporting countries (OPEC) were able to seize and manipulate the oil pricing mechanism in 1973/4. This effectively ended the growth period.

In the 1950s and 1960s the market was generally in surplus with prices being determined by what the oil producers could make from their refining and marketing of oil products. In the 1970s and 1980s with the OPEC leaders capitalizing on the relative scarcity of crude oil, prices rose between ten-and 20-fold from their 1960 levels.

The various 'oil shocks' in the mid- to late 1970s brought about the demise of OPEC. Incidentally, it also brought about the demise of the Bretton Woods agreement used to peg the value of the US dollar to the gold price. It has been argued that OPEC's downfall was self-inflicted. Higher oil prices slowed economic growth and increased fuel conservation. It also meant that oil exploration accelerated, and the search for fresh supplies became ever more important. Importers world-wide would not or could not afford the high price of oil and turned instead to oil substitutes. The various oil crises that followed in those years also allowed other non-OPEC oil producers to compete in the oil export market, where before the cost of their oil had been prohibitively expensive. These factors taken together have led to a downward oil price spiral for both crude oil and petroleum products. Now the 'free market' is not dominated by one group of producers or consumers, but instead volatility and uncertainty are characteristic of today's environment.

The spot market for oil has historically covered only the small amount of oil left over from the fixed price term contracts of the major oil companies. But the collapse of the oil price (West Texas Intermediate) from US$25.60 in December 1996, to US$10.90 in December 1998, led many corporations to discontinue their oil hedging. Now, with prices much higher, the negative impact on the balance sheets will start to show.

Asia and Japan are obvious areas in which the shocks will be felt. The region is short of oil with consumption running at about 19 million barrels a day, while supply is only around 7.5 million barrels a day.

In the words of the NYMEX *Energy Hedging Manual*:

> 'The oil industry is now characterized by stagnant demand, intense competition, volatile price differentials, massive financial and physical consolidation, and declining levels of inventory at all stages of a complex distribution chain. Spot prices have become the *shock absorbers* of the distribution system reacting rapidly to unanticipated market imbalances.'

By the mid-1980s spot and spot-related trading accounted for about half of all the international trade, with the Asia-Pacific region the one area where demand for oil and oil-related products is currently increasing.

What is oil?

Crude oil has a different chemical composition dependent upon a number of factors, including the original biological inputs, the contaminants, the temperature and pressure the oil was subjected to, and the storage conditions over millions of years. Oil is usually described in relation to where it is extracted. Exchange-traded derivative instruments are available based on a small number of different crudes:

- West Texas Intermediate (WTI)
- Brent Blend
- Dubai.

These markets are linked together, however the linkages are not so perfect as to ensure total integration. There are continual tensions between local forces which separate the markets, and the links which tie them together.

Brent Crude oil

Brent Crude is especially important, as it is a marker for other crudes in the North Sea, the Mediterranean, Africa, the Far East and South America.

The Brent Blend of oil comes from a mixture of the production from 19 separate oil fields, collected through the Brent and Ninian Pipelines. As the chemical characteristics of the crude oil vary across the producing fields, Brent is not homogeneous. It is typically, a light 'sweet' (with a low sulphur content) crude oil.

Until the 1980s Brent Blend was only traded on a spot or forward basis. Today the Brent market includes dated cargoes, forward transactions and deliverable futures and options contracts on the International Petroleum Exchange (IPE), as well as futures and options with cash settlement. Over the counter swaps and options can also be tailored to Brent.

Different types of trading

The physical or spot market

The *dated* or *wet* market is a spot market for the trade of cargoes of Brent, which have either been loaded or allocated a specific three-day loading range at the Sullom Voe terminal in the Shetland Islands. Trading takes place up to 15 days before the loading dates, but can continue after loading and during transit. On average there are around 50 to 60 cargoes a month, an average of 800,000 to 900,000 barrels a day. According to the International

Petroleum Exchange (IPE) about 75 per cent of Sullom Voe loadings find destinations outside the UK, mainly in Northern Europe and the USA.

The forward market

The Brent 15-day market was established in the late 1970s. It remains informal in the sense that it is not subject to formal regulations. Instead it relies on self-regulation by means of a set of standard procedures. The number of forward or paper contracts can be many times the volume of physical production, and between 50 per cent and 70 per cent of these contracts are 'cleared' by an agreement between the participants, in the series of trades for a given cargo. This is known as 'book out' and is similar to 'netting out' in FX and interest rate markets. Participants not wishing to enter a 'book out' will be allocated a specific cargo at Sullom Voe during a nominated three-day loading window, which can be accepted or passed on to the next person in the chain. The 15-day Brent market grew rapidly in the mid-1980s, and growth was accelerated by the appearance of the large US and Japanese finance houses. By 1987, within 18 months of their entering the market, these 'Wall Street Refiners' accounted for one-third of the total transactions and brought with them the new derivative products.

The futures contract

The IPE Brent Crude oil futures contract was launched in its present form in 1988, and now trades about 50 to 60 million barrels a day, about 75 per cent of total global oil consumption, for up to 36 delivery months forward. It is a standardized contract and is negotiable only in terms of the delivery month and the price. Participants can choose whether to take or make physical delivery via the Exchange of Futures for Physicals (EFP) mechanism* or they can choose cash settlement. Cash settlement is in US dollars against an index published daily by the exchange. The index is based on outright and spread prices for the 15-day contracts.

EXCHANGE-TRADED ENERGY DERIVATIVES

Introduction

The major exchanges where energy derivatives are traded are the New York Mercantile Exchange (NYMEX), the International Petroleum

---

*For further details on the EFP procedure see the next section on *exchange–traded energy derivatives*.

Exchange (IPE) in London, and the Singapore International Monetary Exchange (SIMEX). NYMEX introduced the first energy-related futures contract in 1978, and now trades a variety of different futures contracts on physical underlyings of No. 2 Heating Oil, light sweet crude oil, natural gas, unleaded regular gasoline, propane, etc. In London, the IPE opened for business in 1981 with a gas oil futures contract, and in 1988 launched their very successful Brent Crude oil futures contract with cash settlement. SIMEX started trading energy futures in 1989, and a Mutual Offset Agreement enables the trading of Brent Crude futures during the Asian time zone. In effect, a 'fungible' futures contract. NYMEX and IPE also trade options on futures contracts to enhance risk management capabilities. Volumes of futures and options contracts traded on exchanges worldwide has grown markedly since the early 1980s. It has been estimated that the total volume of crude oil trading on NYMEX and the IPE is equivalent to over three times world oil consumption (source *Oil Trading*, Shell Briefing Service).

In 1999, trading activity in the NYMEX energy futures contracts alone reached 75.1 million (approximately 301,000 contracts per day), the equivalent of 235 million barrels of oil.

Figure 7.1 gives the total volume of trading on the IPE since 1981. On the IPE, futures contracts are available to hedge or trade Brent Crude oil, gas oil and natural gas with options available on Brent and gas oil.

IPE total exchange volumes 1981–1999

Fig 7.1

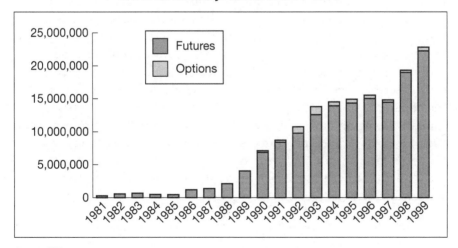

Source: IPE

EXCHANGE-TRADED FUTURES CONTRACTS

As with all futures contracts, positions can be taken to mitigate (hedge) risk or to actively take it as a trader (speculate). A trader may simply have a view on the direction of a particular oil price and wish to take out a futures position that will allow him to profit from his view (or not). A hedger, however, may seek to take an equal and opposite position in the futures market to offset as much of the price risk as possible on his physical contracts. For example, if we pay US$20 for a barrel of oil today and then we sell it tomorrow at US$10, we have lost US$10. If we hedge the position we will try to guarantee the price at which it will be sold, in effect to 'lock in' the price.

To illustrate how futures have been used for risk management and price control, we can look back as far as the Gulf War of 1990–91. Traders were able to manage their price risk using futures to smooth out 'price shocks'. This, combined with the willingness of the International Energy Agency (IEA) to release oil from stocks already held to make up for possible shortfalls, meant that oil prices did not fluctuate as wildly as during the oil crises of the 1970s. Oil prices still moved, as you can see in Figure 7.2, but not catastrophically. The various exchanges world-wide were compelled to raise their initial margins to reflect the increased volatility in the market. Figure 7.3 shows the average annual crude oil price from 1920–99.

For futures and options markets to be successful, they need price volatility and liquidity allowing participants to trade in and out of positions on a regular basis. But for the resulting hedge to be successful, the future (and the option) and the underlying oil price need to move in unison. Unfortunately, as with all futures contracts, but especially in the commodity market, a pricing feature exists called 'basis'. This describes the differential that exists between the futures price of the commodity and the equivalent cash market price. The basis is continually changing and is in practice difficult to hedge. It reflects such variables as storage and transportation costs, interest rates, market sentiment and supply and demand. The only firm certainty is that by the expiry date of the futures the cash market price and the futures price will converge.

Margin rates during the Gulf War

Fig 7.2

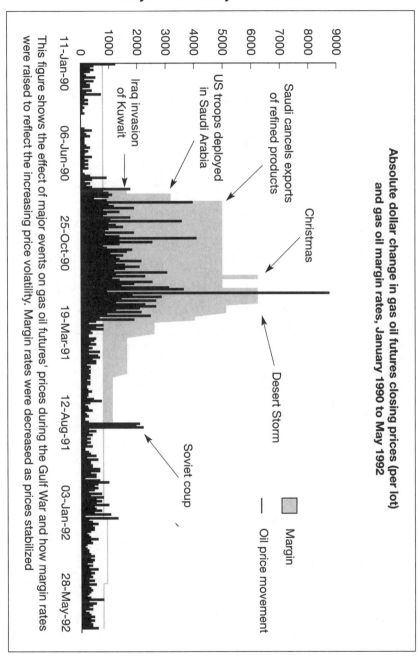

Absolute dollar change in gas oil futures closing prices (per lot) and gas oil margin rates, January 1990 to May 1992

Christmas

Saudi cancels exports of refined products

US troops deployed in Saudi Arabia

Iraq invasion of Kuwait

Desert Storm

Soviet coup

Margin

Oil price movement

This figure shows the effect of major events on gas oil futures' prices during the Gulf War and how margin rates were raised to reflect the increasing price volatility. Margin rates were decreased as prices stabilized

Source: IPE

Fig 7.3

Average annual crude oil price in current US dollars, 1920–90

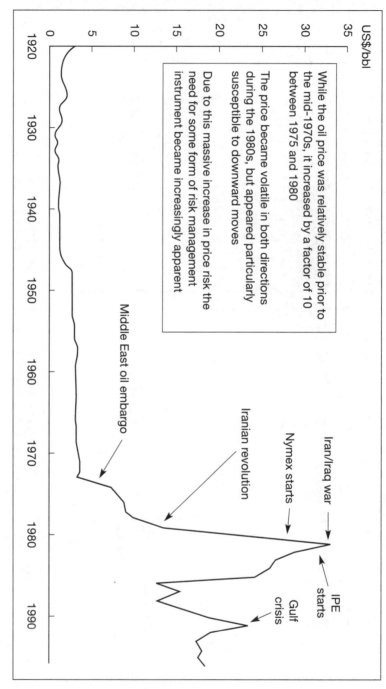

While the oil price was relatively stable prior to the mid-1970s, it increased by a factor of 10 between 1975 and 1980

The price became volatile in both directions during the 1980s, but appeared particularly susceptible to downward moves

Due to this massive increase in price risk the need for some form of risk management instrument became increasingly apparent

Middle East oil embargo

Iranian revolution

Iran/Iraq war

Nymex starts

IPE starts

Gulf crisis

Source: IPE

At this point it is worth defining our terms:

'Long' the physical	A company which produces oil or has bought crude and is holding it in storage for delivery or use at a later date.
'Short' the physical	A company with an obligation to deliver crude at a future date at a fixed price when it does not already own the physical.
'Long' the future	A client who has bought futures to open a position.
'Short' the futures	A trader who has sold futures without previously owning them.

In order for a company to hedge oil price risk, it will need to 'short the futures' if it is 'long the physical', and vice versa. But, by using futures contracts as opposed to options they will not be allowed to participate in a profitable movement, as futures hedge 100 per cent of all risk – profits as well as losses.

Table 7.1 gives a summary of basic hedging techniques using futures.

Basic hedging techniques

Table 7.1

Physical position	Price risk	Futures position	Result
LONG	Falling prices	SHORT	Short hedge
SHORT	Rising prices	LONG	Long hedge

Source: IPE

Exchange of futures for physicals (EFPs)

This is the mechanism used to exchange a position in the futures market for an equivalent position in the physical market, and vice versa. It is a complicated procedure, but in essence it allows the pricing to be separated from the supply. Approximately 5–6 per cent of the volume of the IPE Brent futures contracts are traded out this way. It is also possible to have exchange of futures for swaps (EFSs), which involve a similar procedure whereby futures contracts are exchanged for oil swaps.

> *An* **energy futures contract** *is a legally binding agreement to make or take delivery of a standard quantity of a specific crude or product cargo at a future date and at a price agreed between the parties through open outcry on the floor of an organized exchange. Cash settlement can be arranged for particular futures contracts.*

Definition discussed

As with all futures contracts there is a rigid contract specification that the participants must adhere to. It explains what is expected of the buyer and seller of the future and what obligations they must perform. Each future will also have a fixed 'contract amount' to make it easy to determine how many futures are required for the hedge or trade. The price agreed between two traders today will be for 'delivery' on a particular date in the future. The term 'delivery' is still used, although many of these contracts do not now have to be physically delivered. There is often an opportunity to cash settle the differences between the buying/selling price and the final price at maturity or close out. In fact, 'delivery' really denotes contract expiry. On most of the oil exchanges the 'open outcry' method of trading is used. This conveys an element of price transparency, allowing every trader equal access to the same trade at the same price. For further details on the open outcry method of trading, see Chapter 3 on *financial futures contracts*.

Energy futures contracts

Market
Oil futures are traded on regulated exchanges with standard contract sizes and specific delivery dates. Trades are executed by a member firm or broker physically on the floor of the relevant exchange.

Contracts
Different contracts are available on each exchange; each is standardized to enhance liquidity.

Pricing

It is a competitive auction-based market, and prices are generally quoted as a bid–offer spread, either in dollars and cents per barrel or per tonne, or in cents per US gallon (pricing for propane and natural gas is a little different). Once a futures trade has been executed, the price is then widely disseminated through various information networks, such as Reuters and Bridge Information Systems, providing world reference levels.

Market operations

Both buyers and sellers must put up minimum levels of collateral for each open contract that they hold. This is known as initial margin, and can be viewed as a good faith deposit. The actual level is calculated by the relevant exchange in conjunction with the clearing house. The method used by most exchanges is the SPAN (standard portfolio analysis of risk) system. This was developed by the Chicago Mercantile Exchange to monitor how risky a client's position becomes.

Once the initial margin is placed with the clearing house it will accumulate interest, and will be returned with interest when the position is closed out. The level of margin due on a futures contract can change if market volatility changes. When the Iraq/Kuwait Gulf War blew up in 1990, initial margins had to be reviewed as a matter of some urgency. You can see from Figure 7.2, that just as the US operation Desert Storm commenced the initial margins had increased to US$6000 per contract (lot), equivalent to US$6 per barrel.

Futures positions are 'marked-to-market' daily, and profits or losses are crystallized daily. If the position loses money against the daily settlement price, losses must be paid following the close of the trade. If the position is in profit on that day, then payment will be received. These payments are known as variation margin.

Credit risk

The IPE and other major oil exchanges function in a similar way to LIFFE. The trade is executed on the floor of a regulated exchange, and when the deal is transacted it is entered into a matching system. In London this is known as the Trade Registration System (TRS): it is used by both the IPE and LIFFE. Once a trade has been successfully matched, the London Clearing House (LCH), which is an entity separate from the exchange itself, provides the clearing mechanism for IPE and other futures trades. It is the Clearing House who will call for margin from market participants and their brokers, and ultimately each trade will eventually end up as a trade between the buyer/seller and the Clearing House. This type of order flow is illustrated in Figure 7.4, courtesy of NYMEX.

Availability

There are a number of different oil and gas futures contracts, and it is advisable to check with each exchange exactly which contracts they offer. Tables 7.2 and 7.3 list two separate contract specifications showing the differences between the contracts.

Table 7.2

IPE Brent Crude oil future – abbreviated contract specification*

Unit of trading	1,000 barrels of crude (42,000 US gallons) export quality Brent Blend as supplied at Sullom Voe
Delivery months	12 consecutive months, then quarterly out to a maximum of 24 months, then half-yearly out to a maximum of 36 months
Last trading day	Trading will cease at the close of business on the business day preceding the 15th day of the month prior to delivery
Quotation	US$ and cents per barrel
Minimum price movement	One cent per barrel equivalent to a tick value of US$10.00
Trading hours	10.02–20.13

NB This is a mutual offset contract with the SIMEX Brent Crude oil contract
* For further contract details, contact IPE.

Example

A Brent futures hedging transaction

2 November

A trader has bought a cargo of 500,000 barrels of Brent Blend crude oil, for which he paid US$26.20 per barrel. He has agreed to sell it in mid-January time on a *Platt's*-related basis. *Platt's* is a well-established journal in the market and provides reference rates for many different types of oil and oil products, now owned by Standard & Poor's. A *Platt's*-related trade is based on a continuously variable oil price. It is similar to a LIBOR fix in the interest rate market. He is concerned that oil prices may fall and he will therefore make a loss. To hedge this position he will need to sell futures to protect against this anticipated fall in prices. He will close out the futures position at the time he sells the cargo. The current futures prices from the IPE are shown in Figure 7.5.

Initiating trades and order flow for futures contracts

Fig 7.4

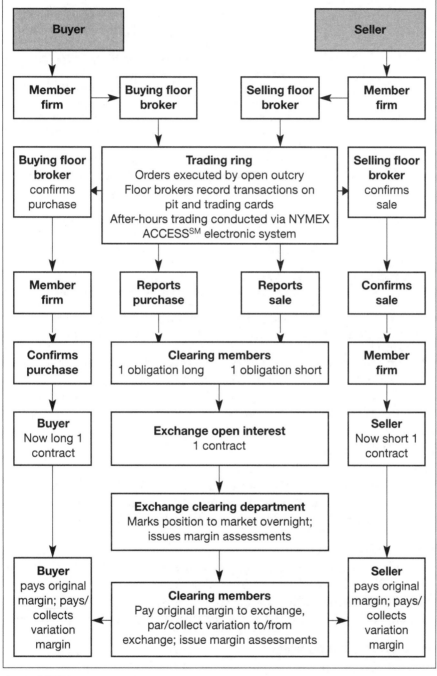

Source: NYMEX

Table 7.3

IPE gas oil future – abbreviated contract specification

Unit of trading	100 metric tonnes of gas oil, with delivery by volume namely 118.35 cubic m per lot, being the equivalent of 100 tonnes of gas oil at a density of 0.845 kg/litre in vacuum at 15°C. It should be of merchantable quality not containing inorganic acids or halogenated hydrocarbons, and should conform to the specification*
Scope	The contracts are for the delivery of gas oil into barge or coaster, or by in-tank or inter-tank transfer from customs and excise bonded refinery or storage installations, in the Amsterdam, Rotterdam, Antwerp (ARA) areas (including Vlissingen and Ghent) between the 16th and the last calendar day of the delivery month
Delivery months	Up to 12 consecutive months, including the current month and then quarterly out to 24 months, then half-yearly out to 36 months
Last trading day	Trading will cease at 12.00 hours, two business days prior to the 14th calendar day of the delivery month
Quotation Minimum price movement	US$ and cents per tonne on an EU duty paid basis 25 cents per tonne equivalent to a tick value of US$25.00
Trading hours	09.15 – 17.27 (local time)

* For further contract details, contact the source, IPE.

Action – 2 November
The trader sells 500 Brent January futures contracts at a price of $25.90. He will put up the initial margin of US$700 per contract – a total of US$350,000 and the position will be marked-to-market on a daily basis with profits and losses crystallized on a daily basis.

Action – 17 November
The trader sells his cargo at a *Platt's* reference price of US$25.30, making a loss of 0.90 cents per barrel or US$450,000. However the futures trade has made a profit which will go some way to offset the loss on the physical position. He buys the futures back at the current market level of US$25.40.

Profit from the futures hedge
2 November	Sell 500 contracts at US$26.20
17 November	Close out position by buying the futures back at the current market price US$25.40
Profit	**(80 ticks × 10 cents × 500 contracts) = US$400,000**

Brent Crude

Fig 7.5

US$ // barrel

Month	First	High	Low	Sett	Chg.	EFPs	Vol	Wtd Avg	Previous business Vol	EFPs	Ope
JAN0	25.90	25.90	25.50	25.78	+0.71	2,467	33,088	25.73	41,209	2,543	91
FEB0	24.83	24.89	24.60	24.71	+0.51	0	12,150	24.77	14,971	1,500	55
MAR0	23.95	23.95	23.62	23.75	+0.40	1,000	8,497	23.80	8,032	0	33
APR0	23.03	23.09	22.89	22.95	+0.36	0	3,327	22.97	3,232	0	18
MAY0	22.15	22.30	22.10	22.21	+0.32	0	979	22.26	807	0	14
JUN0	21.59	21.70	21.51	21.57	+0.29	0	1,936	21.62	953	0	21
JUL0	21.05	22.09	20.92	21.04	+0.28	0	200	21.04	160	0	6
AUG0	20.57	20.57	20.57	20.56	+0.25	0	175	20.57	0	0	4
SEP0	19.98	19.98	19.98	20.14	+0.22	0	40	19.98	0	0	2
OCT0	19.68	19.68	19.68	19.81	+0.18	0	55	19.68	0	0	3
NOV0	19.40	19.45	19.40	19.53	+0.16	0	75	19.43	0	0	1
DEC0	19.22	19.40	19.18	19.29	+0.14	0	1,895	19.29	1,491	0	23
MAR1	0	0	0	18.61	+0.11	0	0	0	0	0	2
JUN1	0	0	0	18.06	+0.07	0	0	0	0	0	
SEP1	0	0	0	17.75	+0.03	0	0	0	0	0	
DEC1	0	0	0	17.54	-0.01	0	0	0	0	0	6
JUN2	0	0	0	17.09	-0.06	0	0	0	0	0	
DEC2	0	0	0	16.64	-0.11	0	0	0	0	0	
						3,467	62,417		70,855	4,043	287

Source: IPE web page

The hedge is not 100 per cent effective but has narrowed the loss on the transaction to US$50,000 (US$450,000 less US$400,000). This loss of US$50,000 can be accounted for by the narrowing of the basis.

EXCHANGE-TRADED ENERGY OPTION CONTRACTS

Introduction

Energy options were launched by all the major exchanges in the mid- to late 1980s. They are options on the underlying futures contract and by using a combination of futures and options, even the most complicated risk scenarios can be hedged.

Readers who are unfamiliar with basic option concepts may find it useful to refer to that section in Chapter 3, for background information. As previously discussed, an option contract is the only derivative instrument that allows the buyer (holder) to 'walk away' from his obligations. With energy options, when the option is exercised, it results in the holder being long or short an energy futures contract, which is then cash settled. In effect the holder of one call option on the energy future will, on exercise, be long one energy future. An upfront premium is due. The option allows a greater degree of flexibility than a futures contract in that it does not completely take away all the risk, i.e., all the losses and *all the profit*. Instead it allows a degree of risk management that allows for risk control not risk removal. Options also exhibit 'asymmetry of risk', such that the most that an option holder can lose is the original premium that he paid, whereas the most he can profit is unlimited, the amount of profit governed only by how far the market has moved in his favour. A seller of options, in contrast, can only hope to keep the premium, but the extent of the losses are potentially unlimited. Put simplistically, buyers of options have rights, but no obligations, and writers of options have obligations, but no rights.

> 'It has been estimated that the total volume of crude oil trading on NYMEX and the IPE is equivalent to over five times world oil consumption.'

Definition

A **traded energy option** *gives the holder the right, but not the obligation, to buy or sell an agreed amount of energy futures at a specified price, on or before a specified date. A premium is due. The option will be cash settled against the corresponding energy future.*

Definition discussed

An energy option gives the holder, who may be an oil refiner, the chance to secure the oil price in advance. The holder of the option will choose his own guaranteed rate (the strike) from those specified by the exchange that are in multiples of 50 cents per barrel. A premium is required, which must be paid upfront, to the seller of the option on the business day following the trade. Energy options are American style, allowing the holder to exercise on any business day in the contractual period.

NYMEX options and futures on light sweet crude oil are used to hedge positions where the underlying is West Texas Intermediate (see Table 7.4).

Most open option positions will be closed out or exercised prior to expiry. Remaining open positions are automatically closed out by the exchange.

Traded energy options

Key features

Insurance protection

The client pays a premium to insure against adverse oil price movements. The clearing house agrees to guarantee the agreed rate if/when required by the client.

Profit potential:

The risk of adverse oil price market movements is eliminated, while at the same time, the buyer retains the potential to benefit from favourable prices. The option can be abandoned or exercised, dependent upon market movements.

Sell-back

Traded energy options cannot be sold back to the exchange, but an opposite position can be transacted at the current market rate with another counterparty.

Exercise

As the counterparty to each deal is the clearing house, if a client wishes to exercise the option, he is assigned a counterparty at random.

Cash settlement

The option is cash settled against the corresponding energy future. This allows participants to take profits from favourable movements without having to deal physically in the underlying cargo.

Table 7.4

NYMEX light sweet crude oil option – abbreviated contract specification*

Unit of trading	One NYMEX division light sweet crude oil futures contract
Expiry months	12 consecutive months and three long-dated options at 18, 24 and 36 months out
Strikes	At least 21 strikes are always available. The ATM (at the money) strike is that nearest to the previous day's close on the futures contract
Exercise/ settlement day	Exercise by a clearing member not later than 17.30 or 45 minutes after the underlying futures settlement price is posted, on any business day, up to and including expiry
Last trading day	Three business days before the underlying future's contract expiry
Quotation	Dollars and cents per barrel
Minimum price movement	1 cent per barrel
Tick value	US$10 per contract
Trading hours (NY times)	09.45 – 15.10 (trading pit) 16.00 – 08.00 (electronic trading through NYMEX ACCESSSM Monday–Thursday) 19.00 – 08.00 (electronic trading through NYMEX ACCESSSM Sunday p.m. to Monday morning)
Delivery	FOB (free on board) seller's facility, Cushing, Oklahoma, *or* buyer and seller can agree different terms, but must notify the exchange of their intentions or by EFPs
Deliverable grades	**Specific US domestic crudes:** West Texas Intermediate (WTI), Low Sweet Mix, North Texas Sweet, New Mexican Sweet, Oklahoma Sweet, and South Texas Sweet **Specific foreign crudes:** Brent, Osberg (carry a 30 cent per barrel discount below settlement price), Forties (carries a 35 cent premium per barrel), and Bonny Light and Columbian Cusiana (carry a 15 per cent premium)

Source: NYMEX
* For further contract details, contact the exchange direct.

Premium determinants

The amount of premium payable by the purchaser of a traded energy option is determined by the following factors:

- underlying price
- strike price
- maturity
- put or call
- cost of carry of the position
- expected market volatility.

(a) Strike price

With energy options, the underlying benchmark against which the strike is measured is the appropriate energy futures price. Strikes are therefore referred to as follows:

Terminology

At the money (ATM)	Where the strike is equal to the current futures price.
In the money (ITM)	Where the strike is more favourable than the futures price, and the option premium higher than that for an ATM option.
Out of the money (OTM)	Where the strike is worse than the futures price and the option premium is lower than for an ATM option.

(b) Maturity

The longer the time to expiry or maturity, the higher the probability of large oil index movements, and the higher the chance of profitable exercise by the buyer. The buyer should be prepared to pay a higher premium for a longer dated option than a short-dated option.

(c) Put or call

This will affect the whether the strike is in or out of the money, and also the final market price due to supply and demand swings.

(e) Cost of carry

As this option is based on the underlying energy future, the cost of carrying the position is a relevant factor. As shown in the previous section on futures, a fair value can be calculated for the futures price. This is a function of the cost of borrowing the money to pay for the oil for the full exposure period.

(f) Expected market volatility

The higher the volatility the greater the possibility of profitable exercise by the customer, so the option is more valuable and the premium is higher. This may well be different from the level of historic volatility, which could be higher or lower.

Various market factors may lead to an increase in the option premium: such events as oil company failures, new taxes, political stability, exchange controls, or general illiquidity in the market.

Terminology

Energy option

Strike price Specified energy futures price where the client can exercise his right to physical settlement. This will be specified as ATM, ITM or OTM compared to the futures price.

Call option The right to buy the underlying future.

Put option The right to sell the underlying future.

Exercise The take-up of the option at or before expiry.

Expiry date The last date when the option may be exercised.

Value date The date of (settlement) as determined by the exchange.

Premium The price of the option, as determined by an option pricing model.

Intrinsic value Strike rate minus the current market rate.

Time value Option premium minus intrinsic value, reflecting the time until expiry, changes in volatility, and market expectations.

Hedging with an option on light sweet crude oil

4 January

An oil producer fears an oil price decline, due to warm winter weather and is worried that he may have to sell his oil too cheaply on the market. He anticipates he will sell approximately 1,000 barrels a day in January at a price of about US$25 per barrel. His expected receipts on 25 days of production are US$625,00. The oil producer could use futures that would cost nothing in terms of an upfront premium, but could actually lose him money if his view of the market was wrong. However, there are certain factors in the market that lead him to believe that there may be a short-term market shortage which may well push up prices temporarily. He wishes to profit if the market moves in his favour, but he also wishes to protect his downside. In order to get an indication of where prices are trading, he screens for NYMEX futures and options (see Figures 7.6 and 7.7).

Action 4 January

The current level of the February future is US$24.67 per barrel. The oil producer decides to buy 25 February put options on the NYMEX light sweet crude oil future with a strike at US$25.00 per barrel. This is slightly 'in the money' and the cost will reflect this. The Telerate page shows that the last trade went through at 59 cents per barrel, the same as yesterday's closing price. Volatility is currently stable, and our oil producer decides to deal through his broker at 59 cents per barrel – a total premium cost of US$0.59 × 25,000 barrels = US$14,750.

February

There are two possible outcomes (see Figure 7.8). Oil prices can rise or they can fall. Let us assume that the oil price can move +/- US 5.00.

First, if oil prices rise to US$30.00 the producer will abandon his option and sell his oil at the higher level. This would realize him 25,000 × $30.00, which equals US$750,000: an improvement of US$125,000 over his original estimate. But his option premium cost him US$14,750, which must be deducted to give the final figure of US$735,250, equivalent to US$29.43 per barrel.

Second, if oil prices had fallen to say US$20.00 from their original level, he would exercise the option to sell his oil at US$25.00, netting an income of US$610,250 after premium costs. This is absolutely the worst case, if oil prices fall to US$5.00 a barrel, the producer will still be able to guarantee a rate of US$610,250 by utilizing the option, an effective rate of US$24.41 per barrel.

Fig 7.6

Light sweet crude oil futures

01/11 04:46 NYC   [TELERATE FUTURES SERVICE]   01/10 16:17 8910

LIGHT SWEET CRUDE OIL – NYMEX

	TIME	NET	LAST	PREV1	LOW	HIGH	OPEN	CLOSE	VOLUME	OP.INT
FEB 00	1545+	45	S2467	S2467	2402	2475	2422	2422	91828	116577
MAR 00	1545+	37	S2413	R2420	2357	2420	2376	2376	50388	81817
APR 00	1545+	37	S2362	R2365	2315	2365	2325	2325	16892	44735
MAY 00	1545+	38	S2313	A2320	2270	2310	2284	2275	4655	26670
JUN 00	1545+	37	S2264	B2250	2224	2248	2235	2227	7259	52198
JUL 00	1546+	38	S2217	2210	2180	2210	2185	2179	3374	32311
AUG 00	1546+	38	S2176	B2152	2144	2154	2144	2138	1255	16676
SEP 00	1546+	37	S2142	2125	2108	2125	2108	2105	1129	14615
OCT 00	1546+	37	S2111	2090	2085	2090	2085	2074	710	12902
NOV 00	1546+	37	S2082	2060	2060	2060	2060	2045	275	9288
DEC 00	1546+	36	S2055	B2036	2019	2035	2025	2019	3950	37232
JAN 01	1546+	35	S2030					1995	93	13442
FEB 01	1546+	35	S2008					1973	253	3821
MAR 01	1546+	35	S1988	B1958	1960	1960	1960	1953	25	3433
APR 01	1546+	34	S1969					1935	50	1529

Source: NYMEX (*courtesy*: Bridge Information Systems)

Light sweet crude oil options

Fig 7.7

[DOW JONES OPTIONS ON FUTURES SERVICE]

NYMEX CRUDE OIL OPTIONS - FEB 00

01/11 04:53 NYC   01/10 16:23 39720

[CALLS] NET LAST PREV1 LOW HIGH	PREV CLOSE	STRIKE	[PUTS] NET LAST PREV1 LOW HIGH	PREV CLOSE
$269	269	2200	$2	12
$171	171	2300	$4	4
$81	81	2400	$14	14
$48	48	2450	$31	31
$26	26	2500	$59	59
$13	13	2550	$96	96
$7	7	2600	$140	140
$4	4	2650	$187	187
$2	2	2700	$235	235
$1	1	2750	$284	284
$1	1	2800	$334	334
$1	1	2900	$434	434
$1	1	3000	$534	534

Source: NYMEX (*courtesy*: Bridge Information Systems)

Fig 7.8

Hedging example using light sweet crude oil traded options

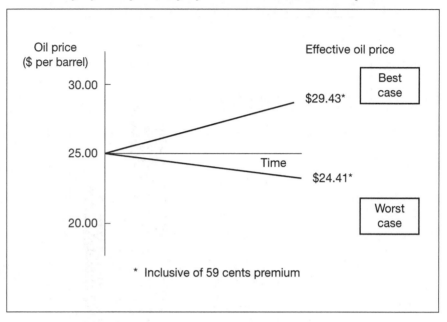

The oil producer has insured against an adverse oil price movement for a limited and known cost, and preserved his right to benefit if the oil spot market rates move in his favour. This option has guaranteed for the client a worst rate of US$24.41. If rates fall lower than the option strike of US$25.00, the oil producer will always exercise the option. So in practice the worst rate is US$24.41. But, if the oil producer is lucky, and oil prices rise, then he will abandon the option and sell his oil at the higher price. There is no limit to the amount of profit he can make, it is constrained only by how far the market may move.

Practical considerations

Using exchange-traded oil derivatives to hedge positions will offer the client liquidity, a tight price and the comfort of dealing with an established exchange and clearing mechanism. Unfortunately, commodities of all sorts can suffer very violent swings in the underlying, and on occasions illiquidity in the spot market will cause problems.

It is very rare to achieve a hedge that is 100 per cent effective, owing to the pricing disparity known as 'basis', which in practical terms is almost unhedgeable.

Commodities are prone to 'backwardation'. In simple terms, this means that the price of oil on the spot market is more expensive than the price quoted for forward delivery. This seems to be the 'wrong way round'. With any commodity, storage, transportation and funding costs almost always mean that forward prices should be more expensive than spot prices which do not include all the above extra costs. But it can happen on some occasions that spot prices are bid up. This relationship needs to be monitored very closely during the life of any hedge.

Listed options and futures can be transferred into the physical commodity, through the trading instrument known as EFPs – exchange of futures for physicals. EFPs allow the traders to choose their trading partners, while retaining their anonymity in the market as a whole.

Documentation for all exchange-traded products will be standardized, although the brokers through whom most market participants will deal will each have their individual terms and conditions for dealing. It is always advisable for the lawyers to have sight of the paperwork before signature, so allow sufficient time for this before dealing is due to commence.

OTC OR 'OFF-EXCHANGE' ENERGY DERIVATIVES

Introduction

Because of the many different types of oil and oil products, dealing 'off-exchange' is popular with users and producers who wish to hedge or trade a particular variety of oil or oil product where there is as yet either no exchange-traded contract available or it has some limitations.

For example, a client may wish to hedge his exposure for a longer period, or to purchase an option with a different strike than that offered by an exchange, or execute an energy swap where there is no exchange-traded equivalent. The providers of OTC energy derivatives will generally be the large oil companies such as BPAMOCO and Shell, together with the US investment banks such as Morgan Stanley and Credit Suisse First Boston.

Available OTC products are energy options and other option related products such as oil caps and collars, and oil swaps which are sometimes known as CFDs – contracts for differences. The credit risks attached to OTC products are always greater than the credit risks attached to exchange-traded derivatives and need careful consideration. An OTC transaction is a bilateral arrangement where each counterparty must bear the other's credit risk. Dealing on an exchange immunizes both counterparties from this risk, as once the transaction is executed, both parties are in legal contract with the clearing house, rather than each other.

OTC OPTION PRODUCTS

The option products that are most frequently used in the oil market are **caps and collars. These have exactly the same structure as those in the interest rate markets, but are typically used to cover a shorter time horizon.**

The cap will have multiple settlements (fixings), with dates that are pre-arranged at the outset. Options with a single settlement are known as puts (the right to sell) and calls (the right to buy), and perform in exactly the same way as options on stocks or options on currency. For further details on options see *basic option concepts* in Chapter 3.

Definition

*An **energy cap** gives the buyer (or holder) the right, but not the obligation, to fix the oil price, on a notional amount of product cargo at a specific rate (the strike) for a specified period. The writer of the cap will guarantee to the holder a maximum price level if/when required, and will reimburse the holder of the cap for any excess cost over the agreed strike rate. A premium is due, payable upfront or monthly.*

Definition discussed

To clarify the picture we need to open up this definition. As with all option contracts there is a buyer and a seller of the option itself. A cap is simply an option with more than one fixing. Mostly, but not always, the cap writers or sellers will be the major oil companies. Usually the buyer of the cap is a consumer or user of oil or oil products, such as an airline, or a transport company, or in some cases an institution looking to risk manage its positions.

The client needs to choose a strike rate for the cap which best reflects his actual fuel costs. One noticeable difference between an interest rate cap and an oil cap relates to the fixing or rollover dates. With an oil cap, the client's floating reference rate is not a particular price on a particular date (as with interest rate caps), such as 6-month LIBOR on 21 March, but the average oil price over the period, usually a month. This strike price, index price or fixed rate will be guaranteed for the client if/when he requires it. A reference rate needs to be agreed at the outset for the floating side of the cap: this can be linked to *Platt's* (now owned by Standard & Poor's), or a futures price +/− some premium. The actual monthly averages in the market, as published in *Platt's* for example, will be compared to the strike rate on the cap, and a payment of the difference will be made by the appropriate party. Caps with average monthly fixings are sometimes known as 'Asian options'. The benchmark used to compare the strike on the oil cap with the current market rates is the equivalent underlying oil swap rate.

Energy caps

Key features

Multiple exercise
A time series of individual energy options with the same strike rates.

Insurance protection
The client pays a premium to insure against adverse oil price movements. Premium can be paid upfront or monthly.

Profit potential
A cap reduces the risk of adverse price movements while retaining profit potential. The instrument can be allowed to lapse (abandoned) if the market has moved in the client's favour.

Cash settlement
Principal funds are not involved. The client is not obliged to make or take delivery from the writing oil company. On exercise, the writer will pay the difference between the strike rate and the average oil reference rate. Settlement is five business days in arrears after the end of the month.

Premium determinants

The amount of premium payable for an oil cap is dependent on the inputs that are:

- underlying price
- strike price
- maturity
- expected market volatility
- market conditions.

(a) Strike price

With energy caps the underlying benchmark is the appropriate oil swap rate, taking into account the correct side of the swap i.e., payer's or receiver's side as appropriate (see the discussion on interest rate swaps in Chapter 4). It is against this that the client's strike rate is measured. Strike rates are therefore referred to as follows:

At the money (ATM)	Where the strike is equal to the current swap rate.
In the money (ITM)	Where the strike is more favourable to the swap rate, and the option premium higher than that for an ATM option.
Out of the money (OTM)	Where the strike is worse than the swap rate and the option premium is lower than that for an ATM option.

(b) Maturity

The longer the time to expiry or maturity, the higher the probability of large price movements, and the higher the chance of profitable exercise by the client (buyer). The buyer should consequently be prepared to pay a higher premium for a longer dated cap than for a short-dated cap.

(c) Expected market volatility

The higher the volatility the greater the possibility of profitable exercise by the client, so the cap is more valuable to the company, therefore the premium is higher. In general terms if there is high volatility in the market, then there is a strong likelihood of erratic oil price movements.

(d) Market conditions

Various market factors may lead to an increase in the option premium and these include events such as government controls, imposition of new taxes, rumours and expectations, or illiquidity in the market. In general terms, anything that can destabilize the oil price will lead to an increase in volatility, so the option premium will increase.

It should also be noted that the level of interest rates also plays an important part in energy option pricing, due to the discounting of the premium (see discussion in Chapter 3 on *basic option concepts*).

Oil caps

Strike price Specified oil price where the client can exercise his right to cash settlement. This can be ITM, ATM or OTM.

Multiple exercise Take-up of the option on various fixing dates.

Settlement date Last business day in the month.

Value date Five business days after the settlement date.

Premium The price of the option, as determined by an option pricing model.

Intrinsic value Strike rate minus the current market rate.

Time value Option premium minus intrinsic value, reflecting the time until expiry, changes in volatility, and market expectations.

Hedging with an energy cap

A small North American shipping company needs to purchase bunkerfuel for one of its subsidiaries. The company estimates that it will need to buy 1,000 metric tonnes (mt) per month for September, October and November, and wishes to 'cap' its fuel costs. The index that best suits this customer is based on New Orleans IF 180 (NOLA IF 180).

Strategy
The company starts to gather prices from the market makers, for a cap with a strike of US$95 per mt. This is a little OTM, and BP Oil International has offered a cap to the shipping company at a premium of US$2.5 per mt, making a total monthly premium cost of US$2,500. This will give full protection starting in September at a price of US$95 per mt.

Outcome
If the monthly average price is below the strike, the shipping company will buy its fuel at a cheaper price in the market; if the average monthly cost is higher than the strike, BP will compensate the company for any excess over and above this rate.

Fig 7.9

Payments under an energy cap

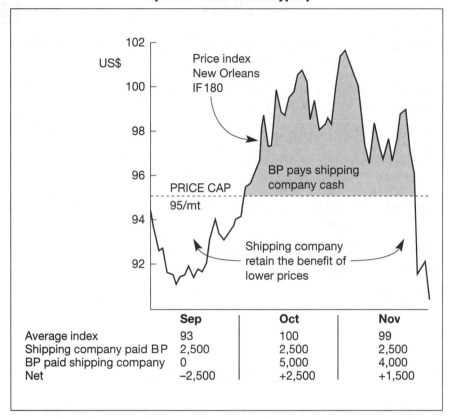

	Sep	**Oct**	**Nov**
Average index	93	100	99
Shipping company paid BP	2,500	2,500	2,500
BP paid shipping company	0	5,000	4,000
Net	−2,500	+2,500	+1,500

Source: BP Oil International

An oil cap will therefore fix the shipping company's bunkerfuel costs at a maximum level of US$95 per metric tonne (see Figure 7.9). The breakeven rate will be achieved at cap price + option premium, a level of US$97.50.

An oil floor is identical in operation to an oil cap, and could protect an oil producer from falling prices by fixing the minimum sale price, for a pre-determined period. However, they are only likely to account for about 35 to 45 per cent of total cap and floor turnover.

Availability

Energy caps and floors are generally available in notional amounts from 1,000 barrels of crude, and 500 metric tonnes for oil products, although deals between market makers will obviously be larger. Increasingly, business is being written in non-dollar-based currencies such as the Euro.

Practical considerations

Most energy caps and floors are for periods up to two years, and occasionally up to five years and will generally have resets every month or every quarter based on the average rate throughout the period. References for the floating rate must be agreed in advance, and there are a number of different oil indices to choose from.

When a client purchases a cap or floor, his only responsibility is to pay the premium required. Once this has been paid, he has no further obligations. However, he could choose to pay the premium by selling another option product to the bank, in effect trying to create a reduced cost strategy. He is then opening himself up to possible risk. These composite products are known as collars, and the premium due can be reduced down to zero. They involve the simultaneous trading of the cap and the floor, and are similar in operation to collars in the interest market (see Chapter 4, on *interest rate collars*).

Where the client buys the cap or floor, a credit line is not required as the client is under no obligation to deliver anything. However, if he wishes to sell the product, or to transact one of the collar strategies, a credit line will be required and this needs to be set up in advance.

Documentation in the oil derivatives market is variable. Most participants are comfortable to deal on major oil company terms, e.g., BP or Elf terms and conditions, which are widely acceptable. Some of the banks in the market are using the ISDA documentation, as this is what they use to document other swap transactions.

> 'Oil swaps have been around for fewer than 15 years and they are one of the fastest growing products on the market.'

OTC OIL SWAPS

Introduction

Oil swaps have been around for fewer than 15 years and they are one of the fastest growing products on the market. The mechanics of oil swaps follow those in other swap markets. The big players continue to be the major oil companies, and the large international banks, most of whom have an interest rate swap capability. Maturities are most likely to be in the one to three year period and are occasionally seen in the five- to ten-year range with quarterly or semi-annual resets.

In Asia, most oil hedging is carried out using swaps, but in the USA more OTC options are transacted.

| **Definition** | *An agreement between two parties to exchange cash flows based on an agreed oil index price for a specified period at agreed reset intervals based on the average price for the period, as noted by a pre-specified independent authority.* |

Definition discussed

This is a legally binding agreement where an absolute oil price level will be guaranteed. One party will agree to pay the 'fixed index rate'; the other to receive this fixed rate, and pay the 'floating rate' based on the monthly average movement of the same index. The underlying sale or purchase transaction is untouched and may well be with another institution. The only movement of funds is a net transfer of payments between the two parties on the pre-specified dates. However, with oil swaps it is possible to link the swap with a particular physical cargo. The cash flows are calculated based on an agreed notional amount with a cargo which may or may not be delivered.

| **Key features** | **Oil swaps** |

Insurance protection
Through a swap a client can guarantee the rate at which he will purchase (or sell) a pre-specified amount of oil or oil products for a pre-determined period. No premium is required.

Cash or physical settlement
It is normally only the index-linked cash flows that are swapped, with the notional amount of cargo not exchanged. However, physical settlement can be arranged but must be agreed in advance.

Funding optimization
As the underlying commitment to buy or sell the oil may be with another institution, the client can deal where he gets the best prices. The swap will be negotiated separately.

Credit risk
The credit risk of both counterparties must be carefully evaluated, as each will bear the other's credit risk.

Premium

Swaps are zero-premium instruments and a credit line will be required. On some occasions the client will need to collateralize the swap, that is, to secure the credit risk with cash, either in the form of a deposit, or by way of a variable letter of credit. These arrangements need to be finalized before dealing commences.

Oil swaps

Fixed payer	The party wishing to pay 'fixed' on the swap, and protect itself from a rise in prices.
Fixed receiver	The party wishing to receive 'fixed' on the swap, and protect itself from a fall in prices.
Swap rate, fixed rate , guaranteed rate	The oil swap rate agreed between the parties at the outset of the transaction.
Resets	Dates when the monthly average floating rate is compared to the fixed rate on the swap. The differences are net cash settled. Settlement is five business days in arrears.

Hedging a bunkerfuel exposure with an oil swap

15 May

A Scandinavian company needs to purchase approximately 1,500 metric tonnes per month of bunkerfuel, from July. The index price that is chosen is *Platt's* Bunkerwire Rotterdam IF 380 as, historically, this has most closely matched the actual cost of the bunkerfuel. The company wishes to protect its costs during the period July to October. The current swap price for the period is US$84 per metric tonne.

Strategy

The company can take out an oil swap which would fix the price of bunkerfuel and remove the threat of rising oil prices. It is important for the swap to match the underlying transaction in all respects. In our example, the company wishes to 'pay the fixed and receive the floating' (rate). The company is happy to hedge at the current levels, and BP Oil International has offered the swap at the current rate of US$84/mt (see Figure 7.10).

Fig 7.10

Oil swap cash flows

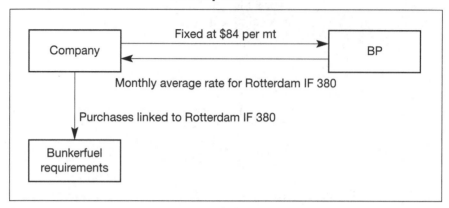

Fig 7.11

Payments under an oil swap

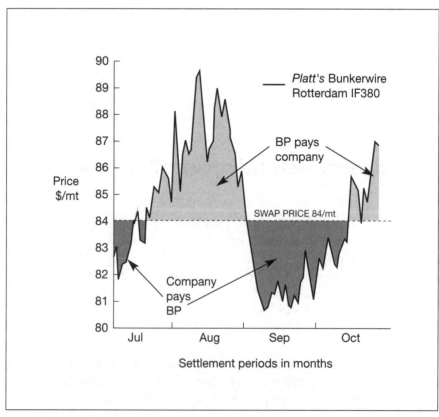

Source: BP Oil International

Outcome

On each of the pre-specified reset dates, the two cash flows will be calculated and offset.

In the white areas of Figure 7.11, the Rotterdam IF 380 was above the swap price, so the swap provider – BP – will pay the difference. In the grey areas, the price of the bunkerfuel was below the swap rate, so the Scandinavian company must pay the difference to BP. So whatever the bunkerfuel price, the company will never pay more than US$84/mt but will never be able to purchase it more cheaply than US$84/mt.

This illustrates that, as with all swaps, the swap rate becomes an absolute guaranteed rate for the transaction. No improvements on the price level are possible. All risk has been hedged away, even the risk of making a profit.

Practical considerations

The OTC market in energy derivatives is growing exceptionally fast and I would advise anyone considering how to manage energy risk to contact one of the providers direct to discuss the possibility of 'off-exchange' hedging.

Further reading

For further reading on products mentioned in Chapter 7:

Brent Crude . . . The International Benchmark, published by IPE, 1999.

A Practical Guide to Hedging, published by BP NYMEX.

BP Oil Ltd *Bunkerfuel Risk Management*, published by BP.

Trading in Oil Futures, by Sally Clubley, published by Simon & Schuster.

Oil Markets and Prices, by Paul Horsnell and Robert Mabro, published by Oxford University Press.

'No longer the exotic playthings of the investment banks, credit derivatives are used to manage and exploit risks and opportunities in credit markets.'

Credit Derivatives

INTRODUCTION

Credit derivatives are among the newest of the derivative products. They comprise a broad range of instruments and have been around for about six to eight years. No longer the exotic playthings of the investment banks, credit derivatives are used to manage and exploit risks and opportunities in credit markets. Essentially, risk is transferred among the various participants using OTC transactions, which may be either 'on-balance sheet' or 'off-balance sheet'.

Off-balance sheet	Credit default swaps, total rate of return swaps, etc.
On-balance sheet	Credit linked notes, CDOs (collateralised debt obligations).

BACKGROUND

The British Bankers' Association (BBA) recently carried out a survey, the results of which are illustrated in Figure 8.1. We see volumes of US$50 billion in 1996 increasing to US$350 billion by end 1998 with projected volumes of US$740 billion for year end 2000. If recent experience is anything to go by, the estimated numbers for 2000 will be seriously understated.

Fig 8.1

Credit derivatives (US $ billions)

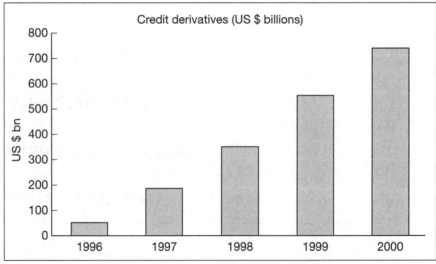

Credit derivatives (US $ billions)

Source: British Bankers' Association

Not surprisingly, banks are the major users of these products, both for their own portfolio management and for trading/arbitraging credit risk across different market sectors, e.g., bonds vs term loans.

WHAT IS CREDIT RISK?

Credit risk can arise in any situation where there is a contract between two counterparties, giving one party a future obligation to the other. The risk being, of course, that the first party will fail to meet its obligations. This means that we are looking beyond a total default situation. Although default risk is important, credit risk also encompasses any waiver, deferral, rescheduling or any adjustment of the terms which is unfavorable to the creditor.

Credit risk actually comprises two different sorts of risk:

1 **Market risk:** that the price of the asset in question will rise or fall, or become more/less volatile.
2 **Client specific risk:** that the firm itself may run into trouble.

For example, a financier may wish to enter into an investment transaction involving corporate bonds issued by a Thai company. He is relaxed about the performance of the company itself, but is more concerned about the possibility of a downgrade in the Thai country risk, which may in turn adversely affect the performance of his investment.

Credit derivatives have applications beyond banks and financial institutions. Consider a manufacturer who sells custom-made machinery to one particular client. What happens if the client goes into liquidation? Not only may the manufacturer be left with the goods unsold, it will be hard to sell them elsewhere as they are designed to a specific set of client requirements.

Typically, banks and financial institutions have more experience in managing credit risk, because they lend money through corporate loans. This means that they have developed ways to manage this risk, e.g., the commercial bank can syndicate the loan or impose covenants in order to mitigate the risk. They could also seek collateral – a cash amount to cover their costs if there is a default. However, collateralization brings its own headaches, notably, has it been paid, is it sufficient, what if the market moves, marking-to-market, etc.

It is very conspicuous that it is the *investment* banks which dominate this market rather than the commercial banks. This may be due to the size of their capital market transactions and/or their tendency to hedge risks more dynamically.

Traditional solutions to credit risk management include factoring (where the company can sell its trade receivables at a discount) and credit risk insurance. This can be very expensive and, typically, only runs for a year, at which point the insurer has the option to cancel the policy or raise the premium.

STYLE OF TRADING

A credit derivative product is an over the counter (OTC) instrument which allows users to manage credit risk in the same way as they can manage currency and interest rate exposure. The 'underlying asset' is usually taken to be a publicly traded debt instrument such as a bond issued by the debtor company.

The market is subdivided into the following sectors:

- investment-grade credits – top-quality government, corporate or bank bonds
- non-investment-grade/high-yield credits/speculative – low-grade, questionable credits
- distressed credits – bonds which are in trouble
- emerging market credits – credits which may not be so freely traded, usually very volatile, often with liquidity/delivery problems.

Ratings

Publicly traded bonds generally have credit ratings assigned to them. The rating agencies are independent bodies, which for a fee, will provide an assessment of the risk associated with the issuer or issue. It should be noted that rating is mandatory in the USA but not in the UK. Some large UK companies do not have ratings, but this does not indicate that they are poor credits. Rather, it shows that they have never needed one. If a bond is so popular it almost sells itself why should the company pay for a rating? Rating agencies include Standard & Poors and Moodys and Ffitch. Large banks often have in-house systems which compute their own default data.

Table 8.1 summarizes the Standard & Poors (S&P) credit ratings – with comments which are my own personal interpretation.

Credit ratings

Table 8.1

Investment-grade paper	
AAA	Triple A credits ... very safe ... often government or supranational bonds
AA+	
AA	High grade, good quality ... safe ... often major bank bonds
AA–	
A+	
A	Upper–medium grade ... Good-quality smaller banks/corporate bonds
A–	
BBB+	
BBB	Lower–medium grade ... Reasonable quality corporate bonds
BBB–	
Speculative paper	
BB+	
BB	Low grade ... Speculative
BB–	
B+	
B	Lower grade ... Very speculative
B–	
Very speculative high yield paper (used to be known as **junk bonds**)	
CCC+	
CCC	Substantial risk ... Vulnerable to non-payment
CCC–	
CC	Possible default ... Highly vulnerable to non-payment
D	Default

DEFAULT DATA

World-wide data on company defaults is patchy to say the least. A trader may have all the public data on a company but if there is no official credit rating (from S&P, say, or Moodys), it is still far less than he would like. In comparison, the rating agencies have access to unpublished data which means that an official rating will often carry more weight.

Many large companies borrow direct from banks in private transactions and publicly traded bonds may be lacking, leading to a certain amount of guesswork.

Defaults also tend to be higher in some parts of the world:

In the Asia-Pacific region, when a default occurs losses can be of the order of 50 per cent of principal, whereas in the USA it is typically around 30–35 per cent.

But let's be realistic. In practical terms, if a company defaults, how do you get any of your money back? The legal system in some countries can tie you up in knots for years, and even then it can be slow to get access to the remaining assets, should there be any.

THE FIRST DEALS

Legend has it that the market started in New York in 1992/3. Various market players claim to have transacted the first deal. Credit derivatives owe their origins to the banks' requirements to manage the large credit risk associated with their swap and bond books. In order to reduce these risks swap houses began to repackage and sell on the credit risk associated with a basket of names. Early transactions were expensive and commanded a large premium, but helped free up capital which could then be used for new or more profitable business.

London tends to be the dominant financial centre, and has been able to further grow this product, for four key reasons:

- the size of the international debt market
- a market-friendly regulatory environment
- liquid asset swap market
- derivative strengths.

TYPES OF CREDIT DERIVATIVE

Definition | A credit derivative allows the holder to isolate and separate credit risk from market risk, thus allowing this credit risk to be either hedged, traded or transferred. A premium may be due.

In essence, although they may be sold by different names within different banks, there are essentially three basic structures for 'off-balance sheet' products:

- credit default swaps
- total rate of return swaps
- credit spread options.

NB: The BBA has estimated that over 50 per cent of all credit derivative transactions are default swaps of one shape or another.

Terminology for credit events

The definition of a credit event or default, which triggers the payout under one of these products can vary from bank to bank and across different transactions but typically include:

- payment default or bankruptcy/insolvency in the case of corporate credits
- moratorium on payments or the rescheduling of payments, as well as payment default itself, for sovereign credits
- Chapter 11 or bankruptcy filing by the issuer
- failure to meet payment obligations when due
- rating downgrade below an agreed level
- change in the agreed credit spread (over a government bond or compared to another government bond).

A materiality threshold (a significant price decline) has also to be breached and independently agreed.

Fee determinants

Credit derivatives are not without cost, and a complex model is used to calculate the fee. In overview the determinants are:

- credit rating of probable swap counterparty
- maturity
- probability of default
- expected value of the asset (post-default).

Market participants.
Protection buyer – party seeking to hedge the credit risk
Protection seller – party (usually a bank) who will take on the credit risk.

Credit rating of probable swap counterparty

Key features

It makes no sense to create a deal where you substitute a weaker credit rating for your original counterparty. Consider a bank writing (or selling) protection on a AA name, when in reality the bank is BBB – would you buy that protection? Or would you seek protection from a better credit? Guess what. You'll pay more.

The concern is that if you substitute in a lower credit as the swap counterparty, you will pay them a premium for the life of the transaction and if the AA name defaults it is quite possible the swap counterparty will as well. Have a care, there are a number of B-type banks in this market selling protection.

Maturity

Obviously, the longer the duration of the transaction, the higher the risk, and the more you will pay.

Probability of default

The higher the probability of default, the more the protection will cost, where possible independent international credit ratings will be used.

Expected value of the asset (post-default)

This is usually looked at two or three months after the default, to give the price a chance to stabilize. There will obviously be opposing views: the protection buyer wants to show it fell a long way, the protection seller that it didn't fall very far. The 'recovery value' of the asset will determine the level of the contingent payout.

Payout process

There are three principal methods by which payment is made after a credit event has occurred:

1 The protection seller pays the protection buyer an amount equal to the difference between the initial price and the post-default price of the reference credit. The post-default price may be calculated via a dealer poll (usually twice a week for up to three months) due to a lack of published information.

2 The protection seller pays the total notional value of the underlying reference credit, in exchange for delivery of defaulted asset.

3 The protection seller pays a pre-agreed fixed percentage of the notional value of the swap.

NB: Physical settlement has become increasingly the standard, as post-default the price of an asset can become very volatile. Physical delivery, of course, protects both parties

CREDIT DEFAULT SWAPS

Credit default swaps enable the separation and transfer of credit risk between two parties, without transferring ownership of the underlying asset itself. They are products that allow the counterparty to hedge/gain exposure to credit default risk. The nature of the default event, the reference asset, and the methods used to calculate the amount payable are specified in the swap contract, and can vary depending on the individual transaction in question. The 'underlying asset' may be a single bond or a basket of assets, and they may be categorized by their seniority or type of issue.

Example

A bank has made a loan for five years to a client, based on a variable rate of interest – 6-month LIBOR plus 50 basis points. Every time the lending bank receives its interest income of LIBOR + 0.50 per cent, they pay 0.25 per cent to the swap bank as the payment on the credit default swap, this is shown diagrammatically in Figure 8.2.

This will continue for the life of the loan. Only if there is an event of default will there be a payout. No default – no payout.

A credit default swap

Fig 8.2

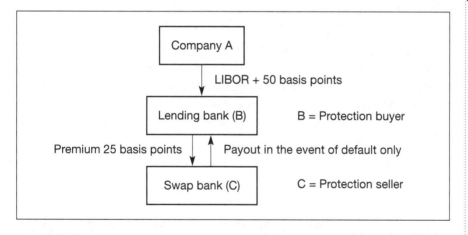

A reference credit is chosen – a publicly traded bond, the price of which must be agreed at the beginning, and must be specified in the documentation.

In this example, the lending bank has paid a premium to insure against default risk – the bank is known as the 'buyer' of the protection but it is also 'selling the risk'. In effect, the risk has been transferred to the counterparty – the 'seller' of the protection or the 'buyer of the risk'. The contingent payment may be a cash settlement amount or the purchase of the defaulted asset as previously discussed.

Why do counterparties use credit derivatives?

Currently, the primary users of credit derivatives are commercial banks, investment banks and insurance companies.

Protection buyer

There are four main reasons why a financial institution may wish to transfer credit risk with a credit derivative:

1 to reduce exposure to a company or bank whose credit rating is deteriorating

2 to free up credit lines so that higher margin business may be transacted

3 to protect against a downgrading below a portfolio manager's internal limits

4 to reduce credit exposures which have exceeded limits, possibly where interest rates or currency movements have exceeded expectations.

Protection seller

Again there are four principal reasons:

1 to synthesize the exposure to a client beyond market constraints, for example, if the market in a particular bond is illiquid

2 to gain exposure to a credit that is not otherwise available, for example, where a company does not issue bonds

3 to benefit from a higher yield which may be offered by the protection seller in a credit swap

4 to choose a specific maturity band that is not available in the bond or loan market.

TOTAL RATE OF RETURN SWAPS

Total return swaps transfer credit risk by swapping an underlying asset's specified total return (capital growth and interest) between two counterparties, in return for regular payments of LIBOR + spread. Instead of a payment in the event of a default, the total return swap guarantees the risk seller (the protection buyer) a specified economic value for the reference credit.

Example

In a total return swap, Bank X pays Bank Y any appreciation on the capital value of the underlying asset as well as any coupons receivable. In return, Bank Y pays Bank X any depreciation of the capital value as well as a LIBOR-linked floating margin. Bank Y is known as the 'receiver' of the total return, and Bank X is the 'payer' of the total return – similar to 'paying or receiving fixed interest' on an interest rate swap.

So, Bank X is guaranteed a specified capital value for the underlying, as well as a LIBOR-linked income for the duration of the swap. The credit risk for the underlying has been transferred to Bank Y, which is the recipient of the income and (any) profits generated by this asset. Bank Y is thus known as the buyer of risk, and Bank X, the seller of risk.

However, Bank X retains ownership of the underlying, and must continue to fund the asset. This is shown in Figure 8.3.

A total rate of return swap

Fig 8.3

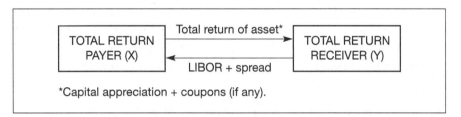

NB: There is no credit event and no contingent payment. At the end of each three- or six-month period, payments are automatically exchanged. In the event of a default, the payment due at the end of the next period is brought forward Net Present Valued and the contract terminated.

Bank X has hedged the economic risk of the asset held on the balance sheet. Bank Y is exposed to that risk, but does not have any of the other problems such as balance sheet, funding, or any of the operational complications of owning the asset.

As well as locking in a specified economic value, total return swaps can be used to transfer the market risk of an asset off-balance sheet and lower the regulatory capital charge. Equally, it can be used for trading credits on a leveraged off-balance sheet basis.

NB: For the technically minded, an interesting analogy for a total return swap is a repo transaction. One leading London house categorizes all its emerging market repo activity as credit derivative business. The primary difference is that a repo transaction is collateralized (the underlying physical credit is actually exchanged during the transaction) whereas with credit derivative products the physical underlying is never exchanged except at the termination of some transactions.

Credit spread options

These are products based on the change of a credit spread.

So what is a credit spread?

Credit spreads are the difference in 'yields' between an agreed reference rate and the specific asset in question. The credit spread is based on market perceptions of the credit quality of the underlying asset compared to a market benchmark. Thus, in the London market, the spread would usually be measured against LIBOR or a specified UK gilt, while in the US market they would normally use US treasuries. To clarify this, if a corporate bond has been trading at 55 basis points over gilts, and then starts to trade at 45 basis points over gilts, the credit spread has narrowed (or tightened), indicating that the credit quality of the bond or bond issuer has improved. A high or wide credit spread would signify a high potential for default, therefore the investor requires a much higher yield on the investment.

Different types of credit spread derivatives

There are two distinct versions of the product:

- the spread relative to a benchmark
- credit spreads between two 'credit-sensitive' assets.

The easiest way to enter into these transactions is through the option route, rather than the swap. Credit spread options enable the trading and hedging of changes in the credit quality of the specified reference credit. Options are usually calls or puts with a strike price at a particular credit spread (in basis points).

Calls or puts

- A call option will have a strike based on a particular credit spread. The option will be in the money (ITM) at expiry if the credit spread exceeds the strike price.
- A put option will compensate the buyer for a decline in the value of the asset below the chosen strike.

Bond vs benchmark

An investment bank may buy a put option from a fund manager and will need to pay an upfront premium. The option gives the bank the right, but not the obligation, to sell a bond at a particular strike price (spread over the bond) to the fund manager. At expiry, if the current credit spread is lower than the strike, the option is worthless. If the actual credit spread is higher than the strike, the option will be exercised, the investment bank delivers the bond in question to the fund manager who pays a price equal to the yield on the strike.

Bond vs bond

A hedge fund might consider that Venezuela risk is preferable to Chile risk, and that Venezuelan bonds will outperform those issued by Chile as Venezuelan credit risk will improve over and above that of Chile.

The hedge fund can take this view without buying or selling either bond. By entering into a credit spread option, using options on both countries' sovereign debt, the hedge fund could profit if after, say, twelve months, Venezuela had tightened more or widened less than the Chilean bonds.

Availability

Most of the investment and clearing banks have some capability in credit derivatives, although this is still a far smaller market than, say, interest rate swaps. It is vital to try and get competitive quotations and liquidity is sometimes a concern. As with any OTC product if you wish to sell it back, or terminate early, you will be dependent upon the original counterparty making you a competitive price. Transaction amounts tend to start at US$10 million and many are in the US$100 million range.

Practical considerations

Learn as much as you can about these products from your bankers and advisors, most of whom will have glossy brochures and will be happy to visit you to discuss potential transactions. But I would suggest as a caveat that you consider these instruments in a similar way to swaps. Don't enter into a credit derivative just because you can. You should see a clear end in sight, either in terms of risk mitigation, or profit, or advantage. Lastly, try not to substitute a weaker swap bank for the original counterparty.

Further reading

Mastering Credit Derivatives, by Andrew Kasapi, published by FT/Prentice Hall, 1999.

Credit Derivatives, by Janet M. Tavakoli, published by John Wiley & Sons Inc, USA, 1998.

Credit Derivatives. edited by Satyajit Das, published by John Wiley & Sons (Asia) Pte Ltd, Singapore 1998.

'If the rocket scientists can't get it right, what hope is there for us normal mortals?'

9

Risk and Managing Risk

Bernard Cowley

Background

To quote Andrew Sparrow in the May 1997 edition of *Professional Manager*

> *'The mere mention of the word risk is sufficient to send managers scurrying for the nearest exit and those who advise them to reach for their indemnity policies. However, the very essence of the board's role is to create tomorrow's company out of today's. Directors have a legal obligation to protect company assets and must prevent failure and ensure survival by succeeding in a rapidly changing world.'*

BACKGROUND

Barings Bank, Metallgesellschaft, Showa Shell, Orange County, London Borough of Hammersmith, Peregrine Investments, Sumitomo Corporation, Barclays Bank, NatWest Bank, Citibank, Salomon Bros., J P Morgan, LTCM – the list goes on. It is no surprise when senior managers, contemplating risk management strategies, regard the whole notion as being fraught with danger. If the rocket scientists can't get it right, what hope is there for us normal mortals?

Human beings have tried for millennia to manage and master risk. For all practical purposes they have never succeeded and almost certainly never will, although conventional risk-management techniques are capable of preventing most potential disasters from overwhelming the risk-manager. From time immemorial people have attempted to forecast the future for one reason or another – perhaps for profit, religious preference, political influence, or just the sheer pleasure of winning.

Brilliant scientists, mathematicians and philosophers have devoted time to the problem of managing risk. But, of course, certainty is an impossibility; the nearest we can get to certainty is that the sun will rise tomorrow, and there is even some doubt about that – not much, to be sure, but still some. The outcome has been some astonishing examples of the folly of human beings – the Russian meltdown, Barings, Metallgesellschaft, Procter & Gamble, Orange County, LTCM.

What has happened during the last 25 or 30 years is that information technology has been able to tackle most of the problems of risk-prevention calculation. But it has not yet been able to substitute the design of formulae and models that can be created by the human mind. Computing has given human beings the freedom to do in seconds what only 50 years ago would have taken months. And such is the state of software development that any business or individual interested in the analysis of risk can buy solutions off the peg. There is almost nothing in the world of finance that cannot be analyzed on an ordinary pc and, alongside the world of finance, in almost any sector of business, industry or pleasure the software now exists, cheaply and easily obtained, that will allow any ordinary person to analyze just about any risk.

The ability to define what may happen in the future and to decide on some alternative action or another is an important part of the behaviour of world society. Now that decision making must be more accurate and precise it is an imperative that managers understand much more about the risks they run. And any manager needs, more than ever before, to have a clear idea about the degree of risk aversion or risk proneness in his or her personality. For many managers, the days when intuition was enough has passed; although intuition still plays a major part in risk management, because the alternatives are probably better, managers need to get a grip on ways in which they can arrive at decisions more accurately, more quickly and in ways that allow them to sleep at night.

When the Arabic numbering system eventually reached the West in around 1200 AD, risk-management philosophy, particularly for gambling and gaming, became more sophisticated. There is even evidence that risk models were built for military purpose by medieval military men. But over time, by far the greatest activity in risk management was the pursuit of winning for pleasure, and many great mathematicians, particularly from the Renaissance onwards, devoted much of their time helping their masters to win at cards. Mathematical thinkers such as Pascal, Fermat and Napier provided fundamental ideas which are still very much in evidence today.

Mathematicians such as Thomas Bayes and Daniel Bernoulli discovered fundamental concepts which laid down the laws for risk management. And these laws rapidly allowed people to make systematic decisions by eliminating as much of the hazard of risk as possible. Over a period of about 100 years, from approximately 1650 to 1750, an incredible move forward in the understanding of risk through statistical analysis took place, and the theories developed then formed the bedrock of all our thinking today.

In the middle of the nineteenth century the agricultural industry in the USA took off. A growing population, fertile plains, and scientific skills were combined in producing a completely new approach to agriculture. Agriculture became an industry rather than a subsistence activity – surpluses were generated. But of course this immediately escalated the risk to the surplus farmer; would he get his expected yield? If he got the yield, what of the price? Into the breach stepped the entrepreneur; the risk taker. And these Chicago-based financiers realized, by taking on the risks run by the farmers, that profit was inevitable, provided that their calculations were anywhere near right. And they mostly were. Much as Dutch merchants of the fifteenth and sixteenth and seventeenth centuries had a clear understanding of international trade risk and, in conjunction with their bankers, were able to devise ways and means of avoiding financial loss which would frequently arise from the hazards of the day, so the Chicago traders were able to use a combination of intuition and mathematical skill to provide services of inestimable benefit to US agriculture, and, for that matter, the rest of us.

The Chicago commodity markets were really the first tangible evidence of the skilful and deliberately systematic management of commercial risk; and the dominance of this market in the world of finance and trade remains undiminished.

Gradually financial managers around the world in banks, in government, in industry, began to realize that there was profit, and loss avoidance, in the management of risk and that the statistical knowledge and calculating skills were available – as crude as they might be – but still remarkably effective.

The great wars fought in the twentieth century led to the even more systematic development of risk management. And, particularly from the end of the Second World War, academic mathematicians and econometricians were able to bridge the gap between the theoretical and the practical. In finance, perhaps the most important signpost to the future was provided by Harry Markowitz in the 1950s with his development of portfolio theory. This is a Nobel prize-winning concept, still very much the basis for managing stock portfolios, that provided the great leap forward for investors. Until Markowitz, an investor in any stock market was forced to use intuition, rather than systematic thinking, in designing a stock portfolio. Of course the 1950s saw the start of the massive development of pension funds, insurance funds, unit and mutual trusts, corporate investment, and world-wide savings movements.

In the world of finance over the last 30 years huge strides have been made in the management of risk in all areas and with all the products which bankers, finance managers and investors need to manage their risk. Probably foremost for financial managers the need to avoid loss, rather than to squeeze out extra profit, is paramount. An enormous amount of thinking and development has happened and even though dreadful mistakes are frequently made, the volume of risk-avoiding financial products and services has escalated in line with the growth of global communications. It is now easily possible for any financial manager, banker, or investor to arrange affairs in such a way as to reduce losses to a minimum and, probably, with careful management, to make a profit. The risk industry is definitely here to stay.

RISK – A PERSONAL CHARACTERISTIC

It is probably worth defining risk and one definition occurs more frequently than any of the others:

> *Financial risk is the possibility of exposure to monetary loss.*
>
> **Definition**

It all revolves around uncertainty and any degree of uncertainty. Risk management starts from the proposition that nothing is certain except uncertainty and it is therefore necessary to calculate the degree of uncertainty in any situation and to take whatever avoiding steps possible. Even then, there will be widely varying individual attitudes to risk and what one manager will consider virtually zero risk as another will see potential disaster. The interpretation of the 'facts' surrounding a risk by one individual or another will vary from optimistic to pessimistic. So it is all intensely personal.

Perhaps the best example of varying attitudes to risk of the past decade has been the attention paid to the Y2K bug. Even at a national level, the problem was viewed completely differently – the USA and the UK spent billions of dollars and pounds taking avoiding action – apparently successfully. Some nations, Russia (and many emerging nations) being the best examples, did virtually nothing. There is no evidence, as I write this, that there have been any devastating catastrophes!!

So it is necessary to accept that risk is a personal experience and attitudes towards the management of risk will depend very much on the individual's perspective. Underpinning this will be the necessity for risk managers always to learn to improve their knowledge of risk information and the value of techniques.

SPECIFIC RISK VS MARKET RISK

Risk can be usefully divided into divided into two distinct sections – **specific risk** which is the risk associated with a particular customer, supplier or financial instrument; and **market risk** which is the risk associated with the sector in which the company does its business and which will probably affect similarly all the other businesses in the market sector.

Specific risk

A manufacturer may be doing business with a particularly important single supplier of vital components which are imported and invoiced in the supplier's currency as a condition of the sale. The risk the buyer faces is not just the exchange risk associated with the purchase, but also the risk that the supplier may fail to deliver on time or delivers substandard components.

In order to manage the foreign exchange risk associated with the order, the buyer purchases currency through a forward contract. If the supplier reneges on the deal in some way, the buyer must still hold to the foreign exchange forward contract and will be left holding foreign currency, but will not have the components.

Market risk

Market risk is the risk associated with the market in which the company does its business. A manufacturer may be prominent in the meat-processing market. A government minister makes a statement in the House of Commons on the subject of BSE and its association with brain disease in humans. As a result any manufacturer or supplier in the beef-processing industry will suffer as the entire market becomes depressed – customers will desert them, their shareholders will sell out, banks will call in loans and there will be a severe loss of profits all round.

STRATEGY

Imagine you are the treasurer of XYZ plc, a large manufacturing business, importing and exporting to a wide range of countries around the world and with manufacturing sites in several different countries, some of which are virtually stand-alone businesses. Many of your customers and suppliers are national and international public companies and others may be government agencies. Some of your customers pay in £ sterling; others insist in paying in their domestic currency; others may demand to buy or sell in US dollars. Although you are frequently cash liquid, your business needs to borrow in several ways – you use bank overdrafts, medium- and long-term facilities; you have issued bonds of varying maturities in varying currencies. The business is large enough to attract international investment and your shares trade as American depositary receipts in New York. As treasurer of a business like XYZ, your whole life will be spent in attempting to manage the various risks to which the business is exposed.

An aware financial management will have clear ideas about the management of risk; and our example company, XYZ plc, would probably have taken definable steps to set up the business effectively to manage the risk process.

- XYZ would define their risk evaluation strategy – they would have a clear idea of where the primary risks lie – in our example this would be pretty much across the range of the company's activities. The areas would include manufacturing and production, capital expenditure, purchasing, sales, shipping, administration. In fact, just about every facet of business activity.

- They would document their risk policies and this would be approved by the board of directors and senior management. There would be clear internal understanding of the corporate risk-management objectives. Communication of risk strategies, at all levels and in all directions, would be unambiguous.

- They would measure their hedging and risk-management performance by using a range of performance measures fully to evaluate risk-management effectiveness historically.

- XYZ would hire only well-qualified experienced people into risk management, well versed in the technicalities of risk control.

- They would segregate their back-office, administrative, functions from the trading function.

- The company would create business-wide service-level agreements, internal and external. They would have firm communications links with customers, suppliers, bankers, auditors, and lawyers. And these connections would be designed to protect against risk both ways.

- Reporting systems would be reliable and centred around the provision of accurate and consistent data, which themselves would flow from intelligent and well-designed information technology.

- XYZ would buy their risk solutions competitively.

- Although as much as possible would be done to prevent disasters, there would still be the need for clear recovery strategies; and teams would be developed to manage and revive if risk problems strike.

Let's look at these risks in some detail.

FOREIGN EXCHANGE RISK

Foreign Exchange probably poses the greatest immediate risk.

The foreign exchange markets are predictable only to a degree and it is perfectly possible to manage dealings in such a way as to virtually eliminate excessive risk. But it can be costly, and it is generally an illusion to imagine that currency exposure can be hedged to zero, free of cost. There are many schools of thought in foreign exchange markets, some of which are more appealing to the treasurer than others. Some businesses, with vast amounts of exposure to currencies other than their own domestic currency, regard the process as being literally the most important element of their activities – almost a reason for existence. It's difficult not to gain the impression with some companies that their trading and manufacturing activities are regarded as being subsidiary to their exchange dealing activities. And many companies are extremely successful at their forex dealings. The very largest global and international businesses are able, through sheer size, to bypass the conventional banking forex markets and to maintain their defences successfully and profitably. They buy and sell forward; they use options, futures and swaps with great skill. And what is more they can move markets because of their sheer size and volume of their trading and dealing activities. In fact, the treasury departments of these global businesses are, for all practical purposes, banks. Examples of this would be the largest oil companies (BP-Amoco, Shell), the great car manufacturers (Toyota, General Motors, Ford), industrial giants like General Electric or ABB) and the global investment banks.

Because XYZ is experienced and well equipped they would be using a wide range of risk and loss-avoidance techniques (you will need to look elsewhere in this book for the full detail, description and appropriate place for these techniques). For instance:

- **Forward currency transactions** – XYZ plc would be able to fix, at the time of a contract or sale, a price for the purchase or sale of a fixed amount of foreign currency for delivery and payment at a specified future time. This means the future payment or receipt will be known exactly, in £ sterling. However, in the real business world, it does not always happen that a payment is made exactly on the expected date; XYZ may decide to cover this uncertain exposure, so they may choose to use:

- **Option dated forwards** – in this case the exchange rate is irrevocably fixed when the contract is made; but the precise maturity date is left open; although there will be a caveat which says the maturity date must fall within a specified period and the other party – a bank – will make a charge. The decision is whether the cost of the protection is greater than the potential loss or vice versa. However, the forward currency option may not be quite what is needed so XYZ plc may set up a:

- **Currency option** – this derivative risk tool is a classical form of hedge. The currency option gives XYZ plc the right, not the obligation, to buy or sell a specific amount of currency at a specific exchange rate, on or before a specific future date; and XYZ would pay a premium. So XYZ has the opportunity to fix the rate of exchange that might apply to a transaction taking place in the future. But the main advantage to XYZ will be that it will not be necessary to go ahead with the option if the treasurer can find a better, more advantageous, rate elsewhere.

- **Currency swap** – this is probably a cheaper alternative and involves the simultaneous buying and selling of a currency for different maturities. Swap deals used for forward cover are usually of two different types –

forward/forward or spot/forward. In either case, XYZ plc begins by covering the foreign transaction forward to an arbitrary, but fixed, date – this would be just as in an ordinary fixed date forward contract. So, if the precise settlement date is eventually agreed before the initial forward contract matures, the original settlement date may be extended to the exact date by a forward/forward swap. If, however, an exact settlement date is not agreed by the date when the initial forward contract matures, the forward cover may be extended by a spot/forward swap.

- From time to time, XYZ would enter the spot market and buy or sell at the current rate, but only when the risk is calculated to be negligible.

INTEREST RATE RISK

The risk here is not only for borrowers but also for lenders and investors. The actual interest rate cost for a borrower will be a substantial element of the business costs, and the opportunity cost of interest rate risk for a company that is liquid will always be at the front of the treasurer's mind as he contemplates the bottom line. The dilemma for the financial manager is whether always to strive for protection against higher interest rate costs – reducing the risk almost to zero through hedging – or to go for profit through a degree of speculation by betting for or against interest rate fluctuations.

There are many ways in which the treasurer of XYZ would protect or hedge against interest rate risk by using a variety of derivatives which could include:

- Forward rate agreements – defined as a legally binding agreement between two parties to determine the rate of interest to be applied to a notional loan or deposit, of an agreed amount to be drawn or placed, on an agreed future date (the settlement date) for a specified term. The bank will guarantee (or insure) a rate of interest for a transaction which starts on a future date. XYZ plc is legally obligated to transact at that rate, so is 'locked' into the FRA interest rate; if rates move adversely, XYZ will be protected and receive a cash settlement equivalent to the difference between the FRA rate and the LIBOR fixing, but if rates move in his favour there will be no profit as XYZ plc is committed to pay a cash settlement to the other party.

- Interest rate swaps – this is where two parties (usually a bank will act as a broker between them) agree to meet each other's interest rate payments when they become due. It may be that XYZ can generally borrow at advantageous fixed interest rates, but takes the view that interest rates will fall below their current rates. Another company takes the opposite view, or finds it impossible to raise fixed interest finance.

The two companies simply swap their interest. The agreement applies only to the interest payments and not to the loans or principal.

- A series of futures and options contracts relative to their interest rate strategies.

COMMODITY RISK

For any manufacturer commodity risk is a constant source of problems. Apart from the really major players, most businesses are primarily helpless in the world of commodities – whether base metals, precious metals, barley, wheat or pork bellies. Commodities are intensely sensitive to market forces and managing the sale or purchase risks demands constant attention. Clearly, as with most definable risks, there are ways to manage commodity risk; but it is at a cost. And it is a foolish manager who contemplates taking on the markets single-handed – some have tried, the result usually being a spectacular catastrophe. The best (or worst) example of this was the fiasco in 1996 when Yasuo Hamanaka, the 'world's most famous copper trader' and an employee of Sumitomo Corporation, disclosed that he had managed to lose his company somewhere in the region of $3bn over a period of about ten years by engaging in unauthorized transactions in the futures and options markets.

INVESTMENT RISK

In our example of XYZ plc, the global manufacturer, the opportunities for profitable and safe investment of surplus capital is an important element in the management of the business. There is little point in storing up reserves of cash in low-interest bank accounts – it may be safe, but there is a high opportunity cost. The techniques for developing managed investment portfolios are well known and well tried.

Markowitz, nearly half a century ago, developed his portfolio theory and transformed the world of investment from a relatively crude, intuitive form of endeavour into a highly sophisticated method of avoiding or managing investment risk. Markowitz postulated that:

- The overall portfolio risk is less than the weighted average of the individual risks.
- The portfolio risk will be lower the more diversified the assets.
- The risk of an individual asset comprises two parts – one which can be diversified away and the other which is ever present and must be carried by the investor.

For any prudent investor, intelligently using the Markowitz principles, selecting a portfolio is reduced to the simple task of producing maximum returns while minimizing the risk. There are few professional investors who prefer intuition to the relatively simple processes of portfolio management. If XYZ plc regards the investment of surplus funds as being a medium- to long-term activity it will certainly enter the bond market, both as investor and issuer. And it will certainly be interested in value at risk as a technique.

VALUE AT RISK (VaR)

VaR measures the maximum loss that a portfolio is likely to encounter over a specific period of time, assuming certain essentials about the behaviour and volatility of security prices. VaR was developed, mainly by investment banks, as a different way of managing and controlling risks through position limits on dealers and traders. The technique is used mainly, in financial institutions, although many supranational, global businesses which are heavily involved in risk management and have their own dealing rooms have adopted VaR as a main tool in the fight against the downside of risk.

There is little doubt that VaR is, in some ways, a technique superior to previously well-used risk-management methods. But VaR is not a panacea. There are many serious problems associated with both concepts and implementation – particularly to do with the gathering of data and the use of third party data bases, which supply the critical information for designing the VaR criteria. But as the data needed for effective VaR can be extremely difficult to manage, the corporate treasurer will need to be aware of the many pitfalls of VaR.

For instance, the technique really only works at its best in highly liquid markets across a wide portfolio of investments. Without liquidity, reliable prices are not available by which to calculate rates of return. If there are wide and large adverse price movements, portfolio managers may find themselves stuck with the need to sell large quantities of a security, so depressing the price further – especially when there are other finance managers out there doing the same thing. VaR has been known severely to underestimate the severity of bad outcomes when markets are less than highly liquid – this circumstance is much more likely to occur with corporates rather than banks. The banks and other major financial institutions will, inevitably, be operating in much wider and more liquid markets than even the largest non-financial company.

There is growing interest in VaR now that the data needed are becoming more and more available and are much more reliable. VaR assesses risk by using standard statistical techniques, for example Monte Carlo simulation. What VaR does is to measure the worst expected loss over a given time interval under normal market conditions at a given confidence level. This means that, for instance, a bank or a dealing company might say that the daily VaR of its trading portfolio is £200million at the 99 per cent confidence level – which means that there is only one chance in 100, given normal market conditions, for a loss greater than £200 million to occur. VaR is a sophisticated technique and will require the treasurer to make complicated calculations about the statistical properties of the rates of return within the underlying portfolio and the consequent decisions as to the confidence levels, and this can only be done by accurate calculation of the standard deviations and the volatility of the components of the portfolio. The resultant single number is a summary of the banks or company's exposure to market risk. And what is more important for general management is that it measures risk using a recognizable unit – £ sterling!

In October 1994 J P Morgan unveiled a new, free, data system called RiskMetrics™. This initially made available risk measures for over 300 financial instruments across 14 countries and has been greatly expanded since and is now a separately marketed entity. There are several sites to visit on the Internet, and probably the most useful is www.riskmetrics. com which is a stand-alone risk site with many valuable references to RiskMetrics.

RiskMetrics has spawned an army of system developers and encouraged rival banks to develop new generations of risk-management systems. Other systems are quickly coming onto the market. In contrast with RiskMetrics, which is basically a data-feed, Bankers Trust made available a system, called RAROC 2020™, which is based on its internal, extensive, risk-management experience. The RAROC system integrates the risk-management calculation with volatility forecasts to produce value at risk measures. The system is sophisticated in that it can incorporate assets not normally distributed or with non-linear payoffs, such as options and collateralized mortgage obligations.

If the treasurer of XYZ plc is keeping a wary eye on the risk ball then a visit to some of the more informative risk-associated web sites on the Internet will be a normal part of the day's function. One of the best places to go is www.intltreasurer.com – this site has an enormous amount of up-to-date information on risk policies and risk management; www.contingencyanalysis.com is equally as informative.

Other excellent sites are:

- www.dc3.co.uk (Delphi Risk Management)
- www.gtnews.com

These sites are global in their context.

'The main approaches to accounting for derivatives are:

- mark-to-market or fair value accounting
- accruals accounting
- hedge accounting.'

10

First Principles of Accounting for Derivatives

Deborah Morton-Dare
ACA, BSc

Introduction

Fundamental accounting concepts

Reporting requirements

Fair value and mark-to-market accounting

Accruals accounting

Fair value vs hedge accounting

Accounting treatment

Recent accounting guidelines

International standards

INTRODUCTION

This chapter provides an introduction to the accounting for derivatives. The principles of accounting and bookkeeping are a large topic in themselves so this chapter assumes that the reader has a basic knowledge of double-entry bookkeeping.

Typically, there are two circumstances where the reader may need to have a knowledge of accounting for derivatives:

- In order to review, understand or prepare accounts. In these circumstances it is important to have an understanding of the disclosure requirements for derivatives.

- In order to make the bookkeeping entries required to account for a derivative transaction that has been undertaken.

This chapter covers the basic accounting principles first, covers the detailed bookkeeping entries required for different types of instruments, and then discusses disclosure requirements. At the end an overall approach to accounting for a new derivative transaction is set out.

FUNDAMENTAL ACCOUNTING CONCEPTS

Statement of Standard Accounting Practice (SSAP) 2 gives the basic accounting principles to be used as a guide for accounting treatment. SSAP 2 defines four fundamental accounting concepts, which underlie the preparation of all sets of accounts:

- **Going concern** – Accounts are prepared on the basis that the enterprise will continue in operational existence for the foreseeable future. This means, in particular, that the profit and loss account and balance sheet assume no intention or necessity to liquidate or curtail significantly the scale of the operation.

- **Matching or accruals** – Revenues or costs are recognized as they are earned or incurred, not as money is received or paid. Revenues and costs are matched with one another as far as their relationship can be established or justifiably assumed and dealt with in the profit and loss account of the period to which they relate.

- **Consistency** – There is consistency of accounting treatment of like items within each accounting period and from one period to the next.

- **Prudence** – Revenues or profits will not be anticipated, but only accounted for when ultimate realization can be assessed with reasonable certainty. Conversely, provision is made for expenses or losses as soon as they are identified, even if precise quantification is difficult.

REPORTING REQUIREMENTS

The derivatives industry is probably the most global industry that exists today. A derivative user in one country might order a futures trade via a broker in another country which gets executed in yet another country. At present the disclosure requirements are different in most countries. Often, an international company or financial institution may have to report in several different accounting jurisdictions. For example, a Swiss bank operating in London, listed in the USA, will have to report in line with US, Swiss and UK reporting requirements. It is not appropriate to cover all the reporting requirements for every jurisdiction in this chapter. However, this chapter does cover the various different approaches to accounting that exist and the reporting requirements for the UK.

The main approaches to accounting for derivatives are:

- mark-to-market or fair value accounting
- accruals accounting
- hedge accounting.

FAIR VALUE AND MARK-TO-MARKET ACCOUNTING

Mark-to-market (MTM) is the term used to describe the market value of open positions held. Any movement in value will result in an unrealized profit or loss on that position.

Mark-to-market accounting values derivatives transactions at the economic or market value of the transaction. This market value is often very different from the impression that you might get from considering the immediate cash flows from a derivatives transaction. For example, cash could be paid out on the next payment of a swap even though it has a positive mark-to-market.

Financial Reporting Standard (FRS) 13, 'Derivatives and other Financial Instruments: Disclosures', is discussed at the end of the chapter. This defines fair value as:

> 'The amount at which an asset or liability could be exchanged in an arm's length transaction between informed and willing parties, other than in a forced or liquidation sale.'

ACCRUALS ACCOUNTING

Many financial instruments are accounted for on an accruals basis, in line with the fundamental accounting concept just defined. For example, a simple loan is typically accounted for as the payment of some principal at the beginning and the end of the loan. During the life of the loan there may be interest payments made, which are normally accrued for over the period between each interest payment. The balance sheet value of the loan will therefore be the principal amounts plus any accrued interest. This value is likely to be different from the market value of a similar instrument such as a bond that has an identifiable market value.

Many derivatives when broken down into their constituent parts can be viewed as if they are made up of simpler financial instruments. For example, a cross-currency swap is essentially a loan in one currency, combined with a deposit in another. It is therefore possible to account for a cross-currency swap as a loan or a deposit on the balance sheet.

A number of European countries require this accounting treatment for derivatives.

FAIR VALUE VS HEDGE ACCOUNTING

One major reason for using derivatives is to provide a hedge against other transactions. For example, a bank may make a five-year fixed rate loan but fund the loan with a floating rate deposit. The bank is therefore exposed to interest rate risk if the rate on deposit increases. The bank could use an interest rate swap to hedge this risk.

It is important that the loan, deposit and interest swap are accounted for on a consistent basis, in line with the fundamental accounting concept defined earlier. For example, if the loan and deposit are accounted for on an accruals accounting basis, while the swap is marked-to-market then the loans and deposit will show a relatively constant value in the balance sheet over time while the swap would fluctuate from day to day. This will give a misleading impression of the economics of the transaction.

In order to avoid this kind of problem all the components of this transaction must be accounted for on the same basis. In this example, one approach would be to account for the loan, deposit and swap on an accruals basis. An alternative approach is to account for all of the transactions on a marked-to-market basis.

ACCOUNTING TREATMENT

When considering the appropriate accounting treatment of derivatives, it is necessary to focus first on the way in which they are used by the reporting entity, considering the management's intention when entering into the transaction. The following distinctions are made:

- Transactions entered into for trading purposes – fair value accounting. If an instrument has been entered into for trading or for speculative positions, then fair value or mark-to-market accounting will be appropriate. This results in the asset or liability being shown and any gains or losses arising from changes in the fair value being recognized immediately in the profit and loss account.

- Transactions entered into for hedging purposes – hedge accounting. A hedge is an instrument that individually, or with other instruments, has a value or cash flow that is expected to move inversely with changes in the value or cash flows of the position being hedged. The intention of entering into a hedge is to reduce or offset a risk to which the entity is exposed. Any gains or losses on the hedge should, therefore, be matched to the same period and accounted for on the same basis as the transaction that is being hedged. This is the application of the accounting concept of matching and accruals.

The significance for accounting of the distinction made is to show a true and fair view in the accounts of the commercial effect of the transaction and whether it gives rise to changes in assets, liabilities, gains or losses for the entity undertaking it. The preference of the Accounting Standards Board (ASB) in the UK is to use fair value accounting unless it does not give a true and fair view. The application of this method of accounting will be illustrated throughout the chapter. Alternative methods are discussed at the end of the chapter.

Determining accounting events

All financial instruments have several accounting events over their lifetime. Accounting events involve:

- cash flows – either money is received or paid
- the creation of future cash flows which are:
  - an asset or liability, or
  - a gain or loss.

The first step in the accounting treatment for a financial instrument is to determine the accounting events involved, and whether these give rise to cash flows or whether they involve an accrual for a future cash flow, either an asset or liability, gain or loss.

Accounting for cash flows is normally an operational accounting event and is usually simple to account for, as the value is known. If the accounting event does not involve cash, valuations will have to be made and this can involve far more complex issues. Valuations of assets and liabilities, gains and losses are normally made by financial accounting departments, often as part of financial reporting requirements. Valuations will usually involve the instrument being marked-to-market. More complex issues over valuations are not covered in this chapter.

The accounting events involved during the lifetime of an instrument will be illustrated by looking at examples of accounting for swaps, financial futures and options. The basic principles illustrated can be applied to accounting for all financial instruments.

It is assumed in all the following examples that the instrument is marked-to-market.

Accounting for swaps

The different types of swaps that exist are discussed in detail in other chapters. To illustrate the key principles of the accounting treatment we will look at an interest rate swap and a cross-currency swap.

Interest rate swaps – accounting events involved

For interest rate swaps the first accounting point to note is that on deal date there is no exchange of principal and so the accounting is not for a cash flow, but for a trading asset or liability which will need to be marked-to-market periodically. There will then be periodic payments for interest rate differentials and these will be cash flow accounting events.

The accounting that follows is for an interest rate swap sold by a bank for trading purposes. The accounting for interest rate swaps entered into for dealing or speculative purposes is on an accruals basis with the asset or liability marked to market, the resulting profit or loss being taken to the profit and loss account in the period in which it arises.

Deal date and each reporting date:

> DR/CR market value swaps
> DR/CR P&L

Each swap payment/receipt date:

> DR/CR net settlement
> DR/CR cash

Example

On 1 April, 2000, you enter into a one-year interest-rate swap to receive fixed at 7.8% pay floating interest rate swap. The floating leg pays 6-month LIBOR + ten basis points (0.1%). The notional principal amount is £15million. Coupons are paid semi-annually.

LIBOR is 7.5% on 1 April, 2000 (this will be paid in October 2000 in arrears) and 8.0% on 1 October, 2000 (paid in April 2001 in arrears).

It is marked-to-market with a value of:

GBP 15,000 on 30 April, 2000
GBP 2,000 on 30 May, 2000

At 30 April, 2000:

DR MTM swaps	15,000	
CR P&L		15,000

Swap receipt on 1 October, 2000 on April, 2000 rate.

Receipt amount $(7.8\% - 7.5\% - 0.1\%) \times 15,000,000 \times 181/365 = £14,959$

DR cash	14,959	
CR P&L		14,959

Note that the mark-to-market on 1 October, 2000, will automatically drop by exactly £14,959 to reflect the receipt of the payment.

DR P&L	14,959	
CR MTM swaps		14,959

On 1 April, 2001, the value of the swap has reversed and there will be a swap payment on the October 2000 rate.

Payment amount $(7.8\% - 8.0\% - 0.1\%) \times 15,000,000 \times 182/365 = 22,438$

DR P&L	22,438	
CR cash		22,438

Mark-to-market valuation

The mark-to-market valuation of interest rate swaps estimates the net present value of future cash flows expected to arise under each swap at current market interest rates. Future cash flows and the notional principals should be discounted to a present value using zero-coupon yield curve rates.

The future cash flows for the fixed rate leg are obviously known. The future cash flows of the floating rate leg are determined by future interest rates, which are not known. The market value therefore has to be calculated from the next known cash flow. This is based on the rate set at the beginning of the interest period, as illustrated in the previous example.

Other factors which need to be taken into account in the marked-to-market valuation are future credit risks, any significant future administration costs and close out costs. Any provisions needed will reduce the marked-to-market valuation and be taken to the profit and loss account.

Cross currency swaps – accounting events involved

The first accounting point to note for cross-currency swaps is that, unlike interest rate swaps, on deal date there *is* an exchange of principal and so the accounting is for a cash flow. On deal date the counterparties will exchange principals in one currency for another, exchanging a debt raised in one currency into a liability in another. The rate of exchange is normally the spot rate at the date of the transaction. The resulting asset or liability will be periodically marked-to-market.

As with interest rate swaps, periodic payments are then exchanged over the term of the swap based on the agreed interest rates on the principal amounts in the different currencies. The interest can be fixed to floating; fixed to fixed; or floating to floating. These cash flows are accounted for as with interest rate swaps.

At maturity, the counterparties re-exchange the principal amounts at the same exchange rate agreed at the outset of the transaction and so there is another cash flow to account for.

Mark-to-market valuation

The mark-to-market valuation of cross-currency swaps estimates the net present value of future cash flows expected to.arise under each swap at current exchange rates and current interest rates in each currency with the resulting profit or loss being taken to the profit and loss account.

The future cash flows for a fixed rate leg are obviously known. The future cash flows of a floating rate leg are determined by future interest rates, which are not known. The market value therefore has to be calculated from the next known cash flow. This is based on the rate set at the beginning of the interest period, as illustrated in the interest rate swap example.

Other factors which need to be taken into account in the marked-to-market valuation are future credit risks, any significant future administration costs and close-out costs. Any provisions needed will reduce the marked-to-market valuation and be taken to the profit and loss account.

Cross-currency swap accounting

The accounting that follows is for a cross-currency swap sold by a bank for trading purposes.

The basic principle behind the accounting is that there is a loan with one set of terms and a deposit with another, the difference being with a swap the resulting balance sheet and profit and loss figures should be netted off.

Deal date – mark-to-market:

DR/CR	Market value currency 1 leg
DR/CR	P&L currency 1 leg
DR/CR	Market value currency 2 leg
DR/CR	P&L currency 2 leg

Value date first principal exchange:

DR	Currency 1 cash
CR	Currency 1 cross-currency swaps
DR	Currency 2 cross-currency swaps
CR	Currency 2 cash

Each swap payment date:

DR/CR	Currency 1 P&L
DR/CR	Cash currency 1
DR/CR	Currency 2 P&L
DR/CR	Cash currency 2

Maturity – principal exchange:

DR	Currency 1 cross-currency swaps
CR	Currency 1 cash
DR	Currency 2 cash
CR	Currency 2 cross-currency swaps

Example

On 1 April, 2000, you enter into a one-year cross-currency swap to receive DEM fixed at 5.1% and pay GBP 6-month LIBOR floating interest rate swap. The notional principal amount is DEM 20 million and GBP 6,451,612. Coupons are paid semi-annually.

GBP LIBOR is 7.5% on 1 April, 2000, and 8.0% on 1 October, 2001. The DEM/GBP exchange rate is 3.1 on 1 April, 2000, and 2.9 on 31 March, 2001.

The mark-to-market on 30 April, 2000, is as follows:

DEM leg:	19,950,322
GBP leg:	6,420,482

Initial principal exchange

DR DEM cross-currency swaps	DEM 20,000,000	
CR DEM cash		DEM 20,000,000

| DR GBP cash | GBP 6,451,612 | |
| CR GBP cross-currency swaps | | GBP 6,451,612 |

MTM at 30 April, 2000

| DR P&L DEM | DEM 49,678 | |
| CR MTM swaps DEM | | DEM 49,678 |

| DR MTM swaps GBP | GBP 31,130 | |
| CR P&L GBP | | GBP 31,130 |

Swap payment on 1 October, 2000

Swap receipt: $5.1\% \times 20,000,000 \times 181/365 =$ DEM 505,802
Swap payment: $7.5\% \times 6,451,612 \times 181/365 =$ GBP 239947

| DR cash | DEM 505,802 | |
| CR P&L | | DEM 505,802 |

| DR P&L | GBP 239,947 | |
| CR cash | | GBP 239,947 |

Swap payment on 1 April, 2001

Swap receipt: $5.1\% \times 20,000,000 \times 181/365 =$ DEM 505,802
Swap payment: $8.0\% \times 6,451,612 \times 181/365 =$ GBP 255,943

| DR cash | DEM 505,802 | |
| CR P&L | | DEM 505,802 |

| DR P&L | GBP 255,943 | |
| CR cash | | GBP 255,943 |

Final principal exchange

| DR DEM cash | DEM 20,000,000 | |
| CR DEM cross-currency swaps | | DEM 20,000,000 |

| DR GBP cross-currency swaps | GBP 6,451,612 | |
| CR GBP cash | | GBP 6,451,612 |

Accounting for futures

A futures contract is an obligation to buy or sell a specific amount of a financial instrument or commodity or a security at a specific time, with the contract traded on an exchange.

Futures contracts – accounting events involved

At inception of the contract no monetary entry is made for the underlying value of the commodity itself. Both parties to the contract have to deposit an initial margin with the clearing house. This cash flow is accounted for and a trading asset recorded.

During the period when the contract is open, a daily mark-to-market valuation is accounted for and an adjustment made to the trading asset or liability account. The net price difference with the previous day's valuation is settled in cash with the clearing house as a variation margin. The party showing a loss will have to pay a variation margin to the clearing house; the party showing a profit will receive a variation margin from the clearing house.

When the contract is closed the resulting cash flows are accounted for. Most contracts are matched off with a reverse contract before the settlement date.

Deal date – Initial margin paid:

| DR | Trading assets – futures margin account |
| CR | Cash |

Daily mark-to-market:

| DR/CR | Trading assets – futures margin account |
| DR/CR | Profit and loss |

Accrual for variation margins due or owed:

| DR/CR | Trading assets – futures margin account |
| DR/CR | Sundry assets/liabilities |

Settlement of variation margins received or paid:

| DR/CR | Sundry assets/liabilities |
| DR/CR | Cash |

A broker buys long 1 platinum (50 troy oz) 6 months @£690.

Example

Value date: deposit initial margin
Initial margin @(£34,500 × 5%)

DR trading assets – futures margin account – initial margin   1725
CR cash   1725

Daily mark-to-market
End of trading Day 1: platinum falls to £689 giving rise to loss of £1 × 50. This becomes a liability to pay the variation margin to the clearing house.

DR P&L	50	
CR trading assets – futures margin account		50

Accrual for variation margins owed

DR trading assets – futures margin account – variation margin	50	
CR sundry liabilities – variation margin		50

Settlement of variation margin

DR sundry liabilities – variation margin	50	
CR cash		50

Closure of contract
If contract is closed @£690

DR cash	1725	
CR Trading assets – futures margin account		1725

Accounting for options

The right, but not the obligation, for the buyer of an option to buy or sell a specific asset or index at a pre-determined price at a specified future date or period. The buyer pays a premium for the option.

Options are accounted for on a mark-to-market basis as with other instruments. It is important to remember the possible values of an option position. If the company has sold an option, the value of the deal can never be greater than the premium received; however, the downside is unlimited. Likewise, if the company has bought an option the value can never be less than the premium paid.

Accounting
The accounting that follows is for an option sold.
Deal date:

DR cash premium received
CR options dealing account

Each reporting date:

DR/CR options dealing account mark-to-market movement
DR/CR P&L

On exercise if out of the money for the company

DR options dealing account
CR cash

On 1 January the company sells a £50,000 three month FT-SE 100 put option with a strike price of 3,000. It is exactly at the money and the premium is £4,000.

On 31 January the FT-SE has gone to 4,000 and the time value is £2,000.
On 28 February the FT-SE is at 2,000 and the time value is £1,000.
On 31 March, the exercise date, the market price is 3,000 exactly.

At 1 January

DR cash	4000	
CR option dealing account		4000

At 31 January

DR option dealing account	2000	
CR P&L		2000

At 28 February

MTM of contract = $50,000/3000 \times 2,000 = 33,333$
Decrease in intrinsic value $50,000 - 33,333 = 16,667$
Total value = $16,667 + 1,000 = 17,667$
Adjustment to balance sheet value = $17,667 - 2,000 = 15,667$

DR P&L	15,667	
CR options dealing account		15,667

At 31 March

Exercise value = 0
Time value = 0

Option is not exercised

DR option dealing account	15,667	
CR P&L		15,667

RECENT ACCOUNTING GUIDELINES

The accounting treatment of financial instruments, and of derivatives in particular, has been under review in the UK by the Accounting Standards Board (ASB) and been the subject of recent guidelines. The ASB was concerned that financial instruments can change very significantly and alter the risk profile of an entity in a way that was not made apparent under previous reporting practices. The value of a derivative can change substantially representing an asset or a liability at a year end, which was not apparent under accounting standards. Under the historical cost accounting convention, potential gains or losses are not reported as they arise, but are deferred until realized.

Financial Reporting Standard (FRS) 13, 'Derivatives and other Financial Instruments: Disclosures'

This was published in September 1998 and is the first instalment of the ASB's rules on financial instruments. The standard only deals with the issue of disclosure and does not cover the more contentious measurement aspects. It is unlikely that an accounting standard will be in place on measurement proposals in the UK and the Republic of Ireland before 2001.

FRS 13 covers all reporting entities:

1 that have any of its capital instruments listed or publicly traded on a stock exchange or market

2 or that are a bank or similar institution or a banking or similar group.

Insurance companies or groups do not have to comply with this standard. The second category means that all banks and similar institutions, whether they are quoted or not, have to comply with the standard. The distinction is made in the requirements of the standard between the following categories of institution:

1 reporting entities other than financial institutions and financial institution groups

2 banks and similar institutions and banking and similar groups

3 other financial institutions and financial institution groups.

The objective of FRS 13 states:

'The objective of this FRS is to ensure that reporting entities within its scope provide in their financial statements disclosures that enable users to assess the entity's objectives, policies and strategies for holding or issuing financial instruments. In particular, such information should enable users to assess:

a) the risk profile of the entity for each of the main financial risks that arise in connection with financial instruments and commodity contracts with similar characteristics; and

b) the significance of such instruments and contracts to the entity's reported financial position, performance and cash flows, regardless of whether the instruments and contracts are on balance sheet (recognised) or off balance sheet (unrecognised).'

The standard aims to achieve this objective by narrative and numerical disclosures, giving a broad overview of the entity's financial instruments and of the risks positions created by them, focusing on those risks and instruments that are of greatest significance.

The standard states:

'The FRS requires specific numerical disclosures to be provided about:
- *interest rate risk*
- *currency risk*
- *liquidity risk*
- *fair values*
- *financial instruments used for trading (including, for banks and some other financial institutions, information on the market price risk of their trading book)*
- *financial instruments used for hedging*
- *certain commodity contracts'.*

Reference should be made to the standard for further details and definitions.

On measurement proposals for which an accounting standard has not yet been issued in the UK, the ASB's discussion paper proposed that the best approach would be for all financial instruments to be measured at fair value. Included are derivatives and non-derivatives, assets and liabilities. This would mean a significant change from present practices, but was also the conclusion reached by other standard-setting bodies, such as the IASC and the FASB.

Hedge-accounting practices were also covered in the discussion paper and the possibility raised of prohibiting or significantly restricting such practices.

INTERNATIONAL STANDARDS

The Joint Working Group of Accounting Standard Setters on Accounting for Financial Instruments (JWG) has been set up to develop an internationally acceptable accounting standard on financial instruments. The group consists of nine national standard setters and delegates of the IASC.

The JWG has adopted the proposal that all financial instruments should be measured at fair value and that all gains and losses arising from changes in those fair values should be recognized immediately in the profit and loss account. The implications for hedge accounting will be considered. If both the hedging instrument and the item it hedges are measured at fair value, all changes will be immediately recognized in the profit and loss account and there is a significant reduction in the need for hedge accounting.

In response to the IASC, the British Bankers' Association (BBA) has accepted that the fair value convention is relevant to financial instruments held in banks' trading books, but objects to its use for non-trading books as these instruments are not actively traded and are entered into over the longer term. Other objections are that in the absence of market prices, estimates of fair value are unacceptably subjective. An aim of fair value and harmonized risk disclosures is more appropriate across a bank's entire balance sheet than universal fair value.

Conclusion – an approach to accounting for a new derivatives transaction

In conclusion, this chapter sets out a step-by-step approach to accounting for a new derivatives transaction.

1 Determine the reason why the organization has entered into the transaction. This will help determine the correct accounting treatment for the transaction. A transaction that is clearly for trading purposes or is hedging transactions that are marked-to-market will normally be marked-to-market. If a transaction is a hedge and the items being hedged are accounted for on an accruals basis then it may be appropriate to use hedge accounting.

2 Check your local jurisdictions reporting requirements and determine how to apply them, based on your knowledge of the transaction.

3 Identify and account for any initial entries required at the date the deal was executed.

4 Identify an account for any initial cash flows, such as the principal exchange on a cross-currency swap, or initial margin on a future.

5 Identify and account for an interim cash flows that may occur. These might include swap coupon payments or variation margin.

6 At each reporting date value the derivative either on a mark-to-market basis or on an accruals basis.

7 At the end of the life of the transaction account for the closing entries.

At each reporting date you should make sure that the valuation is reasonable, given what you know of the commercial intention of the transactions. If you are using hedge accounting you should ensure that, if you look at the total profit of all the related transactions, they have produced the correct overall profit.

'The compliance function must be alert to the danger of ethical creep, or a shifting in the acceptable level of ethics due to a familiarity with the regulations and the innovative atmosphere in a derivatives practitioner, leading to a diminishing of the ethical hurdle over time. '

The Compliance Function in a UK Derivatives Practitioner

Tony Blunden
OperationalRisk.com

INTRODUCTION

A derivatives practitioner has a very broad compliance brief. The content of that brief is primarily determined by whether the practitioner enters into OTC derivatives, exchange-traded derivatives, structured projects involving derivatives or any combination of the three. The practical scope of the compliance function can vary greatly between two similar organizations depending on how responsibility is shared between the compliance, legal, internal audit, operational risk and operations functions.

All derivatives practitioners in the UK are regulated by the Financial Services Authority (FSA) under the financial services and markets legislation. The FSA has replaced a number of regulatory organizations that existed under the previous UK regulatory regime. It has promulgated regulatory principles which must be complied with and which stem, in the main, from normal corporate ethics. It is producing a comprehensive rulebook covering such areas as financial rules, client money, conduct of business rules, complaints and arbitration and enforcement. It is ultimately the responsibility of the chief executive of any UK derivatives practitioner to ensure adherence to these rules. However, the chief executive will generally assign some or all of the responsibility to business management and to a compliance function, although it is recognized that the prime influence on a firm's compliance culture is the leadership of that firm.

THE ROLE OF COMPLIANCE

The task of ensuring that an organization complies with the rules of any relevant regulatory authority is paramount for the compliance function. A practitioner should promote within itself a culture of compliance, a responsibility which should be taken by the chief executive and the highest levels of management, because the culture of an organization flows from the attitudes of those at the top. The compliance culture can then be expected to filter downwards throughout the practitioner. Clearly, the compliance function assists senior management in instilling a positive view of compliance.

However, compliance may also be responsible for ensuring that the organization adheres to the rules of any exchanges of which the practitioner is a member and the applicable rules of any exchange on which it transacts. Additionally, it may fall to the compliance function to assist the legal department in ensuring that the organization adheres to any relevant legislation in any country in which it operates or has counterparties.

It is not unusual for the compliance function to carry out internal audit work. Even if an organization has a separate internal audit department, both the compliance function and the internal audit department should work closely together and, at the very least, the compliance function should be copied on all internal audit reports.

Additionally, the compliance function of a derivatives institution often undertakes operational risk management work. As with internal audit, if a separate operational risk management department exists, both the compliance function and the operational risk function should work closely together. The identification and mitigation of compliance operational risk is a normal part of the work of a compliance function.

The compliance function must be alert to the danger of ethical creep, or a shifting in the acceptable level of ethics due to a familiarity with the regulations and the innovative atmosphere in a derivatives practitioner, leading to a diminishing of the ethical hurdle over time. This situation is very difficult to detect and may only become clear in situations of extreme stress. Regular training on compliance issues may act as a counterbalance together with strong senior management awareness of ethics as well as compliance matters. Further control over ethical creep can be achieved by the regular maintenance of legal opinions and open communications with the regulator.

Transacting in derivatives also raises a large number of technical issues, and compliance with specific regulations often requires the production of reports and the performance of regulatory duties on a daily basis. It is often considered preferable for the compliance function to overview these reports rather than to prepare them, as this then frees it up for alternative work and allows an element of independent review.

RESPONSIBILITIES OF THE COMPLIANCE FUNCTION

There are three principal responsibilities of a compliance function. First, to create and maintain internal rules and procedures to facilitate observance of any relevant regulations. Second, to monitor activities within all parts of the organization on a regular basis, and to ensure that business is conducted in accordance with those regulations. Third, to liaise with sales, marketing and trading staff to influence the design of new products before those products are launched. The greatest value added in the compliance function of a derivatives practitioner is in the third responsibility. Timely intervention by the compliance function is more likely to result in an innovative product that is suitable for the firm to market and appropriate for the target client base.

Other general responsibilities include promoting the awareness and the understanding of compliance rules within the organization, resolving questions of compliance difficulty as they arise and following up any actual or potential, regulatory or related problems uncovered by the monitoring programme or otherwise to ensure that corrective action is taken where necessary.

A regulator's conduct of business rules often provide a good overview of how derivatives business should be conducted. They generally cover a variety of topics ranging from advertising and marketing to customer agreements, customer relations and customer dealing. They often also cover the wider issues including market integrity (for example, insider dealing) and more general aspects of compliance (for example, personal account transactions). All derivatives practitioners should adhere to these rules, and the spirit of these rules, at all times.

One area of responsibility on which there is no industry consensus is whether or not the compliance function has primary responsibility for liaison with the regulator. While this may seem a natural and logical responsibility for the compliance function, some firms view their overall relationship with their regulator as a strategic business responsibility and place this within the chief executive's office. Alternatively, if the operational risk management department has responsibility for strategic business risk then responsibility for the overall regulatory relationship may be placed within this department. It is, however, undeniable that the greatest day-to-day knowledge of how a regulator will react to a given problem will reside in the compliance function. This knowledge is inevitable, especially in a derivatives practitioner, as much day-to-day liaison with the regulator takes place at a working level in the compliance function.

The risks faced by a derivatives practitioner are of a complex nature, and a comprehensive and effective system of internal controls is essential. Such controls are invaluable in assisting the compliance function to perform its duties, and it must take responsibility in this area together with other risk and control-oriented departments such as operational risk management, finance and internal audit. A great deal has been written about internal controls in banks and there is a general agreement that a thorough system of internal controls is a fundamental requirement for sound management.

In addition to these, there are very many specific responsibilities which may fall to the compliance function and some of these may require work to be performed on a daily basis. Examples of such responsibilities are trade reporting (many transactions need to be reported to the regulatory authority within 24 hours of execution), equity position monitoring (holdings in equities above certain percentages may need to be reported to a variety of entities, for example, the company whose equity is held or the exchange on which it is traded, if applicable, according to the legislation of the relevant country) and exchange-traded derivative position monitoring (such positions should be monitored both in the light of any position limits set by the exchange, and with relevance to internal control).

OTC DERIVATIVES INDUSTRY PRACTICE

There are some areas where OTC derivatives practitioners face substantially different risks from those involved with exchange-traded products. This is primarily because almost all of the parameters of an OTC derivative may be individually tailored and negotiated and agreed between the counterparties to the transaction (as an example, in the case of options, the maturity, strike, and size may be negotiated). In addition, because many OTC derivatives may be tailored to meet the specific needs of the counterparties to the transaction, certain OTC derivatives may be more complicated and less standardized than those traded on regulated exchanges.

The general marketing and trading activities of OTC derivatives practitioners have featured regularly in the financial (and non-financial) press. In addition a number of reports have been written attempting to offer guidelines for best business practice. A report was issued by the G30 in July 1993 entitled 'Derivatives: Practices and Principles'. This report focuses on major risks and gives brief guidance on, for example, the role of senior management, marking-to-market, market valuation methods, measuring market risk and stress simulations.

A report was issued in March 1995 entitled 'A Framework for Voluntary Oversight of the OTC Derivatives Activities of Securities Firm Affiliates to Promote Confidence and Stability in Financial Markets'. This was prepared by the Derivatives Policy Group, which includes representatives from CS First Boston, Goldman Sachs, Lehman Brothers, Merrill Lynch, Morgan Stanley and Salomon Brothers with Cleary, Gottlieb, Steen & Hamilton as counsel. This report focuses on management controls, enhanced reporting (for example, on credit risk), evaluation of risk in relation to capital, and counterparty relationships.

Another report was issued in 1995, in August, entitled 'Principles and Practices for Wholesale Financial Market Transactions'. This report includes input from six trade associations and was co-ordinated by the Federal Reserve Bank of New York. It is intended to provide a voluntary code of conduct for participants in the wholesale OTC markets in the USA and includes major sections covering financial resources, participants, policies and procedures, mechanics of transactions and standards of transactions. Even though this report is directed at participants in the USA, as a general set of principles and practices it has been suggested that it might also prove of use to UK derivatives practitioners.

As noted already, the compliance function of a derivatives practitioner will be more heavily involved in the design of new products than its equivalent in a non-derivatives firm. This is particularly so in an OTC derivatives or structured products practitioner, where each new transaction is effectively a new product because of its bespoke nature. Additionally, the compliance procedures of such an institution are likely to cover more material than the regulators' rules and may include substantial guidance on the appropriateness and suitability of OTC derivatives and structured products that include derivatives. In addition, compliance procedures relating to such complex products are also likely to include guidance on ethical conduct.

It should be noted that many regulators have a principle of self-responsibility within their rules or guidance, particularly in relation to institutional investors (i.e. clients that are large or are not individuals). Generally, guidance relating to such a principle is linked either to 'know your counterparty' rules or to a requirement to observe high standards of integrity and dealing and to act with due skill, care and diligence. Occasionally, a regulator may be more explicit, as with the Japanese Financial Supervisory Agency's June 1998 guideline, and require a practitioner to provide a straightforward written explanation of the contents and associated risks of the product or transaction, taking into account the knowledge and experience of the counterparty.

With regard to the principle of self-responsibility, it should also be noted that the obligation for the adequate disclosure of the financial position of the counterparty rests with the counterparty and its external auditors. In particular, the external auditors are required each year to certify that audited accounts present a true and fair view of the financial condition of the counterparty.

Notwithstanding all this it remains good practice to refer unusual OTC derivative transactions to a local law firm for review before contacting the prospective counterparty. Once the counterparty shows interest in the transaction it is also good practice to encourage the counterparty to discuss the transaction with its external auditor and other professional advisers and with its regulator, if appropriate. Steps should also be taken to ensure that a sufficiently high level of senior management of the counterparty is aware of an OTC derivatives transaction (the more complex the transaction, the higher the level of senior management, including possibly the board of directors). Approval at the relevant level and from the relevant departments of the practitioner should also be required.

Although institutional investors should be able to assess properly any OTC derivative, it remains in the practitioner's interest to sell derivatives that are appropriate. There is a need to protect the practitioner from the adverse publicity which accompanies the sale of perceived inappropriate products, even if the commentary is unwarranted or incorrect. However, the derivatives practitioner plays a guessing game in attempting to determine which products will be found to be inappropriate at some time in the future by regulators or politicians who may not even be in office at the time of the sale.

Sensitivity analyses can play a useful role in explaining the effects of a complex OTC derivative to a counterparty. The analysis can take the form of either a spreadsheet or a graph. In either form care should be taken that possible profits and losses (or balance sheet effects, where applicable) are properly and clearly identified and that there is a fair representation of possible outcomes showing both upside and downside exposures. However, it should be made clear to the counterparty that the provision of a sensitivity analysis does not mitigate the counterparty's responsibility to evaluate the OTC derivative independently or to consult with appropriate professional advisers, both internally and externally.

Assumptions will need to be made in order to produce an analysis that is not excessively complicated. Care should be taken to make reasonable assumptions that are clearly stated and that do not present a misleading picture of the potential risks and benefits of the scenarios analyzed. While assumptions should take into account historical movements these should not be followed slavishly. Allowances must be made for movements which might seem extreme today but, for a transaction with a ten-year life, may be viewed as normal in, say, seven years.

Although the practitioner is, by definition, skilled in derivative products, attention should be paid to the overall exposure of the firm to the operational risks of complex and OTC derivatives as well as the market and credit risks. The compliance operational risks will include the relevance of the transaction to the counterparty and the transaction's size in relation to the counterparty's accounts.

It is also important that communications with the counterparty, whether oral or written, should not withhold information. This can happen either through failing to mention relevant information or through failing to correct previous information when subsequent events render that information itself false or misleading. Additionally, care must be taken not to present half-truths or rumours as qualified statements of fact.

While evolutionary rather than revolutionary in nature, the derivatives industry has created two completely new product categories in credit derivatives and insurance derivatives. These categories are in response to counterparties' needs and have developed, and will continue to develop, as the counterparties themselves, as well as the derivative practitioners, identify new uses. The practices outlined here are equally appropriate for credit and insurance derivatives, although careful monitoring will need to take place in order to identify possible additional procedures.

CRIME AND DERIVATIVES

Aside from ensuring compliance with applicable legislation and regulation, the compliance function should take an active role in the prevention, and, if this fails, the detection of crime committed against the organization. Such crime may be committed either by employees or by counterparties. Even if an organization believes that all its employees are honest, all internal controls should be designed with the possibility of crime in mind. It should be recognized that a practitioner will have a cross-section of the community in it and as such will have some potentially dishonest employees. The practitioner will seek to have robust controls to make it harder for such employees to join the firm and to reduce in a cost-effective manner the chance of their being successful. This is again an area of responsibility shared with other functions such as a fraud unit and with operational risk management.

The most likely source of crime that most banks will suffer is crime committed by an employee for his or her own financial benefit. This financial benefit may be sought in a number of ways: there may be attempts at the direct theft of cash – through the misappropriation of funds; there may be attempts at increasing salaries or bonuses – through the mismarking of books or through irregular sales techniques; or there may be insider dealing – through the use of privileged or confidential information for profit.

Apart from the desire for financial benefit, an employee may be driven to crime to cover up an error (perhaps in the misguided belief that this will save his or her job), to gain promotion, or as a result of blackmail. Crimes committed for these reasons are often harder to guard against and detect, simply because they are often less logical.

Crime, of course, is not the sole preserve of the employee. Counterparties may also commit crime against an organization and, once again, it may fall to the compliance function (with assistance from the legal and marketing functions where applicable) to oversee the implementation of safeguards. Many instances of counterparty crime may not cause a problem of detection. The counterparty may deny that a trade was undertaken, claim that the individual acting on its behalf did not possess the relevant authority to transact on its behalf, or claim that the derivatives practitioner failed to adhere to the appropriate marketing or dealing techniques. Procedures such as routine telephone taping of external calls and prompt execution of legal documents together with effective execution procedures can reduce the likelihood of counterparty crime.

Crime is, undeniably, more difficult to detect where there is fraudulent collusion. Such collusion may be between two employees or between an employee and a counterparty. All internal controls must be developed with the possibility of fraudulent collusion in mind. But, it must always be remembered, with sufficient collusion internal controls will always fail! It is therefore essential that management, the compliance function and all the employees do not rely solely on these controls but maintain a vigilant and inquiring mind at all times. Most importantly, an unusual occurrence must not be explained away in the most convenient way by those involved, for example, as a clerical error. *All* unusual occurrences should be investigated. The answer which management wants to hear is not necessarily the right one.

MONEY LAUNDERING

In April 1994 the UK introduced legislation aimed at preventing money from being laundered in or through the UK. Many financial institutions already had comprehensive 'know your customer' procedures in place and, in most cases, this legislation served to formalize what was already standard practice. The prevention of money laundering in many derivatives practitioners has fallen to the compliance department.

There is a possibility that money launderers might focus their attention on the derivatives markets and, in particular, the OTC derivatives markets. There are many reasons why this is the case. For example, OTC derivatives transactions may be of high value and of short duration (either because the hedge is only required for a short period, or because the original transaction is cancelled as the underlying markets move). Additionally, the OTC derivatives markets are global and transactions involving a number of different financial centres are not as unusual as in other financial markets.

There are various commonly discussed events which, it has been suggested, should be cause for a closer review with regard to money laundering. Some of these are:

- requests for payments to third parties which have no relationship to the original counterparty
- settlement instructions that are changed at the last minute
- collateral being delivered from one account and returned to another account
- constant assignment or cancellation of transactions
- dissolution, voluntary liquidation or similar of a counterparty soon after a transaction has occurred
- dealing through a large number of 'offshore' jurisdictions.

To assist in compliance with its relevant obligations regarding money laundering, the OTC derivatives practitioner in the UK can look to a number of documents and, in particular, the relevant guidance notes issued by the Joint Money Laundering Steering Group. These guidance notes cover details such as the requirements of UK law, internal controls, policies and procedures, identification procedures, record keeping, recognition and reporting of suspicious transactions, and education and training. Such guidance notes need to be adapted for individual circumstances.

CONCLUSION

The compliance function of a derivatives practitioner has responsibilities both externally (for example, to regulators and exchanges) and internally (for example, by way of the implementation or review of internal controls and the prevention or uncovering of crime). However, the precise responsibilities of the compliance function should be seen as dynamic, being constantly amended and updated to take account of the derivative industry's innovation and to comply with the regulators' reactions to the industry's innovation. The regulators and the industry are forever evolving!

'All internal controls must be developed with the possibility of fraudulent collusion in mind. But, it must always be remembered, with sufficient collusion internal controls will always fail!'

GLOSSARY

Abandon — Where an option holder chooses not to exercise his option.

American style — An option that may be exercised into its underlying instrument on any business day until expiry (see also **European-style**).

Arbitrage — The purchase or sale of an instrument and the simultaneous taking of an equal and opposite position in a related market, when the pricing is out of line.

Arbitrageur — A trader who takes advantage of profitable opportunities arising out of pricing anomalies.

Asset allocation — Dividing investment funds among markets to achieve maximum return of diversification.

Assignment (futures) — Notice sent by the clearing house to the option writer informing him that his option has been exercised.

Assignment (swaps) — Where the original counterparty to a swap seeks a third party to take his place.

At market — An order to buy/sell a futures contract at the current trading level.

At the money option (ATM) — An option with an exercise price at the current market level of the underlying. For example, this could be ATMF – at the money forward.

Average rate option — An option where the settlement is based on the difference between the strike and the average price of the underlying over a predetermined period. Also known as Asian options.

Basis — The differential between the price of the futures contract and the implied forward price of the underlying commodity.

Basis point — One hundredth of 1 per cent (0.01%).

Basis swap — See **Interest rate swaps**.

BBA — British Bankers' Association.

Bear market — A falling market.

Best	The broker can buy or sell at the 'best' price available at his/her discretion.
Bid	The wish to buy.
Black and Scholes	The original option-pricing model used by many market practitioners, written by Black and Scholes in 1972.
Broker	An individual or a firm that acts as an intermediary, putting together willing sellers and willing buyers for a fee (brokerage).
Bull market	A rising market.
Call option	An option that gives the holder (buyer) the right, but not the obligation, to buy the underlying instrument at a pre-agreed rate (strike rate) on or before a specific future date.
CaR	Capital at risk.
Cash settlement	Where a product is settled at expiry, based on the differential between the fixed/guaranteed price and the underlying instrument.
CBOT	Chicago Board of Trade.
Clearing house	An affiliate of a futures or options exchange which matches and guarantees trades and holds collateral lodged by participants. Acts as a counterparty to every deal, reducing credit risk.
Clearing	The process of registration, settlement, margin and the provision of a guarantee.
CME	Chicago Mercantile Exchange.
Commodity swaps	An obligation between two parties to exchange cash flows, one of which is usually a fixed reference rate, the other based on a floating market rate for oil, bullion, or base metals.
Contract	The standard unit of trading on an exchange.
Convergence	Process by which cash and futures prices converge as settlement or delivery approaches.
Compound option	An option on an option. The holder (buyer) has an option to purchase another option on a pre-set date at a pre-agreed premium.
Coupon	The annual interest paid/received on a bond.
Covered writing	Where an option is sold against an existing position.
Credit default swap	Enables isolation and transfer of credit risk without transferring ownership of the asset.

Credit spread	Difference in yield between an agreed 'benchmark' and a specific asset – usually a bond.
Cross	When an exchange broker has both buy and sell orders. After offering them to others in the 'pit' he can deal with himself to register the trades.
Cross rate	In foreign exchange, the exchange rate between two currencies not involving the dollar, e.g., DM/yen.
Currency swaps	An obligation between two or more parties to exchange interest obligations or interest rate receipts, for an agreed period, between two different currencies, and at the end of the period to exchange the corresponding principal amounts, at an exchange rate agreed at the beginning of the transaction.
Day trade	A position opened and closed within the same trading day.
Default	Failure to perform on a futures contract, or failure to pay an interest obligation on a debt.
Delivery	Final settlement of a futures contract, either cash settlement or physical settlement.
Delta	The sensitivity of an option price to changes in the price of the underlying commodity.
Discount	The amount by which a future is priced below its theoretical price, or below the price of the underlying instrument.
Dividend	The income earned from holding shares.
EDSP	Exchange delivery settlement price. When an exchange-traded contract reaches expiry, the EDSP determines the price for physical delivery or cash settlement.
EFP	Exchange of futures for physical. Common in the energy markets. A physical deal priced on the futures markets.
Equity swaps	An obligation between two parties to exchange cash flows, one of which will be based on an equity or an equity index, the other based on an interest rate such as LIBOR.
EUREX	Amalgamation of DTB (German) Soffex (Swiss) exchanges.
European style	An option which may only be exercised on the expiry date (see also **American style**).
Exchange traded	A transaction where a specific instrument is bought or sold on a regulated exchange, e.g., LIFFE, MATIF, IPE, NYMEX, SIMEX, etc.
Exercise	The conversion of the option into the underlying commodity.

Exercise price/ strike price	The price at which the option holder has the right to buy/sell the underlying instrument.
Exotic options	New generation of option derivatives, including look-backs, barriers, baskets, ladders, etc.
Expiry	The date after which an option can no longer be exercised.
Expiry date	The last date on which an option can be exercised.
Extrinsic value	The amount by which the premium on an option exceeds the intrinsic value, also known as **time value**.
Fair value	For options, this is calculated by an option-pricing model such as that written by Black and Scholes. For futures, it is the level where the contract should trade, taking into account cost of carry.
Forward foreign exchange	An obligation to exchange one currency for another at a pre-agreed exchange rate for a future delivery date.
Forward rate Agreement (FRA)	An agreement where the client can fix the rate of interest that will be applied to a notional loan or deposit drawn or placed, on an agreed future date (the settlement date) for a specified term.
Fungibility	A futures contract with identical administration in more than one financial centre. Trades in various geographical locations can be offset (e.g., bought on the IPE and sold on SIMEX).
Futures contract	A legally binding agreement on a regulated exchange to make or take delivery of a specified instrument, at a fixed date in the future, and at a price agreed at the outset. Positions are marked to market daily.
Globex$_2$	Likely amalgamation of MATIF, SIMEX, CME, BM&F, and Montreal Exchange (French, Singapore, Chicago Mercantile, Brazilian and Montreal) exchanges.
Hedge	A transaction that reduces or mitigates risk.
Hedge fund	A highly speculative investment vehicle.
Historical volatility	An indication of past volatility in the marketplace.
Holder	The buyer of the option.
Index derivative	An equity transaction based on the movement of an index rather than a single stock. Popular indices are FT-SE 100, S&P 500, Nikkei.
In the money option (ITM)	An option with an exercise price more advantageous than the current market level of the underlying.

Initial margin Collateral placed with the clearing house when an exchange-traded position is opened. A 'goodwill' deposit where interest is paid by the clearing house and the deposit is refunded when the open position is traded out. Initial margins change in line with market conditions.

Interest rate cap An option product where the holder (buyer) is guaranteed a maximum borrowing cost over a specified term at a rate of his choosing. A premium is required.

Interest rate collar An option product where the holder (buyer) is guaranteed a maximum and minimum borrowing cost over a specified term at rates of his choosing. A premium may be required, but may net to zero. Involves the simultaneous trading of caps and floors.

Interest rate floor An option product where the holder (buyer) is guaranteed a minimum yield on a deposit over a specified term at a rate of his choosing. A premium is required.

Interest-rate swaps An obligation between two parties to exchange interest-related payments in the same currency from fixed rate into floating rate, or vice versa (vanilla or coupon swap), or from one type of floating rate to another, e.g., eligible bill rate, prime rate, commercial paper (basis swap). New or existing debt can be swapped. The only movement of funds is a net transfer of interest rate payments between the two parties. The interest payments are calculated on an agreed principal amount which is not exchanged.

Intrinsic value One of the components of an option premium. The amount by which an option is in the money.

IPE International Petroleum Exchange.

ISDA International Swaps and Derivatives Association, previously known as the International Swap Dealers Association. Many market participants use ISDA documentation.

LIBOR The London inter-bank offered rate. The inter-bank rate used when one bank borrows from another. It is also the benchmark used to price many capital market and derivative transactions.

LIBID The London inter-bank bid rate. The rate at which one bank will lend to another.

Liquid market An active marketplace where selling and buying occur with minimal price concessions.

LIFFE London International Financial Futures and Options Exchange.

Liquidation The closing of an existing position on the futures market.

Local	A member of LIFFE, or any other exchange, who trades solely for his own account.
Long	Someone who has bought the underlying.
Margin	See **Initial margin** and Variation margin.
Marking-to-market	A process where both OTC and exchange-traded contracts are revalued on a daily basis.
MATIF	Marché à Terme International Français, based in Paris.
Naked option	A short option position taken without having the underlying commodity.
NYMEX	New York Mercantile Exchange.
Offer	The wish to sell.
Open position	The number of contracts that have not been offset by close of business.
Open outcry	The Chicago style of trading where members execute their business via a system of hand signals and shouting.
Option	An agreement between two parties that gives the holder (buyer) the right, but not the obligation, to buy or sell a specific instrument at a specified price on or before a specific future date. On exercise the seller (writer) of the option must deliver, or take delivery of the underlying instrument at the specified price.
OTC or over the counter	A bilateral transaction between a client and a bank, negotiated privately between the parties.
Out of the money option (OTM)	An option with an exercise price more disadvantageous than the current market level of the underlying. An out of the money option has time value but no intrinsic value.
Pit	A designated part of the floor area where a particular exchange contract is traded; can be known as a trading ring.
Premium	The cost of the option contract. It is made up of two components, intrinsic value and time value.
Price transparency	Where a transaction is executed on the floor of an exchange, and every participant has equal access to the trade.
Put option	An option that gives the holder (buyer) the right, but not the obligation, to sell the underlying instrument at a pre-agreed strike rate (exercise rate) on or before a specific future date.
Quanto swap or DIFF swap	A cross-currency swap, where both streams of interest are calculated based on principal amounts of the same currency, and both interest streams are paid in that currency. Often used for yield curve plays.

Rollover	A LIBOR fixing on a new tranche of loan, or the transfer of a futures position to the next delivery month.
Settlement price	The price at which all futures are margined. A representative price for the close of the day's trading.
Short	Someone who has sold the underlying.
Spot foreign exchange	A transaction to exchange one currency for another at a rate agreed today (the spot rate), for settlement in two business days' time.
Strike price/ exercise price	The price at which the option holder has the right to buy or sell the underlying instrument.
SIMEX	Singapore International Monetary Exchange.
Swaps	An obligation between two parties to exchange payments over a specific term at a pre-determined rate. See also **Commodity swaps, Currency swaps, Equity swaps, Interest rate swaps.**
Swaption	An option into a pre-determined swap transaction. Options can be payers or receivers, American or European.
Technical analysis	A graphical analysis of historical price trends, used to predict likely future trends in the market. Also known as 'charts'.
Theoretical value	The fair value of a futures or option contract (see also **Fair value**).
Tick	The standard minimum price movement on an exchange-traded futures or option contract (0.01%). Each tick has a monetary value that is different for each contract.
Time value	The amount (if any) by which the premium of an option exceeds the intrinsic value.
Traded option	An option contract bought or sold on a regulated exchange.
Underlying	The asset, future, interest rate, FX rate or index upon which a derivative transaction is based.
VaR	Value at risk.
Variation margin	Daily movements of debits and credits to/from exchange clearing members, as a result of futures and options positions being marked-to-market.
Volatility	One of the major components of the option-pricing model, based on the degree of 'scatter' of underlying price when compared to the 'mean average rate'.
Warrant	An option which can be listed on an exchange, generally longer than one year. Many capital market issues have warrants embedded in them.
Writer	The seller of an option.

INDEX

Taylor Associates run programmes and tutorials in the following general areas:

Hard Skills

- Capital Markets
- Derivatives
- Money Laundering
- Treasury
- Foreign Exchange
- Fixed Income
- Equities

- Technical Analysis
- Portfolio Management
- Credit Evaluation
- Risk
- General Finance and Accounting

Soft Skills

- Team Building
- Management Development
- Stress Management
- Project Management
- Consultancy Skills

- Presentation and Listening Skills
- Communication Skills
- Managing People
- Interviewing Techniques
- Leadership

To contact Taylor Associates:
Telephone/Fax: 01372 841096
E-mail: info@taylorassociates.co.uk
Web: www.taylorassociates.co.uk